SOUTH HOLLAND PUBLIC LIBRARY

3 1350 00330 0698

W9-BGN-677

Praise for *The Next Gen Leader*

"Robert's 6G Leadership System is a revelation that everyone has the potential to lead in the right environment. *The Next Gen Leader* provides systematic strategies and solutions to accelerating the growth and development of emerging and aspiring leaders, resulting in the creation of high performing teams and organizations. This should be required reading for every employee regardless of position, as an invitation to a seat at the leadership table."

—Dwight V. McMillan, human resource business partner,
Rockwell Automation

"Few organizations develop a universal leadership development system for aspiring, emerging, and seasoned leaders, even though it is the largest area of criticality with major implications for many companies. Robert C. McMillan's *The Next Gen Leader* provides a powerful system with practical strategies that will accelerate change. It is an invaluable tool for that critical time—such transformation."

—Brandon Clairmont, vice president of sales, McCormick

The Next Gen Leader

The Next Gen Leader

Cutting Edge Strategies to Make You the Leader You Were Born to Be

By Robert C. McMillan

CAREER PRESS

Pompton Plains, N.J.

Copyright © 2014 by Robert C. McMillan

All rights reserved under the Pan-American and International Copyright Conventions. This book may not be reproduced, in whole or in part, in any form or by any means electronic or mechanical, including photocopying, recording, or by any information storage and retrieval system now known or hereafter invented, without written permission from the publisher, The Career Press.

THE NEXT GEN LEADER
Cover design by Howard Grossman
Printed in the U.S.A.

To order this title, please call toll-free 1-800-CAREER-1 (NJ and Canada: 201-848-0310) to order using VISA or MasterCard, or for further information on books from Career Press.

The Career Press, Inc.
220 West Parkway, Unit 12
Pompton Plains, NJ 07444
www.careerpress.com

Library of Congress Cataloging-in-Publication Data
McMillan, Robert C.
    The next gen leader : cutting edge strategies to make you the leader you were born to be / by Robert C. McMillan.
        pages cm
    Includes index.
    ISBN 978-1-60163-309-5 -- ISBN 978-1-60163-483-2 (ebook)
    1. Leadership. 2. Executive ability. I. Title.

HD57.7.M399165 2014
658.4'092--dc23
                                                                2013045963

3 1350 00330 0698

Contents

● ● ● ● ● ● ● ● ● ● ● ● ● ● ● ●

Introduction

A Genius in the Making

• • • • • • • • • • • • • • • • • •

This book is for emerging, aspiring, and executive leaders who want to maximize their potential and become the transformational leaders they were born to be. This book contains the complete system for those professionals, teams, and organizations similar to professional athletes and sport teams who want to better not only themselves, but others and teams around them to win and outperform the competition.

I want you to discover the Genius Leader in you. I want to be the coach you always wanted. I want to tell you that you can make it when others say you cannot or when it looks as though you can't go on. You have within you a well of potential that I want to help you discover and unleash on the world!

Hello, I'm Robert, and I'm your leadership coach. What if there was a system where both professionals and organizations could experience extraordinary promotion, performance, productivity, and profits simply by maximizing potential congruently?

What if we all knew, in our own way, that we could achieve the impossible—in our personal lives, our place of work, internally and externally. What if we all realized we could reach our personal, career, and organizational dreams by maximizing our potential and discovering the Genius Leader inside each of us?

How would our lives, organizations, and teams be different? Can you envision what that would look like and mean to your career and life?

The truth of the matter is that you control in your mind, heart, and hands the ability to release your genius in leadership by maximizing your potential and releasing it to the world! *The Next Gen Leader* is the solution that integrates organizational and professional goal congruences, maximizing the leadership potential of every professional through its groundbreaking 6G Leadership System.

For a team or individual to win in any competitive sporting contest, the athletes must be leaders and have the right tools, equipment, and systems to get them there. Whether football, basketball, baseball, soccer, or any sport with or without a ball involved, it is critical that the athletes have the right equipment to realize success as leaders. The same is true in leadership off the field. A leader's success is highly contingent upon having the next generation of tools, equipment, and systems in order to be successful in the business world. Without the necessary tools, systems, and resources, a leader is similar to a talented athlete trying to compete among the best players without the proper equipment; his or her genius gets lost in the chaos.

I will never forget my first year playing collegiate football. It was my freshman year, and I was recruited by Virginia State University, an NCAA Division II athletic program at the time. In high school, I played the running back position and held the rushing record for the most yards per carry. Once I hit the hole, it always took four or more defensive players to bring me down, and often I carried them for 10 yards or more after contact. That is how I earned the nickname Rob Mac. I would either run over or run by people like a runaway MAC truck.

With the hopes of being awarded a scholarship, I accepted the invitation from the head football coach and arrived at camp the summer of 1988. The deciding factor on whether or not I received a scholarship was how well I performed in comparison to the other athletes. After I arrived on campus and settled in the assigned dormitory, I made my way to the stadium for equipment handout for practice that day. As I approached the tunnel heading to the equipment room, I saw a line with more than 100 people. The line was the "equipment line," filled with players who were also there for summer football camp. I quickly stepped in line, only to realize I was dead last.

As I stood at the rear of the line, I saw people coming out of the equipment room, heading to the locker room, with shoulder pads, helmets, cleats, etc. Many of them looked perplexed as they entered the adjacent locker to get dressed for practice. After waiting in line for more than an hour, eventually I made it into the equipment room to find shoulder pads that were too big, cleats that were worn with missing spikes, and a helmet that was too small for my head. Trust me, it was so tight I didn't need a chinstrap.

Given that practice began in 30 minutes, I made my way into the locker room and tried to find someone to trade equipment with. I was successful trading the helmet and shoulder pads for ones that fit, but couldn't get anybody to trade cleats.

Running out of time, I began to suit up, putting on the equipment for practice. After putting on everything except the cleats, I reached down and picked them up: each shoe was a different size. Not only were they worn, torn, and missing spikes, now I had to contend with one shoe being a size 9 and the other a size 9.5. I wore a size 10. I reached down and put those cleats on my feet and noticed that they were so worn my feet rolled over outward because the arch support was nonexistent.

As I walked toward the field, I noticed I wasn't the only one with bad equipment. I saw other rookies wearing worn cleats, old helmets, and oversized shoulder pads. I later found out that veterans received new equipment one day earlier and the rookies were left with the hand-me-downs from the University of Virginia, the school that donated their used equipment to Virginia State University.

As everyone approached the middle of the field, the head coach blew his whistle three times—commanding silence—and began to communicate the summer camp schedule and the performance evaluation process. Immediately after the announcement, the coaches began placing players into groups to perform drills used to assess speed, strength, and agility. I was placed in the running back group. The problem was I could not run because those shoes were so worn and they were killing my feet. With little to no support in them, I performed the drill as best as I could, feeling blisters forming each step I took.

Each drill, exercise, and play I ran was viewed by the coaches as poor because I could not demonstrate quickness, balance, or agility. I remember one drill—the obstacle course—where the player had to run top speed and cut in, out, and around a set of cones, which would demonstrate ability to accelerate and change direction instantly. During the drill, I slipped, fell, and ran outside the obstacle course cones because of the inadequate equipment. Out of the corner of my eye, as I performed the drills, I could see some coaches shaking their heads and others laughing. I became so frustrated during the drill, as running back coaches yelled at me to pick it up. I kicked off those cleats because I felt I was better off without them. There I was in summer camp, performing drills, attempting to make the team barefooted. At the end of practice, because of my poor performance, I was pulled aside by the coach, cut from the running back position, and moved to third-string defense as a corner back, a position I had never played before.

That is how leadership can be. Without the right resources, tools, and systems, a leader can often be taken out of a position on a team, as a result of not being able to perform, and moved to a position of unfamiliarity. It is no fun to be in the game—any game—without the right equipment or resources to help you achieve success. This book contains the 6G Leadership System, which can be your internal resource to help you maximize your leadership potential and help you to compete against all competition in the global economy.

Several weeks later and understanding the high risk of being cut from the team, I decided to take my last few dollars and buy football cleats at a sports store in the local mall. The next day at practice, my feet could not thank me enough! I stepped on the field wearing my new cleats; that day would be very different from all the others. I tackled the biggest and strongest running backs, covered and ran alongside the fastest receivers, and intercepted passes thrown by the star quarterback.

After practice, impressed by my performance, the coach walked up to me and said, "I didn't know you were one of the fastest on the team. Keep up the good work!" Little did he know I was always the fastest on the team, but it was the equipment that allowed me the opportunity to demonstrate it.

In leadership, the difference from being underestimated and stereotyped as a low potential leader is often tied to the internal tools, resources, and equipment that an individual uses to play in the game of leadership. Becoming extraordinary can often be as simple as having the right system, equipment, and tools at your disposal. This book is your resource to enable you to maximize your leadership potential and compete on a level playing field. I invite you to take hold of this system and leverage it to become the next generation you.

Here is what I know. I believe there is a Genius Leader in you! A leader who is waiting to be discovered and released to the world! To help you discover that Genius Leader in you, I have developed a leadership system that will prepare, place, and promote your destiny: to be the leader you were born to be. The 6G Leadership System creates extraordinary promotion, performance, productivity, and profits for professionals and organizations congruently, simply by maximizing the genius in each leader.

How do I know this system can prepare, place, and promote you to new levels of unfound success? Well, because the life and career strategies, solutions, and techniques described in this book transformed my life. I was not always an executive leader for one of the largest Fortune 500 companies. This book contains the secrets that unleashed my potential through multiple stages of my life: a child with a severe speech impediment, marked as "special needs"; a struggling staff professional as an adult, attempting to climb the imaginary corporate ladder while working nights as a comedian trying to "find myself"; to discovering the secrets to leadership and becoming a consultant, coach, and thought leader on leadership, and an executive Leader of Significance for some of the world's most-admired Fortune 500 companies. This is how I know there is a Genius Leader in you, because I studied the traits of great leaders and discovered ones in me!

There are many secrets I discovered during my journey, which I will share with you in this book. But, generally, there are three things you need to know straight off. First, organizations cannot be successful unless they have successful leaders, and leaders cannot be successful unless their organization is successful. Therefore, organizations and leaders need to come together in order to be successful.

Second, if you want to be invaluable and irreplaceable, and have true security in a career and not just a job, the secret is not to master a job but to master leadership. Leadership can be transported to any environment, but a job is stationary and limited in nature. This book provides a process to master leadership and connects the goals of the individual, creating a success ecosystem for the organization and its leaders. In addition, the book reveals the secrets of converting existing professional roles into empowering leadership roles. It also challenges the traditional power-and-control philosophy, replacing it with a distributed leadership model where everyone is empowered to be a leader.

Third, because leadership is ambiguous, challenging, and complex, many professionals and organizations do not have a clear definition of leadership or a transparent process that is shared and understood for developing, growing, and promoting leaders. The fact is, most companies only promote and reward the top 20 percent of their organization's employees and forego investing in and developing the remaining 80 percent. This results in attrition, frustration, limited growth, and a strained talent-supply system. From a professional and career development perspective, many people do not understand the process for growing into broader leadership roles, often learning through unwritten rules or going through a continuous loop of learning bad behaviors from bad leaders. Ultimately, they crash and burn. For that reason, this book also provides a complete system to help professionals achieve growth and promotion by focusing on maximizing their leadership potential and becoming engaged, committed, and instrumental in helping their organization achieve extraordinary results.

Finally, the system solves the age-old quandary of producing, placing, and promoting leaders while increasing organizational performance, productivity, and profits. The system easily overlays the existing job/family hierarchy, job titles, and assignments that typically typecast employees into roles and limit their ability to grow into an all-inclusive leadership structure where everyone is recognized as a leader. Leaders are developed using a standardized system that grows and develops leaders to become Genius Leaders, regardless of position, authority, or power. The 6G Leadership System is a leadership network that creates and fosters a positive culture and environment where every professional is empowered to be a leader, resulting in professional and organizational promotion to newfound success.

Since discovering my true leadership potential, I have blended my gift and passion to entertain, inspire, and educate into a career as an expert in the field of leadership and maximizing potential, a thought leader on leadership, a coach, and an author, all while maintaining a career as a chief executive leader for one of the world's largest healthcare corporations with direct accountability for the Federal Employee Health Benefit Program—an account totaling $27 billion.

Several years ago, as one of the former chief executives of the Federal Employee Health Benefit Program, I had the honor of serving more than 5 million federal employees, members of Congress, White House staff, and the President of the United States and his cabinet. Often I am asked how I felt about serving President Barack Obama and his family as members of the federal employee health insurance program as a number-one priority. My response has always been the same: the President and his family are my second priority. My mother, a recently retired federal employee, made sure she was the first during my years with the Blues! I love you, Mom, for your commitment, sacrifices, and leadership to your family and the federal government. Congratulations on your 40 years of service with the U.S. Department of Health and Human Services!

I have learned in life that in order to soar in leadership, you must face your fears, embrace your failures, recognize your inherent gifts, and make the choice to fly to new heights of success. With that revelation, I started the Next Gen Leader Institute and the Circles of Dreams Foundation in 2007 with the goal of touching 10 million lives and helping organizations, leaders, teams, and professionals soar to new heights. In this book, I will share secrets uncovered during more than 20 years of experience working in Corporate America as an executive leader and consultant with some of the world's most-admired companies: General Electric, Motorola, more than 50 Blue Cross Blue Shield plans, Ernst & Young, PriceWaterhouseCoopers, Command Packaging, PaineWebber, T. Rowe Price, AT&T, BellSouth, small-, mid-, and large-size organizations, and other Fortune 500 companies. I will also share the secrets to maximizing your potential in life and in leadership. By soaring—and growing wings on the way—I have been fortunate enough to author several books, and share solutions and secrets with organizations, companies, and professionals all over the world. Now I want to share them with you and coach you on how to maximize your potential as a leader in your personal and professional life.

It is my honor to share *The Next Gen Leader* with you, your team, and organization! You have in your control a system that can transform your ability to become a Genius Leader and to lead others to extraordinary success. I encourage you to take the challenge and soar to your maximum leadership potential. There is a Genius Leader in you, and if you dare to discover, cultivate, and unleash it on the world, it will change your life! It has changed mine forever!

I also encourage you to begin journaling your transformational journey. As you read through the coming chapters, invest quality time using your journal to respond to questions, take notes, complete chapter coaching exercises, and to reflect on your transformational journey. It is just as important to note introspective thoughts and watershed moments, and write down your goals and actionable steps that will help you to reach you individual team and organizational goals. Often the key to transformation is changing our perspectives, which requires us to make a decision and to take action. Use the book as the roadmap and leverage your journal as your tablet for taking actionable steps to become the genius leader you were born to be! Now let's begin exploring the 6G Leadership System and how you, your team, and organization can become transformational and leaders of high significance.

Part 1

The 6G Leadership System

You Are a Leader!

● ● ● ● ● ● ● ● ● ● ● ● ● ● ● ● ●

Believe it or not, if you are reading this book, you are a leader, regardless of position, pay, or power. You are a leader; there is no doubt about it! Here is what I know: Each of us falls within the 1G to 6G leadership networks (similar to cell phone and iPad networks). We all are born with leadership hardware and software, but we require constant maintenance and application upgrades in order to operate at our maximum leadership potential. With that visual in mind, and understanding that everybody is a leader, there are five critical questions that every professional, team member, individual contributor, supervisor, manager, director, and officer within an organization must ask:

- What kind of leader am I?
- How do I become a leader of High Significance?
- How can I upgrade my leadership hardware and software?
- Do I understand others' leadership expectations of me?
- What is my true leadership potential?

The Next Gen Leader: Cutting Edge Strategies to Make You the Leader You Were Born to Be was designed to answer those complicated leadership questions and to provide a leadership system to help organizations, teams, and individuals maximize leadership potential. Centuries of research have shown that the concept of leadership has been one of the most misunderstood yet most critical capability gaps in business. However, once the true meaning of leadership is discovered and a universal system is adopted to grow and nurture leaders, the potential for individual, team, and organizational success is limitless.

The concept of leadership sounds simple yet is complex. The challenge is that each organization, team, supervisor, and employee has its own unique definition and description of the term "leadership," which makes it a complicated concept to define, measure, and evaluate. For more than two decades, I've been in the business of helping professionals, teams, and organizations become better leaders. That's my passion, my sweet tooth: helping others reach their maximum potential.

Through the years of consulting, training, coaching, and working in leadership and individual contributor capacities for Fortune 500 companies (General Electric, Motorola, BP, Blue Cross Blue Shield, and many others), I've observed and profiled the traits and characteristics of successful professionals and leaders in various roles—from project managers, individual contributors, analysts, team leads, supervisors, directors, executives, and C-level executives. I have also held leadership positions in challenging organizations and worked alongside difficult people who operated in negative cultures, resulting in self-created titles many people carried on their foreheads (along with their title Chief of CYA—Chief of Cover Your Ass). To help leaders and aspiring leaders looking to maximize their potential, this book also sets out to provide solutions to the negative aspects of leadership and its unfortunate challenges in dealing with difficult people, organizations, and teams.

Leadership Is Action, Not Position

The fact of the matter is, regardless of position, title, or appointment, we are all leaders. We are naturally born to lead. The successful professionals I observed used what I later refer to as the Six Secret Leadership Applications, which I will share with you in this book. I have applied these concepts and credit them with much of my success in reaching the C suite as the youngest executive within the world's largest healthcare conglomeration. Through the use of these applications, it is clear that it is not position, pay, or power that produces leadership results; it is action that results in leadership. Bottom line, as I always say, "Leadership is action, not position."

What Really Is Leadership Anyway?

The concept of leadership—an excessively used word to describe a desired action—is one of the most misunderstood yet most critical capabilities required in business. Each person, team, organization, and culture has its own unique definition and description of this term, which makes it a complicated concept to define, measure, and evaluate in comparison to the goals and objectives of teams, organizations, and individual contributors. Let's consider a few illustrative questions:

- **How do you rate leadership?** Leadership success cannot be solely determined based on achieved business goals and objectives noted on an organizational scorecard describing desired results. For example, one may be able to achieve goals and objectives while demonstrating poor leadership. Many organizations make the error of judging leadership solely on achieving business goals and objectives, often creating casualties resulting from the behaviors used to meet those goals.

- **How does one know leadership when they see it?** Can you take a picture of leadership with your iPhone? If I were to ask you to go find leadership and bring it back, what would you return with? Most people believe that you cannot see, hear, touch, taste, or smell leadership because it is not a person, place, or thing. I am of the opposite belief. I believe you can always find leadership; it is both an action and a thing that can be found in people. Leadership is a network of applications embedded in each of us, which I call the 6G Leadership System.

- **Can anyone be a leader?** Many thought leaders who embrace the traditional view of leadership would suggest that everyone is not a leader and that leadership is merely a vertical climb concept. They envision a climb up an imaginary corporate ladder in which one steps from one level to the next, eventually elevating to greater responsibilities and oversight and never revisiting the previous "steps" or "roles" they've climbed to reach their desired level of success. If this view on leadership was truly proven, tried, and tested, leaders would never fall, would they? The truth of the matter is just the opposite; under this concept, many leaders have fallen quickly. Because this concept lacks footing and balance, it is unsustainable with the constant motion of leadership. Throughout history we have seen leaders fall on their own sword. Leadership is not a vertical climb; it is a horizontal pull in the format of a network constantly rotating like the earth—the 6G Leadership System.

The Best-Kept Secret About Leadership

The best-kept secret about leadership is that everyone is a leader! Every person was born with the innate talent and gift of leadership. In the 6G Leadership System, this is referred to as the Genetic Leader—those who have leadership potential but simply have not stepped into awareness of their leadership potential. They have it within them, but the application is just not turned on; it's on "hibernate." Leadership is complex because its networks are constantly revolving, and many people operate on different network frequencies. Some are operating on 1G, and others at 6G capacities. The question becomes, what leadership network are you operating on?

A leadership foundation built on the vertical climb model is unsustainable. Leadership of significance consists of a network of leader applications operating in parallel with our human minds, then carried out in the form of actions in pursuit of a desired result. Many leaders are in leadership positions but have no network app. It's like having a GPS system with no application—you have the hardware but no application to know where you're going. True leadership is a network of leader intelligence applications that run within our core—mind, body, and spirit—always in operation mode. Many people believe leadership is something you can turn on or off. You can never turn leadership off. It is always online. Most leaders operate from a leadership level or hierarchical concept of artificial success rather than navigating through a perpetual leadership growth network that propels success. The fact is, anyone can physically step up to the next level on a ladder—that is just as easy as walking. But the question is, once you step up, do you have the appropriate leadership application to perform and sustain your position?

Simply put, leadership is a system of leaders. In order to be successful, an organization—in today's competitive environment of accelerated change and overwhelming complexity—cannot afford to have an enterprise of followers. The traditional leadership concept, that in order to have leadership you must have someone willing to follow and someone willing to lead, is antiquated and outdated. In today's global economy, organizations, associations, and companies need everyone to be a leader. They need more leaders and fewer followers.

Organizations need thinkers, leaders who foster influential thought and action toward achievement of a desired vision, objective, and goal. Traditionally, followers don't think; they do as they are told. In today's competitive world of doing more with less and becoming more effective and efficient, followers will not be the competitive force that innovates, breaks ground, or discovers more effective ways of doing business. This will come from leaders. Again, every person is born with the innate talent and gift of leadership. There just happen to be six networks of leadership that people operate within.

What Is the 6G Leadership System?

6 Networks + 6 Apps = The 6G Leadership System

In order to effectively lead, leaders must operate in a leadership network infrastructure designed to identify, cultivate, and build leadership aptitudes within an existing network of leaders that allow behavioral replication and synchronization of the desired leadership state. For example, to be effective and meet market demands, cell phones have to be adaptable to operate on multiple cellphone carrier networks. Similarly, leaders must be able to operate on various leadership networks based on a specific scenario or situation. Through time, people have morphed into different types of leaders. With so many different leadership models, styles, and approaches—and the significant increase of external leadership recruiting—a clear leadership model is much needed in today's challenging times.

In leadership, there are varying styles, experiences, and behaviors. The 6G Leadership System has been narrowed down to six networks that provide insight on the features, benefits, and limitations of each network, consisting of network to 6G: 1G–Genetic Leader, 2G–Generic Leader, 3G–Go-To Leader, 4G–Growth Leader, 5G–Gateway Leader, and 6G–Genius Leader.

Professionals have different experiences, and many are in different places in their career journey. The 6G Leadership System provides a tracking system to identify exactly where you are, and it provides a pathway forward. As stated earlier, the philosophy is that everyone is a leader and the difference between leaders is simply where they fall within the leadership network.

There are leadership applications that each leadership network operates on. Success is dependent on optimizing the right applications of Awareness,

Acceptance, Acknowledgement, Achievement, Acceleration, and Agility within the leadership network to foster influence and success.

Your responses to *What Is My 6G Leadership Aptitude?* will reveal your aptitude in the *Genetic Leader, Generic Leader, Go-To Leader, Growth Leader, Gateway Leader,* and *Genius Leader* categories and also help to assess how well you are optimizing those life and leadership apps (Awareness, Acceptance, Acknowledgement, Achievement, Acceleration, and Agility).

The next section provides a system overview of the 6G Leadership System and defines in broader terms the various leadership networks that will assist you in understanding the necessary keys to maximizing your leadership potential.

Overview of the
6G Leadership System

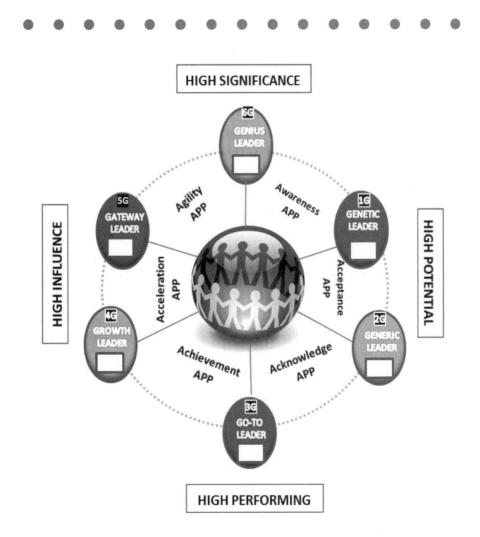

Six Applications to Maximize Leadership Potential

One of my goals in writing this book is to share with you what I have branded as the 6G Leadership System. These six leadership applications, if understood, practiced, and universally applied, will maximize your leadership potential beyond your imagination. These applications help us understand what truly makes us leaders and also provides solutions to help improve our ability to lead through the leadership apps that most often lay dormant in us all. Listed next is a summary of the six maximum potential leadership applications, accompanied with descriptions of why others allow us to lead:

- **Awareness App:** We are leaders because our actions demonstrate awareness of our innate ability to lead others.

- **Acceptance App:** We are leaders because we are accepted as leaders by others based on actions.

- **Acknowledgement App:** We are leaders because others acknowledge our actions.

- **Achievement App:** We are leaders because our actions are recognized as business achievements.

- **Acceleration App:** We are leaders because our actions accelerate business performance and results.

- **Agility App:** We are leaders because our actions create agility to grow the business or organization and its people, simultaneously.

Leadership Is Not Flat; Leadership Is Round

This breakthrough in bringing clarity to the true meaning of leadership explains why leadership is often misunderstood and its potential is rarely maximized.

For many centuries, we have been taught that leadership is a linear and vertical process, which is far from the truth. Like those who argued that the world was flat only to conclude it was round when they failed to fall off the edge, so it is with the misrepresentation of leadership. Simply put, leadership is round, not flat. Through observations and experiences, I discovered that leadership is not a linear or a vertical process. In fact, it is the complete opposite: leadership is a system of various networks and frequencies that each of us operate on within a circular motion.

Leadership Network Styles

In addition to the Six Leadership Applications described previously, there are Six Leadership Networks, 1G to 6G, that coincide with the applications. These Leadership Networks—which I also refer to as "Leadership Network Styles" when I speak to audiences and organizations—help us understand the various leadership networks, the type of leaders we are and the value of each:

- **1G–Genetic Leader Network:** People value you because they see potential.
- **2G–Generic Leader Network:** People value you because you accept leadership.
- **3G–Go-To Leader Network:** People value you because they recognize your results.
- **4G–Growth Leader Network:** People value you because of your consistent achievements in business performance and growth.
- **5G–Gateway Leader Network:** People value you because you create opportunities and change for others.
- **6G–Genius Leader Network:** People value you because they respect your leadership agility and ability to influence success.

The leadership networks described above will be discussed in much greater detail in later chapters to assist you and your organization in discovering and maximizing your leadership potential. Now, let's discuss briefly how applying the system concepts and features can provide a sense of extraordinary outcomes for you and your team.

System Concept and Features

The system concepts and features of *The Next Gen Leader* are applications, leadership networks, and an operating system. If understood, practiced, and universally applied, the system will maximize the leadership potential of individuals, teams, and organizations, resulting in measurable improvements in the areas of shared employee and organizational success;

increased customer satisfaction; improved employee engagement and commitment; reduced High Performer/High Potential attrition; and opportunities for goal congruence.

All of these quantitative values have positively impacted the performance, productivity, and profits of organizations, teams, and professionals that have taken the bold challenge to soar to new heights of leadership potential.

Why This Is the Right System for You and Your Organization

Through the years, the successful professionals and organizations I have observed accessed many, if not all, of the applications and leadership networks that are introduced in this book. Contrarily, the applications were either nonexistent or inconsistently used by less-admired leaders, professionals, and organizations that I have studied. In short, what I have found using these leadership principles is that the stronger the usage of the Six Leadership Applications and Networks, the more success you will have in becoming an individual, team, and organization of High Potential Leaders, High Performance Leaders, High Influence Leaders, and High Significance Leaders, in that order.

The concepts in this book are proven, tried, and tested. The values and the benefits of adopting these leadership concepts, applications, and systems are summarized in the following system features.

Next Gen Leader System Features

1.   The Next Gen Leader Provides a Clear Vision of Leadership.

Leadership is not predicated on a stagnant hierarchical structure, such as leadership levels or ladders of success that most traditionalists on this subject subscribe to. Leadership is not a vertical climb. Leadership ladders do not exist. They are figments of our imagination like the genie in the bottle who makes dreams come true by fulfilling a simple wish. In leadership, you are that genie in the bottle. And you have to find a way out of the bottle to take action and realize your leadership aspirations. It is my belief that leadership is not flat; it is round—a round network system comprised of various frequencies that leaders operate within. Their leadership potential is only limited by the ability to connect to other leadership signals and frequencies. The Law of Leadership, as I call it, operates within a network system of frequencies, much like a wireless network that works best when it connects to a strong signal. Leadership is not as simple as climbing a ladder positioned against a wall made of people and then becoming the leader by reaching the top. Leadership is much more complex than that. Leadership is connecting to others, regardless of position, pay grade, or power, thereby achieving mutual beneficial outcomes for all parties. True leadership systems afford the opportunity for everyone to be the leader he or she was born to be.

2. **The Next Gen Leader Asks and Answers Tough Leadership Questions.**

In the competitive marketplace with overwhelming business complexities, the fundamental question that every organization is wrestling with is "How can we effectively solve complicated business problems?" The answer is simple but challenging to implement: you solve problems with leadership, which is why, when I consult, speak, train, and coach organizations on leadership, I repeatedly state, "Leadership is everything." All outputs, inputs, outcomes, opt-ins, and opt-outs are actions and decisions based on the good, the bad, and the ugly of leadership. Considering the complexity of the answer to the Fortune 500 question, "How Do You Measure Leadership?" the next question obviously becomes, "How can one create more leaders and expand leadership capabilities to solve complicated business challenges and problems more effectively and efficiently?" Perhaps a "twin" question in the minds of every person working in any organization is "How can I become a Leader of Significance and expand my leadership capabilities?"

3. **The Next Gen Leader Shares the Secret Success Formula for Effective Leadership.**

"Leadership" is the most commonly used term to describe desired actions one wants to see in solving a specific problem or challenge. Think about it. Whenever there is a problem in any organization, the first words out of anyone's mouth are usually, "How do we fix this?" People throw their hands in the air, look toward the sky, and cry out "Leadership!" In all my experiences, if leadership is not the solution, then it is the problem.

The problem is that many people refer to leadership as if it is some talent, special gift, or assigned command of power that only those with authority, position, or status have. The fact of the matter is that leadership is not any of those things. Leadership, simply put, can only be as good as its leaders. The good news is that all of these things I am describing are not gifts or talents, they are skills that exist in each of us and can be developed using a universal system that creates an environment where *everyone is a leader.*

4. **The Next Gen Leader Reveals Strategies to Overcome Politics in Leadership.**

A good example of leadership politics is what occurred in Washington, D.C., in 2012. From the wars in Iraq and Afghanistan, to the economic environment, loss of American jobs, deficient reduction debates in Congress, to the failure of the Super Committee and the Supreme Court's review of the constitutionality of the Health Care Reform Law, all eyes are on leadership.

The question being asked by everyone, regardless of party lines, is "Do we have the right leadership system in Washington?" Americans are questioning the leadership abilities of both Democrats and Republicans. For example, President Obama, a first-term president who inherited the worst economic environment since the Great Depression, record high unemployment rates, and the Iraq and Afghanistan wars, is being questioned about his leadership ability. His American citizenship and Harvard University education are often questioned. Regardless of his successes in stimulating the economy, resuscitating the auto industry, saving the financial industry from catastrophic collapse, and re-engineering America's healthcare, his leadership is continually questioned.

In addition to questioning the president's leadership, Americans are questioning the leadership of every elected official. According to the January 2014 Gallup polls (available on Gallup.com), Americans ranked their satisfaction with Congress at a mere 13 percent, and President Obama at 43 percent, respectively. There was one word that described their dissatisfaction in both polls: leadership. Both Democratic and Republican leaders argue that they are waiting for the other party to show leadership while problems continue to grow and go unsolved.

Sound familiar? In your organization and professional experience, how do "corporate theater" and "corporate politics" influence your leadership success or failure? Have you questioned someone's leadership? Has anyone ever questioned your leadership because of politics? If the media were granted access to your world, would people see parallels to the leadership behaviors in Washington? What would be your individual, team, and organizational leadership job approval rating by internal and external customers and suppliers when it comes to transformational leadership?

The observation I would like you to consider, as you draw your own conclusions from this example, is that leaders of High Significance do not allow politics to drive actions and decisions. That is what leaders of Low Significance do. They make decisions based on politics that implode the system of leadership, just like what is happening in Washington.

To address this highly relative issue, I have specifically dedicated a chapter in this book to dealing with the challenges of politics in the workplace and provided applicable strategies to help professional teams and organizations solve their political challenges.

5. **The Next Gen Leader Ignites Action to Pursue Leadership Growth Opportunities.**

The Washington, D.C. leadership complexity parallels and exists in every organization, whether for-profit or nonprofit entities. Leadership never escapes criticism. Often influential people are attacked because others are threatened by their potential.

Leadership is the number-one challenge in any and all organizations. According to leaders of Fortune 500 companies, as well as small businesses and organizations, leadership competencies are one of the biggest risks in any organization, yet 70 percent of organizations rate their leadership development efforts as ineffective, according to Development Dimensions International Inc.'s Global Leadership Forecast 2011.

I am amazed that with all of the leaders in Washington, D.C., it can be a single vote and the voice of the American people that creates true change. That same dynamic exists in your organization.

You, too, have the ability to pursue your leadership growth opportunities, but it will take a decision, a vote, and your voice to change your predicament, just as it does in Washington. It starts with believing in your potential and recognizing that you are a leader.

6. **The Next Gen Leader Provides a System to Maximize Leadership Potential.**

The good news: Leadership is a system that encompasses learnable skills. The bad news: Leadership is full of complexities—with confusing jargon that requires the development of a new baseline. I wrote this book to inspire you to your infinite greatness and to bring clarity on this topic. This system shares strategies and solutions for:

- Identifying and assessing leadership potential.
- Becoming a leader of significance.
- Creating a leadership culture to produce better leaders.
- Implementing a universal leadership system to convert followers to leaders.
- Measuring leadership success outcomes.

7. **The Next Gen Leader Provides a Leadership Assessment.**

To assist organizations, teams, and individuals on their journey, a leadership assessment is included in this book. In the assessment, leaders will learn the Six Leadership Network Applications, which will help them understand how their strengths, weaknesses, opportunities, and potential can make them better leaders.

It is essential for leaders, aspiring leaders, teams, and organizations to weave a universal leadership system into their culture, allowing their talent supply to self-assess routinely and create opportunities to operate in an environment that encourages them to pursue their full potential.

Because of business priorities, organizational theater, fear, intimidation, and a lack of confidence in the potential and abilities of others, much too often the cultural environment of organizations does not allow leaders to flourish, discover, or explore leadership qualities. Aspiring leaders can be stuck in the past or present with no avenues to pursue the future.

This assessment provides an opportunity, in a safe environment, to assess professionals' leadership aptitude and, through coaching principles, helps them develop a Fastforward Action Plan to maximize their leadership potential.

Summary of the Next Gen Leader

This Leadership System of applications and networks, if integrated within the culture, heart, mind, and actions of all, will create leaders—regardless of position, pay, or title—who produce extraordinary and transformational results. I am inspired to write this book for several reasons: First, to provide solutions to those career-limiting leadership challenges and difficulties we all face on a daily basis. Second, to inspire those who have made the courageous decision to maximize their potential, not be-cause of appointment but rather because of anointment. And, finally, to share success lessons, stories, and strategies in a coaching role to guide you and your organization through the journey of maximizing your true lead-ership potential.

Through *The Next Gen Leader*, you have access to a system that can bring extraordinary success and change your life!

To assist you along your journey, we have included a Leadership Aptitude Assessment in the next section to help you begin the process of assessing your current Leadership Network Aptitude. The assessment has helped many people discover their leadership aptitude, identify leadership growth areas, and operate on a leadership system that is shared and used by others. I look forward to receiving e-mails, letters, and phone calls from you and your teams as you take the journey to maximize your leadership potential.

I would encourage you to review the next section very carefully, un-derstand the material, and take about an hour to complete the assessment in a quiet place. You should reflect on your behavior, your actions, and the personality traits displayed to your peers, teams, and management in the workplace.

What's My Leadership Aptitude?

· · · · · · · · · · · · · · · · · ·

What Is the 6G Leadership Aptitude?

Like cell phones and tablets, we all operate on various leadership networks, as described in the previous pages. This four-step assessment process is designed to help you determine your leadership aptitude and assess capabilities, attitudinal intelligence, and skills to lead others. Our leadership aptitude, more often than not, is defined by others, based on their reaction to our leadership behaviors and actions—so much so that often you can literally predict how an individual will react to scenarios based on prior observations. Think about a person you know whom you have worked with for more than a year. If that person was asked to lead a challenging new project, initiative, or assignment, you could probably determine his behaviors, style, or strategies in leading the effort. This is the leadership network they operate on when working with others.

What if that person is you? Your ability to leverage your full leadership aptitude will determine your success or failure. The 6G Leadership Aptitude Assessment evaluates how you measure against the aptitude styles of a Genetic Leader, Generic Leader, Go-To Leader, Growth Leader, Gateway Leader, and Genius Leader.

The *What's My 6G Leadership Network Aptitude?* assessment provides you with an opportunity to increase your potential, performance, influence, and significance as a leader, helps you understand how your peers assess your leadership network bandwidth, and how your style manifests itself in leadership scenarios and opportunities.

To begin evaluation of your 6G Leadership Aptitude under the categories of 1G–Genetic Leader, 2G–Generic Leader, 3G–Go-To Leader, 4G–Growth Leader, 5G–Gateway Leader, and 6G–Genius Leader, follow the instructions on the next few pages.

Assessing Your 6G Leadership Network Aptitude

Step 1: Open your mind and eliminate all negative preconceived notions about yourself—5 minutes.

Step 2: Think about your leadership preferences and how you actually lead yourself and others—4 minutes.

Step 3: Make a decision to commit to answering each question with serenity—1 minute.

Step 4: Take the assessment in one sitting—25 minutes.

Assessment Guidelines and Ground Rules

For each leadership action presented on the Assessment Form, assign a total of 7 points by allocating points between the three behaviors you demonstrate most often. Use whole numbers. Your total must add up to 7 for each—no splitting hairs or using fractions, whole numbers only.

- Do not pre-read aptitude definitions in an effort to predetermine the scoring results.
- Respond to the questions on the 6G Leadership Aptitude Assessment Form.
- Self-calculate your total scores by category of 1G to 6G Leadership Aptitudes and enter the results on the Leadership Aptitude Results Scorecard.

Leadership Aptitude Assessment Form

Instructions: For each leadership action presented on the Assessment Form, assign a total of 7 points by allocating points between the three behaviors you demonstrate most often. Use whole numbers, no fractions. Your total must add up to 7 for each of the 20 listed behavior actions. (*Example:* _4_ *Focus on predetermined goals.* _1_ *Redefine success.* _2_ *Define scope. 4+1+2=7*)

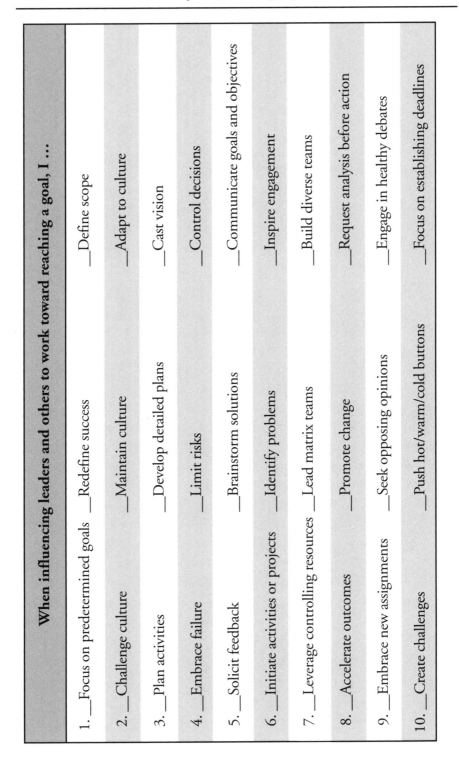

When influencing leaders and others to work toward reaching a goal, I ...

1. ___ Focus on predetermined goals ___ Redefine success ___ Define scope

2. ___ Challenge culture ___ Maintain culture ___ Adapt to culture

3. ___ Plan activities ___ Develop detailed plans ___ Cast vision

4. ___ Embrace failure ___ Limit risks ___ Control decisions

5. ___ Solicit feedback ___ Brainstorm solutions ___ Communicate goals and objectives

6. ___ Initiate activities or projects ___ Identify problems ___ Inspire engagement

7. ___ Leverage controlling resources ___ Lead matrix teams ___ Build diverse teams

8. ___ Accelerate outcomes ___ Promote change ___ Request analysis before action

9. ___ Embrace new assignments ___ Seek opposing opinions ___ Engage in healthy debates

10. ___ Create challenges ___ Push hot/warm/cold buttons ___ Focus on establishing deadlines

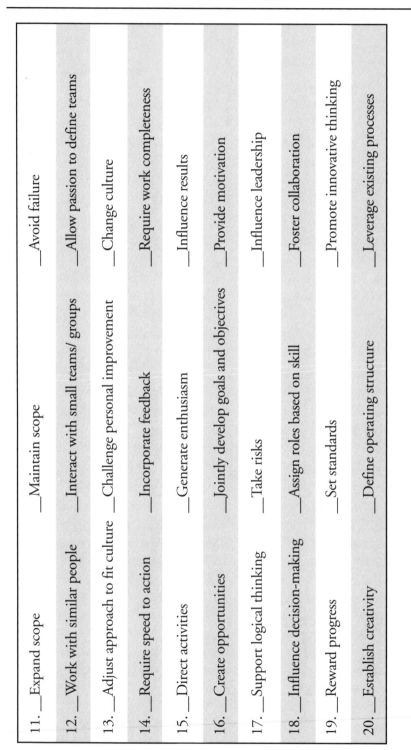

11. __ Expand scope   __ Maintain scope   __ Avoid failure

12. __ Work with similar people   __ Interact with small teams/ groups   __ Allow passion to define teams

13. __ Adjust approach to fit culture   __ Challenge personal improvement   __ Change culture

14. __ Require speed to action   __ Incorporate feedback   __ Require work completeness

15. __ Direct activities   __ Generate enthusiasm   __ Influence results

16. __ Create opportunities   __ Jointly develop goals and objectives   __ Provide motivation

17. __ Support logical thinking   __ Take risks   __ Influence leadership

18. __ Influence decision-making   __ Assign roles based on skill   __ Foster collaboration

19. __ Reward progress   __ Set standards   __ Promote innovative thinking

20. __ Establish creativity   __ Define operating structure   __ Leverage existing processes

EXAMPLE:

1. **1** Focus on predetermined goals   **5** Redefine success   **1** Define scope

2. **5** Challenge culture   **1** Maintain culture   **1** Adapt to culture

3. **1** Plan activities   **1** Develop detailed plans   **5** Cast vision

4. **4** Embrace failure   **2** Limit risks   **1** Control decisions

5. **3** Solicit feedback   **3** Brainstorm solutions   **1** Communicate goals and objectives

6. **5** Initiate activities or projects   **1** Identify problems   **4** Inspire engagement

7. **1** Leverage controlling resources   **1** Lead matrix teams   **5** Build diverse teams

8. **4** Accelerate outcomes   **2** Promote change   **1** Request analysis before action

9. **2** Embrace new assignments   **1** Seek opposing opinions   **4** Engage in healthy debates

10. **2** Create challenges   **1** Push hot/warm/cold buttons   **4** Focus on establishing deadlines

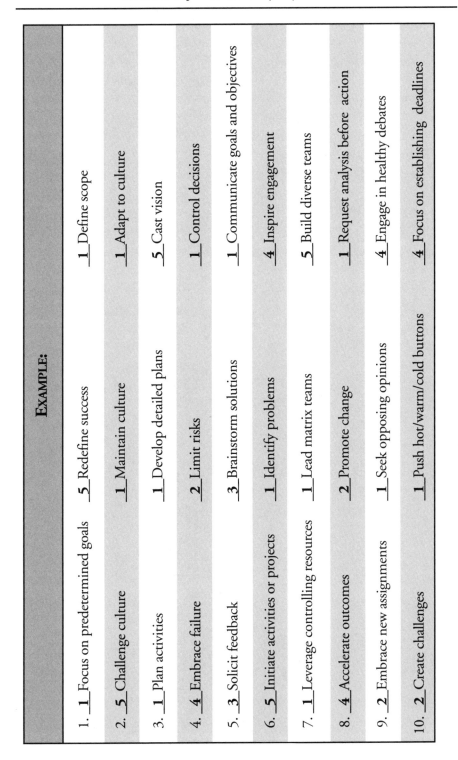

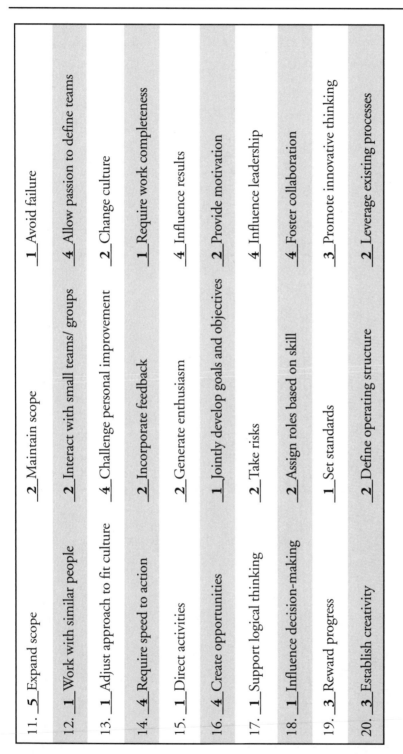

11.	**5** Expand scope	**2** Maintain scope	**1** Avoid failure
12.	**1** Work with similar people	**2** Interact with small teams/ groups	**4** Allow passion to define teams
13.	**1** Adjust approach to fit culture	**4** Challenge personal improvement	**2** Change culture
14.	**4** Require speed to action	**2** Incorporate feedback	**1** Require work completeness
15.	**1** Direct activities	**2** Generate enthusiasm	**4** Influence results
16.	**4** Create opportunities	**1** Jointly develop goals and objectives	**2** Provide motivation
17.	**1** Support logical thinking	**2** Take risks	**4** Influence leadership
18.	**1** Influence decision-making	**2** Assign roles based on skill	**4** Foster collaboration
19.	**3** Reward progress	**1** Set standards	**3** Promote innovative thinking
20.	**3** Establish creativity	**2** Define operating structure	**2** Leverage existing processes

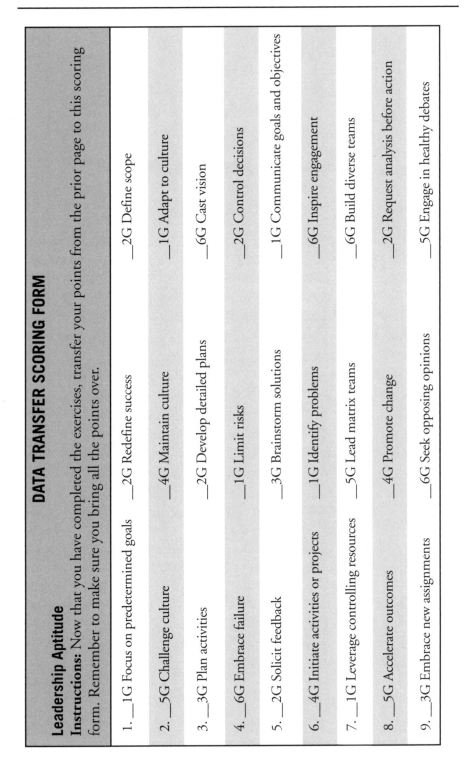

DATA TRANSFER SCORING FORM

Leadership Aptitude

Instructions: Now that you have completed the exercises, transfer your points from the prior page to this scoring form. Remember to make sure you bring all the points over.

1. ___1G Focus on predetermined goals   ___2G Redefine success   ___2G Define scope

2. ___5G Challenge culture   ___4G Maintain culture   ___1G Adapt to culture

3. ___3G Plan activities   ___2G Develop detailed plans   ___6G Cast vision

4. ___6G Embrace failure   ___1G Limit risks   ___2G Control decisions

5. ___2G Solicit feedback   ___3G Brainstorm solutions   ___1G Communicate goals and objectives

6. ___4G Initiate activities or projects   ___1G Identify problems   ___6G Inspire engagement

7. ___1G Leverage controlling resources   ___5G Lead matrix teams   ___6G Build diverse teams

8. ___5G Accelerate outcomes   ___4G Promote change   ___2G Request analysis before action

9. ___3G Embrace new assignments   ___6G Seek opposing opinions   ___5G Engage in healthy debates

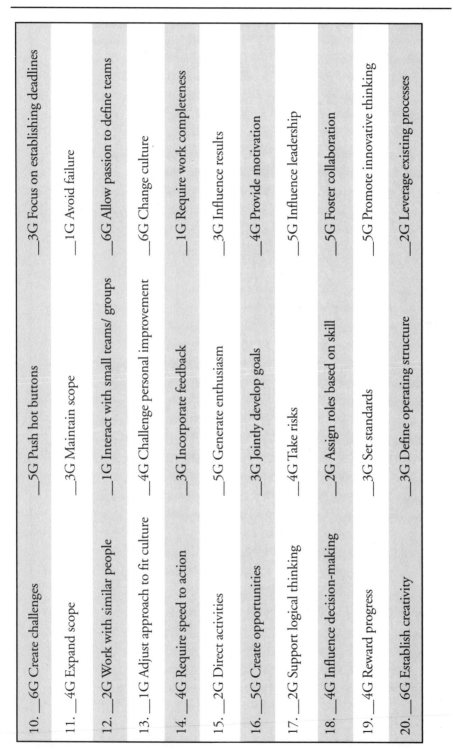

#			
10.	___6G Create challenges	___5G Push hot buttons	___3G Focus on establishing deadlines
11.	___4G Expand scope	___3G Maintain scope	___1G Avoid failure
12.	___2G Work with similar people	___1G Interact with small teams/ groups	___6G Allow passion to define teams
13.	___1G Adjust approach to fit culture	___4G Challenge personal improvement	___6G Change culture
14.	___4G Require speed to action	___3G Incorporate feedback	___1G Require work completeness
15.	___2G Direct activities	___5G Generate enthusiasm	___3G Influence results
16.	___5G Create opportunities	___3G Jointly develop goals	___4G Provide motivation
17.	___2G Support logical thinking	___4G Take risks	___5G Influence leadership
18.	___4G Influence decision-making	___2G Assign roles based on skill	___5G Foster collaboration
19.	___4G Reward progress	___3G Set standards	___5G Promote innovative thinking
20.	___6G Establish creativity	___3G Define operating structure	___2G Leverage existing processes

EXAMPLE:

1. **1** 1G Focus on predetermined goals	**5** 2G Redefine success	**1** 2G Define scope
2. **5** 5G Challenge culture	**1** 4G Maintain culture	**1** 1G Adapt to culture
3. **1** 3G Plan activities	**1** 2G Develop detailed plans	**5** 6G Cast vision
4. **4** 6G Embrace failure	**2** 1G Limit risks	**1** 2G Control decisions
5. **3** 2G Solicit feedback	**3** 3G Brainstorm solutions	**1** 1G Communicate goals and objectives
6. **2** 4G Initiate activities or projects	**1** 1G Identify problems	**4** 6G Inspire engagement
7. **1** 1G Leverage controlling resources	**1** 5G Lead matrix teams	**5** 6G Build diverse teams
8. **4** 5G Accelerate outcomes	**2** 4G Promote change	**1** 2G Request analysis before action
9. **2** 3G Embrace new assignments	**1** 6G Seek opposing opinions	**4** 5G Engage in healthy debates
10. **2** 6G Create challenges	**1** 5G Push hot buttons	**4** 3G Focus on establishing deadlines

11.	**5** 4G Expand scope	**2** 3G Maintain scope	**1** 1G Avoid failure
12.	**1** 2G Work with similar people	**2** 1G Interact with small teams/ groups	**4** 6G Allow passion to define teams
13.	**1** 1G Adjust approach to fit culture	**4** 4G Challenge personal improvement	**2** 6G Change culture
14.	**4** 4G Require speed to action	**2** 3G Incorporate feedback	**1** 1G Require work completeness
15.	**1** 2G Direct activities	**2** 5G Generate enthusiasm	**4** 3G Influence results
16.	**4** 5G Create opportunities	**1** 3G Jointly develop goals	**2** 4G Provide motivation
17.	**1** 2G Support logical thinking	**2** 4G Take risks	**4** 5G Influence leadership
18.	**1** 4G Influence decision-making	**2** 2G Assign roles based on skill	**4** 5G Foster collaboration
19.	**3** 4G Reward progress	**1** 3G Set standards	**3** 5G Promote innovative thinking
20.	**3** 6G Establish creativity	**2** 3G Define operating structure	**2** 2G Leverage existing processes

Leadership Aptitude Network Scorecard

Instructions: Using a calculator, add the points awarded for the behavioral actions identified as 1G, 2G, 3G, 4G, 5G, and 6G on the Scoring Form on page 47. Enter the sum totals in the Leadership Aptitude Results within the 6G Leadership System. The maximum score is 140 points when you total all Six Leadership Network categories; your results will range based on your leadership preferences identified. At the end of the process, you should have scores in each category. The score with the largest number is your dominant preferred leadership style; others are secondary based on the scoring results.

Translation of Your Scores into Leadership Meaning

Next is a short summary of definition and description of each leadership network from 1G to 6G. Enter your score as a reference point and review each description, paying particular attention to your scoring results. In upcoming chapters, we will go into greater detail on each network leadership style and application to help you to understand your current strength zone, provide strategies and solutions to grow to the next network, and create action plans to aid in maximizing potential.

The results of your aptitude leadership assessment can be summarized into four distinct leadership quadrants. The full 6G Leadership model lends a good visual of how this looks while also helping you compare your scores between leadership styles. Following is an example of how to fill in your assessment scores.

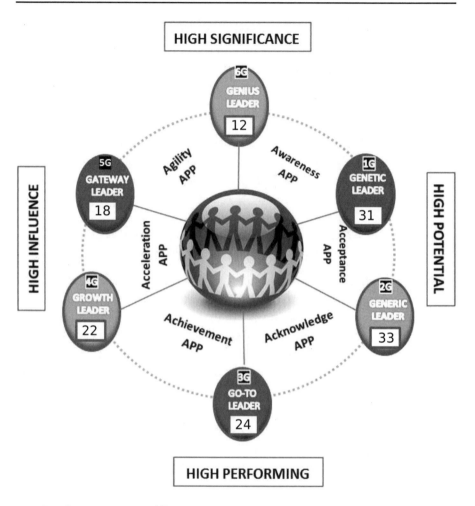

On the next page, fill in your scores on the model. After that, read a more detailed description of each leadership style. It might be a good idea to fill in your scores there, too, in order to keep them readily available.

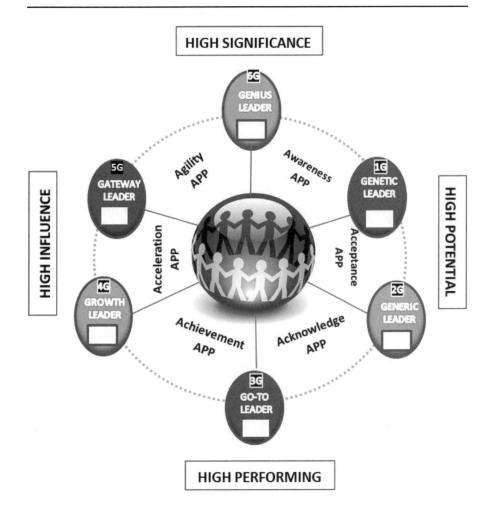

Genetic Leader: High Potential Leader, with awareness of ability to lead tasks and others. Leaders allow you to influence them because they see potential.

Awareness App: *Awareness* is an individual state of knowledge of leadership potential.

Generic Leader: High Potential Leader, with acceptance of ability to lead. Leaders allow you to influence them because you accept leadership.

Acceptance App: *Acceptance* is embracing leadership and others embracing you.

HIGH PERFORMING LEADER

Go-To Leader: High Performing, with the ability to lead others and produce a desired result. Leaders allow you to influence them because they acknowledge your results.

Acknowledgement App: *Acknowledgement* is others' recognition of your individual leadership accomplishments.

HIGH INFLUENTIAL LEADER

Growth Leader: High Influence, with the ability to drive and influence measurable business improvements. Leaders allow you to influence them because of consistent achievements in business performance growth.

Achievement App: *Achievement* is recognizing your business successes through leading others.

Gateway Leader: High Influence, with the ability to accelerate positive business results by influencing decisions. Leaders allow you to influence them because you create opportunities and accelerate change.

Acceleration App: *Acceleration* is creating success and wins while improving business processes and teams.

HIGH SIGNIFICANCE LEADER

Genius Leader: High Significance, with the ability to redefine success through vision, inspiration, and embracing failure. Leaders allow you to influence them because they respect your leadership ability and connect with you.

Agility App: *Agility* is achieving business, organizational, and professional outcomes.

Understanding the Results

As we have already established that everyone is a leader, more often than not, leaders use styles they have learned through observation or training, or have developed through time. As a result of taking this Leadership Aptitude Network Assessment, you should see your style correlated to a leadership network. For example, a Genetic Leader operates on a 1G Network. This assessment summarizes your leadership network and style preferences, as well as hindrances according to your scoring results based on a most-to-least point system within the Leadership Network categories.

Given the situation, these styles are often interchanged by leaders. As a result of successful or failed experiences, most leaders become comfortable with a style that provides the least resistance, strain, or work—the dominant style. To illustrate this, review your Leadership Aptitude Assessment and you will see that the style with the greatest number of points allocated is your dominant or preferred style of leadership. On the contrary, if you take a look at your results, you will also notice lower scores. These are styles that you often do not prefer, and may be an action-oriented behavior you treat not as a preference, but as a hindrance, in your dealings with people, therefore unconsciously or consciously relying on the dominant network.

In some cases, there are a few leaders who find themselves with a relatively even distribution of points throughout the Leadership Style Network, which simply means they use a variety of styles based on the leadership situation. This is completely outside the norm and is rare for someone to have mastered each network, but it is possible with enough practice and dedication to maximize potential.

More often than not, what I have found in my consulting, leadership experiences, and while presenting leadership strategies and solutions at conferences and events, is that most people find themselves consistently leading within their comfort zones. They rely on their most dominant style and network, even if it does not provide the value and results the other leadership networks offer. The downside here is that a person will not tap into his maximum potential. And weakness in leadership growth is directly linked to dependence on a dominant network.

Diagram 1 summarizes the maximum and least potential benefits of each of the defined leadership networks and styles.

• •

DIAGRAM 1: Summary of the 6G Leadership Network

1G–Genetic Leader

• Focuses on predetermined goals.

• Limits taking risks.

• Demands work completeness.

Maximum Potential—realized in a scenario with tight timeframes, structure, and predefined tasks.

Least Potential—created in an environment that requires flexibility, risk-taking, and working with large teams.

2G–Generic Leader

• Directs activities and assignments.

• Controls decision-making.

• Solicits feedback.

Maximum Potential—realized in routine complex situations requiring specialized knowledge or skill.

Least Potential—created in an environment that requires creativity, collaboration, and diverse teams.

3G–Go-To Leader

• Embraces new assignments and direction.

• Brainstorms solutions.

• Driven by deadlines and urgency.

Maximum Potential—realized in situations that require planning, structure, and setting standards.

Least Potential—created in a scenario that is routine, mundane, and unchallenging.

4G–Growth Leader

• Takes risks and influences decisions.

• Promotes change and delivers business results.

• Motivates and rewards success.

Maximum Potential—realized in scenarios requiring innovation, motivation, and transformation.

Least Potential—created in an environment that requires consistency and mediocre business goals.

5G–Gateway Leader

• Creates opportunities for improvement.

• Promotes innovative thinking.

• Challenges the culture and status quo.

Maximum Potential—realized in initiatives requiring accelerated outcomes and matrix team collaboration.

Least Potential—resides in situations with rudimentary activities structure, urgency, and complexity.

6G–Genius Leader

• Redefines boundaries of success.

• Embraces learning through failure.

• Changes culture through challenging leaders.

Maximum Potential—realized in scenarios requiring agility, extraordinary results, engagement, and visionary thinking.

Least Potential—created in situations that limit creativity, risk-taking, and agility.

• •

Applying the six applications will produce the above leadership profiles and the following outcomes for aspiring leaders:

• **Awareness**—Individual state of knowledge of leadership potential.

• **Acceptance**—Embrace leadership as others embrace you.

• **Acknowledgement**—Recognize others' leadership accomplishments.

• **Achievement**—Experience business successes through leading others.

• **Acceleration**—Create success while improving business processes and teams.

• **Agility**—Achieve business, organizational, and professional outcomes, simultaneously.

What's the Point?

Research supports that leadership aptitude can be best understood by evaluating the extent to which a leader's preferred behavior illuminates potential and performance based on a desire to achieve an outcome. Potential describes the degree to which leaders have the potential to lead—it evaluates their leadership awareness. Performance describes the aptitude for a leader to accept accountability for achieving results.

The message is simple. To be effective, influential, and significant, leaders need to be able to navigate and operate on all 1G through 6G Leadership Networks. Regardless of your results on the Leadership Aptitude Assessment, the fact is, you are a leader! The same is true in your leadership role in your organization; regardless of power, position, or pay, you are a leader! The bottom line is that you fall somewhere on the Leadership System Network, and my goal is to help you get better.

Before you advance to future chapters, I'd like you to think about your scoring results. Regardless of how you scored in each Leadership Network or Style category, make it a goal to find ways you can improve on all Leadership Networks.

We will go into much more detail in the upcoming chapters on each Network Leadership Style and the application to help you understand your current strength zone, provide strategies and solutions to grow to the next network, and create action plans to aid in maximizing potential.

But before we do that, let's talk a little about leadership—the good, the bad, and the ugly.

It is important that in Part II of this book, you fully recognize and understand that you were born to lead. Embracing this section is foundational to becoming the genius leader you were born to be.

Part 2

You Were Born to Lead!

The Truth About Leadership

• • • • • • • • • • • • • • • • •

What Is Leadership?

To truly understand leadership, let's break it into small, understandable parts. When you look at the word *leadership*, what do you see?

If you were to ask The Leadership Institute at Harvard University (one of my partnering organizations) what the word *leadership* means, they would define it as the skill of motivating, guiding, and empowering a team toward a socially responsible vision. The *American Heritage Dictionary* defines leadership as 1) The office or position of a leader; 2) Capacity to lead; 3) A group of leaders; 4) Providing guidance and direction.

The definitions are general in nature, however, my definition and what I envision as leadership is slightly different from both good definitions. As a leadership practitioner, coach, consultant and tranformationalist, I envision and define leadership in three words and in three separate parts.

First, as I asked previously, what do you envision when you see the word *leadership*? I recognize that there are four distinct words with similar meanings but different impacts that make up the word *leadership*. The words I see in leadership are: **lead**ership, **leader**ship, **leaders**hip, and **leadership**.

To understand leadership, we must first break down and define each word separately. Most traditional and institutional universities do not take that into account when defining or explaining this most complicated business term. To be clear on definitions, let's take a few moments to clarify each of the terms, one by one.

First, the word *lead* is defined as: 1) To show the way by going in advance; 2) To direct the performance of activities; 3) To serve as a conduit; 4) To have charge of.

Second, the word *leader(s)* is defined as: 1) A person who leads or guides; 2) One who is in charge of others; 3) One who has influence or power over others; 4) A person who has commanding authority or influence.

And finally, as defined earlier, *leadership* is: 1) The office or position of a leader; 2) Capacity to lead; 3) A group of leaders; 4) The act of providing guidance and direction.

As you review the definitions, how do you picture yourself in your work, family, or social settings? Consider the following questions:

- Do you show others the way?
- Are you in charge or do you take charge of others?
- Do you create things (i.e. events, work products, meetings, assignments)?
- Within your being, do you have the capacity to lead?
- In some shape or form, do you have influence or authority over others?
- Do people look to you for guidance and direction?

If you answered "yes" to any of these questions, welcome to leadership. That's right—you are, by default, a leader. You were born with the ability to do all those things noted above.

Leadership Is 3D

Here is how I know you are a leader. Leadership is three-dimensional, just as you are. There are three parts to humans: the mind, the body, and the soul, all working together to produce one you. That is how leadership works.

If you examine closely the four words *lead, leader, leaders,* and *leadership*, you'll see that each word is contingent on the other. If you really think about it, leadership is the composite output of the definitions of *lead*ership, *leader*ship, *leaders*hip, and *leadership*. Simply put: 1) Leadership is only as good as an organization's *leaders*, 2) the leaders of the organization can only be as good as their current *leader*, and 3) a leader is only as effective as their ability to *lead* others, beginning with him or herself. So the message is simple: leadership starts with the leader in you! If there is no leader, there are no leaders. If there are no leaders, then leadership does not exist.

To have leadership, you have to be aware that regardless of rank, power, status, or pay, you are a leader. If a child can be a leader, so can you!

Daddy, Am I a Leader?

One of the most beautiful things in the world is to be a parent. Little children love you no matter how you look, how old you are, or what your job is—they just love you!

I'm the husband of a beautiful wife and the father of two lovely children, Journee, 12, and Jalen, 10. There isn't enough time in the day for me to tell you all the things I have learned from my children, but I will share with you one thing I recently learned from my son, Jalen, about true leadership.

A few weeks ago, my son came home from school. I was in my office with the doors closed, writing the outline for this book. Now you must understand our house rules. There are 10 rules that we have communicated to our children that they must follow.

Rob Mac's Rules of the House

1. Wash your hands before you go into the refrigerator!
2. Don't play on the furniture!
3. Say "excuse me" before you interrupt a conversation!
4. Ask permission before going outside!
5. Be inside the house before it gets dark!
6. Clean up after yourself!
7. If you're not using a light, turn it off!
8. Never drink the last swallow of anything!
9. No running in the house!
10. Knock before you enter a room!

Just like most parents, we are serious about the 10 rules. But for some reason, our children are not. Even though we constantly remind them of the rules, it amazes me how much they teach us when they break them.

On the first day of school, he barged into my office, immediately breaking the 10th rule. He threw his book bag on the floor and screamed at the top of his lungs, "Dad, you won't believe this. I'm a leader!"

Jalen went on to tell me that his third-grade teacher, Mrs. Jefferson, asked if there were three volunteers in the class interested in being classroom and hallway leaders. There was complete silence. Nobody moved a muscle. When nobody raised a hand to volunteer, his teacher looked at him and asked, "Do you want to be a leader?"

"Yes, I'll be a leader," my son replied.

Then the teacher looked at another child and asked the same question, trying to get more children to participate, "Do you want to be a leader?" she asked a child named Kevin.

Kevin was shy, shook his head "no," and put his head on his desk.

Then a child across the classroom screamed, "I'll be a leader!" And then another child. And then another. As the children saw others raising their hands, they all began to raise their hands. "I'll be a leader," they all jumped and screamed as loud as they could to get Ms. Jefferson's attention.

As Ms. Jefferson got control of the room, one child asked, "How can we all be leaders?"

"Everybody is a leader, and we will just take turns," Jalen answered. The kids screamed for joy at the top of their little lungs.

That day I learned four truths about leadership from my son:

1. Leadership is a choice.
2. Leadership is exciting.
3. Everybody is a leader.
4. Be leaders, not followers. It's a lot more fun being a leader than a follower.

Leadership Is a Choice

In today's workforce, there are questions asked every day, such as, "Who wants to be a leader?" Although this may go unsaid and unwritten, this is asked every day by associations, agencies, and companies around the world. Why? Because organizations are looking for true leaders at every level to step up into their natural leadership roles. Sometimes that requires volunteering to be leaders.

Simply put, *leadership is a choice.* My son's story illustrates that there were choices related to leadership given by the teacher to the children in her class. They could decide to be leaders or not to be leaders. It was as simple as that. One child even made the conscious choice not to be a leader.

Offices and cubicles are filled with both people who choose to lead and those who choose not to lead. That same choice is given to us each day as we live our personal and professional lives. Will we lead or will we choose not to lead?

True leadership does not start with the acquisition of power, position, or pay. It starts with the conscious choice to be a leader. If you are a professional, an aspiring leader, or already a leader, I would ask you to step up into your natural leadership potential by accepting leadership each day. If no one formally asks you to be a leader, then volunteer to be a leader. If people do not accept your volunteerism to lead, lead anyway. Remember—as my son's lesson taught us—*leadership is a choice*, not a position.

Leadership Is Exciting

When you make a conscious choice to lead, leadership can be an exciting place. It is where the action is. Leading others is exhilarating for both the leader and the people being led. Because of the excitement and positive energy that the first few children displayed to Ms. Jefferson, more children volunteered to be leaders.

Leadership should be exciting to all of us. To be excited about leadership requires a positive attitude. None of the children displayed a negative attitude about leadership; leadership was exciting to them. They saw leadership as a reward—inclusive and fun.

As professionals, we must have the same perspective about leadership that those children had. Often, professionals view leadership in a negative way, using the terms "areas of responsibility," "everything is on my shoulders," and most commonly, "the buck stops here" to describe leadership. These adjectives are depressing, rather than exciting, to non-ego leaders; however, these same adjectives somehow make leaders with egos feel validated and important.

Leaders have to be excited about leadership. No one wants to associate with leaders who are not excited about the journey they are leading. Remember, leaders should see leadership as an opportunity to influence actions and outcomes, a gift of help and inspiration, and a reward to share with others, placing egos aside. That is an exciting place to be!

Everybody Is a Leader; Take Turns Doing It

What does true leadership look like in action? Envision everybody in your organization leading and taking turns doing it. That is true leadership and what those third-graders envisioned leadership to be. They were 100 percent right. After that lesson, my son added rule #11 to our list of house rules: *Everybody is a leader; take turns doing it!*

The lesson my son and his third-grade class taught me is ever so valuable and has changed my outlook on leadership and life. If you think about it, there are similarities in a classroom setting that consist of a leader (the teacher) leading leaders (the students). In the professional workplace, a leadership system is critical to the success of professionals and organizations. In the third-grade classroom situation, there were many volunteers. Quite frankly, professional organizations need more volunteer leaders.

More often than not, the leaders you find in the workplace are appointed. It is the appointed leaders who often have responsibility for the issues, challenges, and complexities found in the operation of the business. Those issues, complexities, and challenges exist primarily for two reasons: a lack of leaders and too many followers who watch, wait, and debate before taking action. For example, have you ever witnessed someone respond to a requested action or decision to solving an issue say, "That's above my pay grade! I don't have authority to provide feedback on that! I don't make those calls. Let me check with my boss first."?

Don't get me wrong. It is not that all appointed leaders are bad. The fact is there simply are not enough people stepping up to take their natural place in leadership. *Leadership is a choice*, and there is always the option to volunteer if no one has been appointed.

This begs the question, "Why are there more followers than leaders in the workplace?"

There are experts in the field who have written millions of best-selling books on the subject of leadership, and they often refer to leaders having followers. "Leaders lead followers and followers follow the leader" is their philosophy. The majority of books are predicated on how to get more people to "follow you"—in essence, how leaders can make more followers.

I believe it is that mindset that has created what I refer to as the "Organizational Followership" dilemma. "Organizational Followership"—a term I have coined—is the situation that occurs in an organization when there are more people training to become followers than leaders. Think about your organization for a second. How many people would you classify as followers? How many as leaders? When I consult and speak to organizations, I often use the 80-10-10 illustration to explain this phenomenon.

With respect to percentages of leaders and followers, organizations typically consist of 80 percent followers, 10 percent leaders, and the remaining 10 percent are neither followers nor leaders. They are on the sidelines watching the game; they're the bystanders. They stand by idly and watch things happen.

So, if you have more followers than leaders, you are in an Organization of Followership. If you have more leaders than followers, you are in an Organization of Leadership. Which environment are you operating in?

The followership system, mindset, and organizational design are outdated and invalid. Here is what is wrong with the followership traditional system of management: as a leadership futurist and thought leader in the new economy, I predict that followers will become obsolete and extinct, replaced by automation, expert systems or (as I refer to them) *smart cubicles*. *Smart cubes* will be the old sitting locations of employees who formerly reported to work and followed a leader's every command without exercising thought, ideas, or judgment; future "followers" will be replaced by expert and intelligent systems doing the work of humans.

A recent study by a well-known institute predicts that in the near future, humans will be replaced in the workplace by smart computers. Logically, if there are no thoughts, ideas, or judgments required on an assignment or work product, then a computer, drone, or robot could accomplish the same thing faster, better, and cheaper. Remember, computers were designed with the intent of reducing the dependence on human assets, so the best position you can be in is in the mindset of a leader, not a follower.

Organizations and professionals that do not adjust and introduce an all-inclusive leadership system—where everyone is empowered to lead—and take turns doing it, will likely be out of business, and you'll be out of a job. Organizations and professionals must shift from a followership system to a pure leadership system due to the competitive economy, business complexities, and industry challenges. It all starts with believing you are a leader and empowering others to become the same.

Think of it this way. If 27 nine-year-olds on their first day of third grade can figure out they are leaders and not followers, what is stopping professionals and adults from realizing the same thing and stepping into their maximum potential as leaders?

I'd like to suggest that what is stopping them is tradition—an archaic leadership model that maintains order and, at the same time, restrains morale, growth, and business performance. Many of us are waiting to be appointed to lead rather than recognizing our anointment to lead. I want you and your organization to have a nontraditional system that creates the flexibility for everyone to be a leader.

I challenge you as you read this book to begin asking yourself, your team, and your organization if you are leading from your leadership potential. Are you allowing others to lead, and are you taking turns leading others? If you are an aspiring leader, I'd ask that you start leading today and wait for the appointment to come tomorrow.

That's how leadership works. Leadership is opportunity. You start leading where leadership is needed. Eventually someone will recognize your value, and opportunity will find you.

Leadership Opportunities Are Dressed in Overalls and Look Like Work

Several years ago, I attended a C-level meeting with Fortune 500 executives wrestling with significant challenges and issues resulting from heightened market pressures, regulatory changes, and overwhelming business complexities. In attendance were people in various roles and positions of authority, including CAEs, CEOs, CFOs, COOs, senior vice presidents, vice presidents, executives and directors with responsibilities for sales, operations, finance, marketing, information technology, communications, and strategic planning functions.

Once a year, the brightest minds in the organization gather to discuss their most challenging, complex business issues. As the meeting progressed, each person outlined his concerns and views on the organization's most complicated issues. It became clear that the attendees of the meeting could not resolve the issues by themselves; they would need an infusion of new leadership blood to assist in solving them.

As the meeting unfolded, I realized that those people not in attendance would be challenged and tasked to solve the complicated organizational problems uncovered by these leaders. As each issue arose, the discussion quickly morphed into defining issues and identifying ownership of those issues. A facilitator began capturing the unique challenges and business uncertainties on a flip chart in front of the room. He transcribed the issues, action items, and next steps, as discussed by the vocal C-level executives.

As the meeting progressed, the facilitator listed the most significant issues brought to light in the four-hour meeting. There were approximately 10 issues on the flip chart. The chart was organized into columns: the left column—issues; the middle column—challenges; the right column—actions steps; and the far right column—ownership of the issues.

The facilitator summarized the meeting. All parties agreed on the issues, actionable next steps, and the persons identified in the column of "issue ownership" as accountable for solving the problems listed. The funniest thing was that none of the owners listed on the matrix were present in the meeting. How interesting....

The meeting was viewed as another success. The participants began exiting the room, expressing how well they thought the meeting went. They commented on the process, effectiveness, and value of spending time tackling and talking about the tough issues. One participant described the meeting results by stating, "Confronting issues and assigning ownership are the keys to our success."

Returning to my office, I wondered why similar complex business issues and themes arose or resurfaced, year after year. I also wondered why similar themes and issues reoccurred in other organizations and companies as well, causing the creation of an "issues resolution day"—a day set aside for leaders to inventory and assign others to solve complex problems and issues. I envisioned a matrix that identified the issues, "the keys to our success," as one participant described them. I realized that the keys to success had become the keys to our failures.

The truth is, those issues identified by the leaders that day were issues that had escalated and now required attention. True leadership, strong leadership, network leadership resolves issues before they become problems. Our leadership system failed. Those in the trenches did not operate in their natural leadership potential, and leaders did not create an environment of empowerment for aspiring leaders to step up into their infinite greatness. It was clear that, in order for resolution of those problems to be realized, leaders would have to become more aware and create solutions. Professionals, regardless of level, would have to step into their true leadership potential to become decision-makers and influence organizational success.

I realized that the issues and risks identified in the meeting did not leave the meeting anchored to a leadership system; the issues left the meeting tied to an ownership system. As a result, what were thought to be the keys to success inadvertently became barriers to discovering leadership; they allowed an ownership system to get in the way of igniting a leadership system.

In today's complex business environment, business challenges and issues are so significant that ownership is never enough to resolve or transform them into solutions. It requires leadership in each and every one of us.

Leadership competencies are the biggest risk in any organization. How often have you attended a meeting when most of the time was spent on understanding an issue and identifying issue ownership, never focusing on solving the problem? How many meetings have you attended that focused on developing a leadership system to address business issues at their roots?

Some may say I am arguing semantics—*ownership* is often confused with *leadership*. *Ownership* recognizes an individual's acknowledgement of a problem and, hopefully, the necessary commitment to tactically resolving the matter. *Leadership*, on the other hand, is influencing decisions and directions, and initiating changes associated with a problem, regardless of ownership, responsibility, or authority. Leadership can result in the creation of innovative solutions through others, turning a problem into a future capability or opportunity. The key to success is not found in finding an "owner" of an issue; success is found in identifying a "leader" to resolve the issue.

Summary

That day, the executives adjourned their meeting assigning issue ownership, failing to take advantage of the leadership opportunity. The name of the company described is not important, but I will tell you that on that day I was the meeting facilitator. Based on my work in this field of leadership and maximizing potential, it is clear that this dilemma plagues small, medium, and large organizations all across the world.

Leadership is the number-one capability gap in talent supply, and more than 70 percent of organizations rate their leadership development efforts as ineffective, according to the 2011 Global Leadership Forecast Study. This explains why the same industry challenges and issues resurface year after year.

To take advantage of opportunities to grow and develop leaders, organizations must create an environment where *leadership is a choice, leadership is exciting, everybody is a leader,* and *leaders convert followers to leaders.*

Here are the Seven Leadership House Rules of Engagement that you, your team, and your organization can apply in your daily actions to build leadership behaviors and a system that maximizes potential. Hang this in the lunchroom, break room, or water-cooler area.

The Seven Leadership House Rules of Engagement

1. Everybody is a leader!
2. Be a leader, not a follower!
3. Act first, then ask!
4. Choose to lead.
5. Seek growth opportunities.
6. Leadership is always greater than ownership.
7. Leadership is 3D = lead, leader, leaders.

Now that we have talked leadership, let's talk potential.

Let's Talk Potential

● ● ● ● ● ● ● ● ● ● ● ● ● ● ● ●

Now that we have defined leadership, let's talk potential. As we have discussed, in order to reach the expectations of leadership, it is important to recognize your potential.

Potential is something that every human being uses each day to survive and succeed. Some of us use a lot, and some use a little. The amount used determines our aptitude of success.

A professional athlete—whether a football, baseball, or basketball player—uses his potential—made up of mind, body, and soul—to compete against opposing teams consisting of players with just as much potential. So it is with leaders in the workforce. Leadership potential is the driving force and deciding factor on who comes out on top. The best way to guarantee victory in any athletic or business competition is to maximize potential. In order to maximize it, you have to believe you have it and release it! This chapter is designed to help you do just that.

There are many books on the subject of maximizing potential. Through the years, I have observed that very few scholars, professors, or business consultants tackle the definition of *potential* in a way that is applicable in our professional and personal lives. This chapter will help you define what potential means to you, what you envision your maximum potential to be, and give you insights on how to maximize it.

Potential has several meanings. It can be defined, according to The Free Dictionary, as 1) Possible, as opposed to actual; 2) Capable of being or becoming; 3) A latent excellence or ability that may or may not be in use or fully developed.

As starters, based on that definition, let me ask you a few basic questions: What is your leadership potential? What inherent ability in you is latent, untapped, or marginalized? What opportunities and leadership qualities do you possess that can be released to the world in the form of actions?

Here is what I believe. I believe we are all born with the potential to be extraordinary in our professional and personal lives. Each of us is gifted with the greatness to achieve the desires of our heart. We have the potential of the Creator. In fact, the Creator has told us we are cut in His image like a diamond from a rock. To give you a picture of our potential, consider the script of life that says, "Then God said, 'Let us make man in our image, in our likeness.'" (Gen. 1:26–27 NIV). This means that our potential is made in the likeness and image of God! Our souls are wells of infinite greatness, but in order to realize greatness, we must have the courage to pump our well.

Pump the Well of Potential

Too often, many of us fail to fully utilize our natural resources to realize life's possibilities. The natural resource I am referring to is the natural resource of potential. Potential is like a well that never goes dry. The trick is understanding how it operates, learning how to pump it, and, of course, eventually releasing water through it. Rather than pumping the well and slowly drawing water, we would rather buy bottled water because it appears to be cleaner, faster, and more accessible. The operative word is "appears." However, if we took the time to pump from our well of potential, we would find that it is so plentiful that there are not enough water bottles to contain it.

Being a country boy, spending the summers down south in Hallsboro, N.C., I know a little bit about wells. I remember a recent story about two brothers in their 40s, their wives, and their children between the ages of 6 and 13, working on a farm. You see, with fall coming, they had driven that morning about 60 miles from home, in no man's land, to pick crops on a farm they rented to grow their own food. It was a family activity that they could all enjoy, experiencing the process of growing their own food. This was their first time picking the harvest they planted several months ago.

They arrived at the farm and worked for about an hour picking tomatoes, peas, and butter beans, and placing them in buckets. A 6-year-old cried out, "I'm thirsty." As they continued to work, the child called out again, "Mama, I'm thirsty."

The mother looked at the child. "When I was your age, we didn't get water until we finished, and sometimes two days passed before we got water."

Then one of the men said, "And it wasn't a bottle of water, either. We had to walk three miles and drink from a well!"

"What's a well?" the child replied. They all laughed.

The mother then asked one of the older children to go to the car and get a bottle of water for the 6-year-old. The older child was picking vegetables and listening to Jay-Z on his iPhone and didn't hear his mother. So much for family bonding!

She went to the minivan, looked in the trunk and saw about 30 empty water bottles in a bag. "Where is the water for everyone?" she yelled. "And why are all these empty water bottles in the trunk?"

Everybody looked at the older child who was still listening to Jay-Z. His father walked up to him, pulled his ear-buds out, and said, "Where are the water bottles I asked you to put in the car?"

"In the car where you asked me to put them, Dad."

"Well, all the water bottles are empty," said the dad.

"You asked me to put *water bottles* in the car, you never said anything about *bottles of water*." The teenager had placed the recycling bag of empty water bottles in the car rather than the new box of water the father had just purchased at Sam's Club.

Not saying a word, the father looked at his son, placed the buds back in his ears and poured the bucket of butter beans over his head, calling him a bean-head as he walked away.

Frantic, the mother yelled, "We don't have any water?"

The children started crying and screaming. One of the children yelled, "We are going to die from 'thirstvation.'"

"We are only 60 miles from home, and you won't die if you don't have water for two hours or so," the older brother said, trying to calm the situation. His statement did not help matters. It only made the children cry louder.

Looking around for a solution, one of the men remembered that about 300 yards back was a well in the middle of the field. Two men grabbed the bag of empty water bottles and headed for the well.

After they caught their breath from the sprint to the well, one of the men grabbed the pump handle and started pumping as fast as he could. The other brother placed a water bottle under the well spout.

Five minutes passed and the man pumping the well was drenched in sweat. "I don't believe there is any water in here," he said.

"Yes, there is. Keep pumping," the second man yelled. A few more minutes passed, and the pumping became slower and slower. "Let me pump. If you stop, the water will drop back to the bottom."

Shoving each other out of the way, they switched positions, one pumping while the other held the empty water bottle under the spout. With the heat beating down on them, exhaustion set in. As they continued unsuccessfully to try and pump water out of the old well, a man in his 80s appeared, joined by the rest of their families. "You'll die out here before you get any water out of that well pumping like that," he said.

From the bag of empty bottles, the old man pulled out a bottle that had about two ounces of water in it. He instructed the brother to pump faster. As they pumped, the children and family started to yell, "Pump, pump, pump," repeatedly.

Encouraged, they started pumping faster and faster. With everyone looking on, the older gentleman poured the bottle of water into the well. In an instant came a gushing stream of water. When the bottles were filled, and everyone had as much as they could drink, the brothers looked at the old man and asked, "How did you do that?

And the wise old man said, "You have to prime the pump! To get something out, you have to be willing to put something in."

Isn't it amazing that a few ounces of water can produce more water than you'll ever need? Potential works just like that. Your potential is like a well of unlimited water. In order to reach your maximum potential, you have to know the well exists, understand how to prime it, then release it by priming the pump.

We all have a well of potential within us. But often it is not fully tapped because of our limited ability to recognize our well of potential and our ability to release it to the world. How are you maximizing your well of potential?

I'm going to share with you a strategy to help you pump and prime your well so that you can reach your maximum potential.

Pump Your Well of Potential

First, to reach your well of maximum potential, you must start pumping. You must start pumping your mind with positive thoughts about your abilities. With all of the negative feedback we receive on a daily basis, we have to make a conscience effort to remind ourselves that within each of us exists an untapped well of infinite potential.

To tap into our potential, we sometimes need to just pump ourselves up, reminding ourselves that we can do all things through the potential that resides in us. Like the experience the farm family had with the well, if you don't pump, then you don't drink. I like how the script of life puts it: "He that does not work does not eat."

The pumping of your potential is based on your degree of confidence and faith in your untapped abilities. As with a well, just because you can't see the water does not mean it does not exist. In order to tap into your potential, you have to begin pumping what you want out of it. Potential is based on how hard and how much you are willing to pump to get the results you desire. The key is to start pumping today, and tomorrow you will overflow with potential.

Prime Your Well of Potential

Second, you must prime your well of potential. A well, which is another name for a water table, is based on a system of underground streams, rivers, and undercurrents that create an open source of water. Similarly, our well of potential is based on our abilities and skills, and it grows and develops within each of us.

In order to retrieve our potential from the well and release it to the world, we are required to make the decision to use our God-given potential in all we do. Confidence, skill, information, and positive proclamations will multiply potential. Fear, complacency, negative thoughts, and non-productive environments will reduce potential. What you put into your well of potential is what you will get out of it. That is called "priming the well."

Leadership Potential Pre-Exercise

Ask yourself the following questions:

- How are you pumping your well of potential?
- How would you better prime your well of potential?
- List in detail how several of your closest colleagues, friends, or family members view your well of potential.

Maximize Your Potential

Potential is something inherent in each of us. At the same time, it is something we can build, grow, and develop, which makes it really cool. It is our secret weapon, but most of us do not fully utilize it.

The fact is that no one can control your potential but you. No one can release your potential but you. No one can grow your potential but you. I love the saying, "Anything worth doing poorly is worth doing until you can learn to do it well." That is how leadership potential works. You work at it until you learn how to do it well.

From a leadership standpoint, I like to think of potential as both a horizontal and vertical diagram resembling a cross, as portrayed next. The horizontal axis from left to right is a measure of your current leadership ability and skills compared to what your maximum potential truly is. The vertical axis is the measure of your absolute belief in your leadership potential.

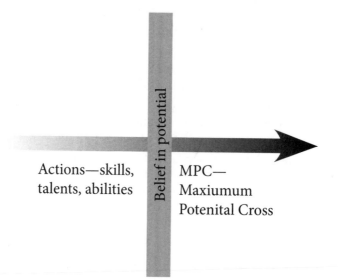

Actions—skills, talents, abilities

Belief in potential

MPC—
Maxiumum
Potenital Cross

Both the "belief in potential" axis and the "skills, talents, and abilities" axis produce both current and maximum potential. To explain further, the realization of your skills, talents, and abilities directly correlate to the level of belief you have in your leadership potential. For example, if you demonstrate a low usage of your innate talents, abilities, and skills, your leadership potential will be low. But if you demonstrate high usage of your innate talents, abilities, and skills, your leadership potential will be high!

Similarly, the vertical axis, the level of belief you have in your potential, impacts the release of talents, skills, and abilities as it relates to leadership. If you have a low degree of belief in your potential, then you will release less of your innate skills, talents, and abilities, resulting in low realization of your maximum leadership potential. However, if you have a high degree of belief in your potential on the vertical axis, then you will spread more of your leadership skills, talents, and abilities across the horizontal axis.

Most theorists, intuitionalists, and motivational experts suggest that reaching your maximum potential requires you to reach the top of your game. Most people picture potential as an image of an individual with an imaginary level on him, usually at a peak, marked in bold words, *"Your Maximum Leadership Potential Is Here."*

Theoretically, this makes sense. However, in reaching your maximum potential, there is no top level to reach because potential is infinite and immeasurably great! The goal is not to reach a maximum potential level but to enter the maximum potential zone. To reach that zone, you need to work from both the horizontal and vertical positions on the Maximum Potential Cross Axis, with your goal being not to reach the top but to reach the intersection of both the vertical axis (our belief in our potential), and the horizontal axis (the utilization of our skills, talents, and abilities). Once these two elements intersect at the center of the Maximum Potential Cross Axis, we begin to maximize our results.

When speaking, coaching, and consulting with professionals and organizations, I define potential as "the inherent ability or capacity for excellence, growth, development, or coming into being with a possible goal, desire, or aspiration." I also communicate that there are two types of mindsets: the *mindset of impossibility* and the *mindset of potential*.

It blew me away when I came to truly understand this definition, along with the script of life. It forced me to confront those people who taught me the mindset of impossibility as a child and as an adult.

Have you ever shared with someone a dream, aspiration, or goal, only to hear a list of reasons why your aspirations are impossible to achieve? That is a person with a mindset of impossibility. I can't tell you the number of times I have heard children, teenagers, adults, and elders use the word "impossible" when responding to someone sharing dreams, aspirations, or desires. This term is deadly. It cuts, derails, and marginalizes potential. If we look at the word *impossibility*, it is the complete opposite of the word *potential*.

Impossibility, according to Dictionary.com is defined as 1) Not possible, unable to be, exist or happen; 2) Unable to be done, performed, or effected; 3) Incapable of becoming true; 4) Not to be done, endured, with any degree of reason or propriety; 5) Utterly impracticable.

I know how a mindset of impossibility can impact a person negatively. How do I know, you may ask? Well, because I didn't always think with a mindset of potential. Through the years in my personal and professional life, I have been in the presence of a lot of people who operated in a *mindset of impossibility*. Because of that, up to age 30, I didn't push myself to extreme limits to try to discover my well of potential. I thought I didn't have a drop of potential, let alone a well. Just like many others, I was conditioned to think I wasn't smart enough, good enough, or charismatic enough to be a successful leader or professional. Why? Because I had a lot of people—including supervisors, leaders, friends, family members, as well as myself—telling me that my aspirations, dreams, and goals were impossible to achieve.

Let me tell you what that mindset did. It produced fear that left me mentally paralyzed to aspire, dream, or believe in my potential. It paralyzed my inherent skills, abilities, and talents. My Maximum Potential Cross was virtually untapped because I let others' beliefs in my abilities become my reality. Impossibility is a dream killer, a journey destroyer, and a weight on the soul that can anchor you to the ground, never to rise again, if you allow it.

I cannot begin to tell you the number of times I was told by elementary, middle, and high-school teachers and even college professors that I did not have the potential, talent, skills, or ability to be successful in school or college, let alone Corporate America.

In elementary school, my fourth-grade teacher suggested that my parents place me in special education and move me back one grade because of a speech impediment and my difficulties learning to read and write. Because my parents refused to place me in special education and hold me back, the teacher reacted negatively to prove a point, often requiring me to read aloud in the classroom. My classmates snickered while I struggled with reading difficult words. I had a tendency to look up when I concentrated to pronounce a word that I didn't recognize.

I remember it as if was yesterday—the teacher yelling at me in front of the class. "I don't know why you are looking in the air," she said. "God isn't going to help you." All of the children burst out laughing.

When she called on me the following day, I told myself that I wasn't even going to try to pronounce challenging words. She had killed my belief in my own potential. I decided if she called on me to read, I would read aloud, but when I got to a word I didn't recognize, I would improvise by ad-libbing the story. Within minutes of beginning to read aloud, I got to a sentence of words I could not pronounce, then started to ad-lib. As the teacher and the other children read along, they quickly realized I was adding my own words, creating a new story.

When I finished with the story, *Goldilocks and the Three Bears*, they were in a homeless shelter. The children roared with laughter, and I was sent to the principal's office. It was then that I fell in love with making people laugh by telling stories.

The next day, I raised my hand to read. The teacher saw my hand, looked the other way, and called on other children. I remember she sometimes asked for volunteers to read and my hand would be the only hand raised; she would ignore it and call on others who did not volunteer to read. She had a mindset of impossibility that caused me to become disinterested in learning. I guess she didn't want to take the risk and hear my creative storytelling, either.

In my senior year of high school, I remember deciding to fill out college applications. Because of my low belief in my potential, skills, and abilities, my grades were average. My teachers did not see potential in me, and they made that clear.

Just a drop of belief in my potential pushed me to consider going to college. I went to both my English teacher, Ms. Hamilton, and guidance counselor for help in filling out the college application, only to have them both look at me with pity and tell me that I did not have the potential for college. They told me that no college would accept me, and that I should sign up for trade school.

What I didn't realize was that they were looking at my grades and the results of my PSAT score. When they were reviewing my results, I overheard one of them say, "You get 500 just for filling in your name on the test; he only got 515."

Little did they know that I did not read one question on the test. Because I was affected by a mindset of impossibility, I simply marked all the answers "C" and handed in my test.

I did not encounter a wise coach or influential figure who untapped the well of potential in my life. There was no principal or teacher who took me under his wing. Rather, I was often thrown under the bus. I was left to figure it out alone, just like you may be doing right now. But one day I heard a voice, an inner voice saying, "You are going to be great!" It was a combination of the voices of my parents and close family members.

One thing I did have was a set of old-school parents and a family that sat me down each time others rejected my potential. They reinforced their belief in me by simply uttering the words, "You can do better than that. There is greatness in you!" It was at that point when I began to discover this well called potential.

Somehow, some way, a college did accept me. Throughout college, I had more professors, friends, and classmates with mindsets of impossibility than I had with mindsets of potential. I vividly remember each of my professors talking about the complexities and challenges of being successful in Corporate America as an African-American. I remember asking myself, "How would they know if they never worked in Corporate America? And if they were so good, why are they here teaching what in effect they have never done?" I would discover later that they had mindsets of impossibility. Because of their own failures, it was difficult for them to help anyone else succeed.

Many of my classmates' only purpose for attending college was to graduate and get a job. And many of them were successful in doing just that—getting a job.

But the true question is, "Are you maximizing your potential? Does your job pump and prime your well of potential, or does it minimize your potential, causing your well to run dry?"

I know what it is like being in a position that minimizes potential. Graduating college with a 3.2 GPA, I began working for a CPA firm performing foreclosure audits under a contract with the U.S. Department of Housing and Urban Development. After nine months of traveling all over the United States uncovering foreclosure errors charged to the government by mortgage lenders, I realized I was just going through the motions of fulfilling a job description for a paycheck, rather than pumping and priming my well of potential.

I had an epiphany and believed I could do far more than the company allowed me to do. I believed I could be promoted into leadership and ultimately become the CEO of that company. Nobody convinced me that I could achieve this; nobody said to me that it was possible; nobody put the idea in my head. It was my personal belief in my potential—that inner voice. The problem was that my supervisors, coworkers, and peers did not see it that way.

I shared this with a few of my peers and was again met with the mindset of impossibility. What a mistake. Some of the questions and comments launched by my peers and leaders were:

- Who would make you a CEO?
- You just got here and you think you can get promoted above us?
- Do you think you are better than we are?
- He is really too ambitious for his age!
- Who does he think he is?

Although I was never promoted beyond the staff level I was hired for, internally I believed I had the potential to be a leader. Because they didn't see the leadership potential in me, I resigned and went to another organization that viewed me through a different lens. I learned that sometimes in order to become a leader, one must remove himself from toxic positions.

During my lifetime, I have constantly run into this mindset of impossibility. And I have discovered that there are two types of people: those who operate in the mindset of potential and those who operate in the mindset of impossibility. Here is the difference. (It is big and wide, but I will make it short.) People who operate in the mindset of potential grow and people who operate in the mindset of impossibility become stagnate.

Operating in the mindset of potential provides an almighty current that roars with greatness into your life, freeing you from despair and unleashing you into the waves of possibility. Potential allowed my wings to open and for me to soar under the current of hope!

Here is what a mindset of potential will do for you. It will allow you to overcome those things that appear to be insurmountable. Potential will allow you to accomplish those things that others can't imagine or dream of. For example, when I set out to become a speaker, author, and leadership coach to help others maximize their potential, countless people (i.e., friends, family, coworkers, bosses, and associates) stated:

- You can't become an author.
- Why would you want to help others become better? So they can take your job?
- You can't become a motivational speaker. You don't have experience.
- What makes you think you're an expert?
- You don't have the potential to train and grow others.
- Nobody is going to buy your books.
- You are pretending to be someone you are not.

All of these statements came from people who had a mindset of impossibility. My good friends and mentors, Simon T. Bailey and Willie Jolley, and others, including my father, mother, and wife, are people with mindsets of potential and balance the negative mindset with the following statements:

- You can become an author. Just start writing!
- You should help others get better. It will make your life easier!
- You have more than enough experience to be a motivational speaker!
- You're an expert because you are unique!
- You have more potential than you are aware of!
- Everybody will buy your book!
- You are becoming the person you were created to be!
- You are going to be great!
- Your best days are ahead of you!

And the same is true for you. Your potential is designed to take you anywhere you want to go. You just have to fuel it with a positive mindset.

The mindset of potential will give you the ability to do anything you set your mind to, including maximizing your potential and becoming a great leader. Potential is the desire that defeats fear and the fire that ignites action. Once you discover the mindset of potential, you will recognize your potential to be a leader of infinite greatness in both your professional and personal life.

Pumping and priming your well of potential is the secret to your success. That is what was and still is behind my success as one of the few successful minority C-level leaders for the largest healthcare contract in the world, the federal employee program. Believe it or not, after I accepted the position offered, my previous boss told me I had no idea what I was getting into, and that I did not have the potential or experience to be successful.

Five years later, not only was I a successful leader but also became a successful thought leader, speaker, coach, and author on leadership. I bet Ms. Hamilton and my elementary-school teacher are rolling over in their graves, saying, "Robert McMillan, an author and speaker?" They miscalculated my success by looking at my past performance instead of my future potential.

It is amazing what happens when you pour a few ounces of water, sweat, and tears into your well of potential.

That same well of potential is available to you, but you have to have the mindset of potential to release it! Here are several mindset potential affirmations and action strategies to help you realize and maximize your true leadership potential. Each morning when you open your eyes, repeat each affirmation three times before going to the next affirmation:

- I am a leader.
- There is greatness within me.
- Each day is an opportunity to become better than I was yesterday.
- Within every failure is a hidden opportunity.
- I have a well of potential that never runs dry.
- Leadership is action.

- I control my destiny.
- Negative comments feed my aspirations.
- I can soar on wings like eagles.
- Everybody is a leader.

Leadership Is All About Connecting

● ● ● ● ● ● ● ● ● ● ● ● ● ● ● ● ●

As I mentioned, there are positives and negatives in leadership. The positive part of leadership can be found when you work with good people in a good culture producing a good connection. The negative part of leadership is when you are a good person who has to maneuver and navigate around bad people in a bad culture that, in turn, creates a bad connection.

If you don't know what I mean by "good leadership connections" and "bad leadership connections," and have never had the joyous opportunity to work in both environments, let me give you a few real-life examples with practical learning points.

Bad Leadership Connections

I am a true transformationalist and do not want to be negative, but I am also a practical realist and a leader in Corporate America. When it comes to motivating others, I don't believe you can put sugar on poison and call it sugar cane.

I don't want to start sugarcoating leadership to get you to swallow the medicine that may help you temporarily but will eventually cause your career to die a slow death. So to ensure that you reach your maximum potential, I will do the opposite—point out the poison that can kill your career. To do that, I am going to give it to you straight with no chaser—bad people, mixed with bad cultures, produce bad leadership connections, which can make leadership suck!

There it is—the naked truth that leadership can suck when you have to deal with these elements. A lack of trust and truthfulness, and self-interests, can cause leadership to have a bad connection that no one wants to connect to or embrace.

Sometime ago in my role as a leader for a Fortune 1000 company, I met with a former colleague and friend who had recently transitioned to a new organization. Tom was a person I had known for about five years and previously had the privilege of working with. As a result of job realignment, Tom and I would meet and exchange advice on how to survive in a culture of bad leadership connections.

Bad leadership connections are made up of leaders who use and leverage others to attain compensation, bonuses, and recognition goals that are tied to their performance plan and the organizational scorecard. What is wrong with that, you may ask? Well, to begin with, their decisions and actions are not based on a desire to grow others while growing the business. Their motive is to grow the business at the detriment and expense of others. This is a bad leadership connection.

As I met with Tom over dinner, he expressed that he had a great relationship with the new C-level executive who would be taking over a division of the organization I reported under. Tom had worked with this leader in the past and thought very highly of him. He described how he knew the new leader and how he thought I could build a stronger relationship with him. Tom described how close they were and how they continue to meet routinely; they shared the same values and perspectives about leadership. He also mentioned that this person was a personal mentor and coach of his and was the reason behind much of his success.

A few days later, the person we were talking about, the new C-level leader of the division, attended a meeting I was also invited to. As the meeting progressed, the new C-level executive began to ask all of the meeting attendees to tell him all of the issues they had with a particular organization we received support services from. He wanted to communicate the areas they could improve on during an upcoming strategy and operational meeting with that division's president.

After collecting that information, he asked for a complete list of all of the negative concerns the attendees had with how the services were provided, specifically by the senior vice president who provided the services to our division.

As he opened the floor up for comments, many people who appeared to have a good relationship with that senior vice president began to make negative and unprofessional comments about him. The C-level executive threw gas on the fire with his own commentary and asked for specific examples of concerns raised.

He gathered several pages of negative feedback from those who provided comments. A few people tried to make positive comments, only to be cut off. He never inquired about the positive values or benefits the person and the organization provided. Clearly this was a witch-hunt.

The C-level executive met with the division's president and presented his invalidated listing of all of the negative concerns and issues collected in an attempt to assassinate the senior vice president's character. Within 24 hours, that senior vice president was raked through the coals and told his position was in jeopardy if he did not change the perceptions of the division.

That senior vice president was my friend Tom. To this day, I still can't believe that Tom viewed this person as a peer, colleague, mentor, and friend.

It turns out that this all happened because of leadership insecurity and envy. Tom was promoted to senior vice president over the C-level executive, who had also interviewed for the position. Because of his insecurities and job envy, he set out to destroy Tom's career via sabotage.

After a series of other events, many people began following negative leadership styles and behaviors, attempting to climb the so-called "leadership ladder." Distrust, envy, jealousy, and a lack of respect immediately became the fabric of the culture. An organization consisting of backstabbing, infighting, and turf wars was born because of countless bad leadership connections throughout the organization.

Good Leadership Connections

Good leadership connections are found in organizations that put people ahead of the achievement of organizational or personal goals. Don't get me wrong: it's not that personal and organizational goals are not important, but good leaders recognize that attaining goals cannot be achieved at the expense or detriment of others.

Early in my career, there was a particular company that nobody wanted to work for. I asked a friend who worked for the company how it was to work there. His response was, "If you work here, you better wear a sweat-suit."

I asked why and he replied, "Because it is a sweatshop." The organization was branded by its own employees as a "professional sweatshop."

A sweatshop is an organization that uses its resources to achieve a goal, then fires those resources after burnout or when the goal is obtained, then hires new resources to achieve the same goals. This is similar to the consulting model where firms hire talent for a particular contract or project at a fixed rate and require the talent to work overtime at that fixed rate to achieve a desired project goal and outcome. Once the goals and outcomes are reached, the project is over and so is the future use of the resources leveraged to achieve the goals.

Today's professionals view "sweatshops" as organizations, departments, and divisions headed by leaders who make considerable compensation but require employees to work long hours to achieve the organization's goals in exchange for fixed wages and low rewards. How many people do you know who work for leaders of departments or organizations that operate like this? This is another example of what a bad leadership connecting organization looks like.

A good leadership connecting organization operates in the exact opposite way. Good leaders engage employees to define goals, they promote and recognize their employees once the goal is obtained, they share in positive financial and social recognition, and they invest and retain resources to achieve future goals. Good leadership connecting organizations, teams, and leaders take considerable amounts of time and effort to ensure that employees are operating in the optimal work environment, have clear roles and goals, and are provided a work-life balance to limit attrition, morale erosion, and talent depreciation.

You can usually spot a good leadership connecting organization when you have the following occur on a routine basis, which can be quantifiably measured:

- Low employee saturation.
- Low attrition.
- Low termination.
- Low waste, errors, and defects.
- Low distrust and infighting.
- High employee satisfaction.
- High leadership conversions.
- High quality and outcomes.

- High customer satisfaction.
- High profits.

Consider the following:

- How do you stand with your boss, colleagues, teammates, and peers? What would they say about you if what was said was sworn to secrecy?
- How would you assess the type of environment you are in? Are you in good or bad connecting leadership organizations? Explain why you feel the way you do.
- What behaviors do you demonstrate that influence perceptions of you?
- Have you had a 360-degree assessment done on you, and what was the feedback?

Tom's situation can happen to any person regardless of position, pay, or title. The root cause of this type of dilemma in the workplace is called "bad leadership connections." The objective of this chapter is to provide solutions for this dilemma.

People with the objective of "self-survival" at the expense of others produce a toxic culture that not only destroys professionals' careers, but also causes the implosion of organizations and teams. The "Survivor Leadership System" from the TV show *Survivor*, adopted by many professionals, does not work in business because of one thing: ultimate success is not based on a single individual winning and taking home all the recognition; it is based on a single individual helping others to win. Reward and recognition are given based on team accomplishments, not the accomplishments of a single individual.

Achieving a desired outcome at the expense and detriment of others is not the essence of true leadership.

If you really want to understand and control your organization's leadership, consider using what I have developed—the 90° FeedForward System over the 360-degree feedback tool, which is currently used by many organizations.

90° FeedForward!

Have you ever wondered why the 360-degree feedback survey is so named? Probably because after you spend time administering it, getting feedback, and analyzing the results and understanding what they mean, you end up in the same spot where you started. You end up going in a complete loop that evaluates past performance rather than future potential.

Another flawed term used by traditionalists is "feedback," which is often used to describe constructive criticism. The message and process takes a person backward rather than forward. Constructive criticism is still criticism and is rarely accepted as positive.

For centuries, psychologists have done studies on strategic methods to influence desired behaviors in humans. It is scientifically proven that the best time to correct or reward behavior is in the present rather than in the past. If you correct a child a week after a behavior was observed, child psychologists will tell you it is highly unlikely that the child would be able to relate the correction to a particular behavior in the past. The same holds true for recognition of positive behavior. After too much time has gone by, the acknowledgement—whether negative or positive—becomes ineffective.

Similarly, a 360-degree feedback survey released greater than 360 days after performance was observed is highly unlikely to provide reliable, valuable, and practical information for a professional to leverage in maximizing leadership potential. The potential must be observed, analyzed and coached in real time and not 360 days later.

Can you imagine any professional athlete not being evaluated day by day, week by week, game by game but being evaluated 360 and 360 days after a game? What's wrong with that picture? It does not give the professional athlete the opportunity to maximize his potential in the present moment. A professional athlete would be making the same mistakes in practices, scrimmages, and games if corrective action and communication of the desired behavior or action were not done in the present moment. As a result of the one-year performance evaluation and use of the 360-degree feedback tool, many employees are making the same mistakes hour after hour, day after day, month after month. If feedback is given at all, it is provided a year after performance and communicated backward in time rather than forward to the future. This is why 360-degre feedback tools don't help you maximize your potential, but minimize it instead.

In order to provide valuable information about a professional's future and potential, the term should be changed from "feedback "to "feedforward," and 360-degree feedback to 90° FeedForward.

Why 90° rather than 360 degrees? It's simple. Most companies who use the 360-degree process go back in time about a year, dust off the 360 feedback evaluation and send it out to people who have worked with you more than 360 days before evaluating how you performed. Also, 360 degrees is a complete circle. I do not believe we want our professionals to be going in circles when it comes to performance and growth. The direction we want them to go is 90° North—up in growth and in development.

I am not sure about you, but I can't remember exactly what I ate or wore 360 days ago, and I am unlikely to recall an individual's performance vividly enough to provide performance feedback. So simply put, 360 degrees looks backward rather than looking forward toward future potential.

In coming chapters, you will find a brief 90° FeedForward System you can you use in real time to provide a cultural reading of your organization and the perceptions associated with your leadership skills. In addition, this system provides you with transparent and professional questions that allow others to not only analyze your performance but, more importantly, to help you define actionable steps for maximizing your potential in the future through the FeedForward process.

Circle of Life Apps

• • • • • • • • • • • • • • • •

Finding Life Balance

Before you can truly maximize your leadership potential, you must have universal balance in your life. If your Universal Faith, Moral Purpose, Intellect, Self-Awareness, Relationships, and Wealth Life Applications are out of balance, chances are your professional life is as well. That imbalance will minimize your leadership potential rather than maximize it.

Life can be hectic, confusing, tempting, chaotic, painful, and sometimes just downright boring. But maximizing your potential can change your life. With the right applications, information, and systems, life can become prosperous, exciting, joyful, and a complete blast.

In early 2001, a company's leadership team set out to do something that had never been done. They bet on potential and not performance. They decided to just go for it. About 11 years ago, this company decided to make four investments that planted the seeds for their 21st-century success story.

The four investments were spread across research and development, market exploration, and product development, during a time when companies were getting out of the technology sector because of the hi-tech bust. The company's "potential" investments were made at a time when the company's stock value was at an all-time low, around $10 a share. There was much skepticism about their leadership from the media, shareholders, and investors. Only a few leadership visionaries held true to the potential envisioned.

The company entered the retail market when other technology companies were exiting. They invested substantially in online music content and music stores. In addition, the company created a unique operating system.

Today, the company's market value is $421 billion, and its share price has soared. Remember that 11 years ago it was at an all-time low of $10 a share with a dismal market cap. If you haven't figured it out yet, the company I am referring to is the legacy of Steve Jobs, Apple Inc. Their investments more than 11 years ago resulted in today's generation of iPods, iPads, and iPhones. What makes Apple's success authentic and unique is their creative ability to integrate the necessities of life into technology.

As the famous psychologist Abraham Maslow illustrated through many of his works, humans have several hierarchical needs that must be fulfilled in order to live. Those needs consist of:

- Physiological.
- Security.
- Social.
- Esteem.
- Self-Actualization.

Apple, through its iPhone and iPad products, has been able to assist in providing four out of the five hierarchical needs to its customers, resulting in phenomenal success: a sense of security and protection from danger; the ability to communicate on any social media; feeling value and recognizing others by way of photo and information sharing; and fulfilling the self-actualization need of accessing information based on desire. The only thing the iPhone is not is a shelter, even though some people are so enamored of their iPhone that they go into an anti-social shell, blocking out all others.

It is clear that Apple's success did not come overnight. From its humble beginnings in the 1970s, it took the organization more than 42 years to reach its true potential in 2012, redefining success in the smart-device technology industry.

Humans vs. iPhones

Of all of the products that Apple produces, we as human beings resemble the iPhone the most. The iPhone has the ability to operate on any network, it has memory and data storage, operates on an operating system, processes information, communicates with other devices, and has more than 10,000 applications that can be accessed on demand. I don't know about you, but that sounds awfully close to what a human being is. We are like iPhones but much better; there is no technology that compares to the human brain.

In terms of processing power, it is estimated that the human brain's processing power is about 100 million MIPS (million instructions per second). The brain's memory capacity is estimated to be about 750 gigabytes. An Apple MacBook Pro has 2.4GHz processing speed and a computer hard drive of 750 gigabytes. Simply put, the brain is like a 168,000 MHz Pentium computer. In fact, brain capability is estimated to be 10 times greater than these numbers, because muscle movement, body regulation, unconscious processing, and many other functions are not mathematically calculated into the equation. As humans, we have the ability to do everything and more than an iPhone or computer can do. But like computers and smart devices, we require maintenance, upgrades, and sometimes deprogramming in order to maximize our potential.

Maximizing your potential requires what I call the Life App System, which consists of six applications similar to those on iPhone and tablets. I discovered its importance while pursuing a career that was not pursuing me. The secret is that we all have applications embedded in us, and we must master and maintain them in order to reach extraordinary success in our lives.

Like Apple's story, life's successes do not happen overnight. There are no overnight success stories, just stories written by people who just discovered the success you have been working on for years. There is no secret sauce or magical recipe to success. It takes time and patience. But if you are willing to apply the six Life Apps I will share with you, you can increase your value to others, achieve extraordinary success, and influence organizational growth while living a life of significance. Just as professionals and leaders work hard to achieve organizational goals, that same effort must be applied to achieving success in each application in your life. If you truly desire to maximize your God-given potential, you must evaluate how you are applying the Life App System. You must also become aware that God designed you to be a system of excellence and, in order to realize your true potential, you must optimize the use of your life applications.

You must decide that you control your destiny and that your destiny is contingent upon monitoring, evaluating, and upgrading your life applications based on what you aspire to become. I encourage you to look at each application and assess:

- How do the applications manifest themselves in your life?
- Are there areas you can improve on by applying the applications?
- What life viruses are bogging down your potential?

Evaluating your life and determining if you are maximizing your potential can be a daunting exercise. But if you honestly look for application failures, viruses, and inoperability, you can replace them with application upgrades that will make your life more successful, healthy, and extraordinary. Your initial discomfort and pain are valuable in this exercise. Just as in athletics, if there are muscles you haven't used for some time, you will initially experience some discomfort and pain on your way to becoming stronger and faster. With this exercise, that same discomfort and pain will produce both short-term and long-term values, rewards, and benefits that can be sustained throughout your life.

Today, I challenge you to evaluate your performance and invite you to explore maximizing your potential using the Life Apps System:

- **Universal Faith App**
- **Moral Purpose App**
- **Intellect App** (Mind)
- **Self-Awareness App**
- **Relationships App** (Family, Friends, and Associates)
- **Wealth App** (Finance & Health)

Universal Faith App: How are you doing in terms of viewing the world? Do you see the world as an open field or a maze that traps you in a box? How you view the universe is the essence of you. The core of your potential is based on abundance, not on a limited view of life. Are you universally connected to those who have a different value system, belief, spirituality, or religion than you have? Oftentimes, diversity provides the answers to complicated questions, issues, life challenges, and mysteries that will never be discovered if we only operate in our comfortable environment.

To truly get the maximum out of life's experiences, we must operate in a universal faith that offers us similar truths. Are you satisfied with your journey in life? What universal truths can you adopt to live a spirit-driven life that navigates you to reach your destiny?

Operating in a universal faith takes dedication, utilization, and solidity of principles that connect your mind, heart, and soul with the universe. By applying the application of universal faith to your daily actions, your potential will be aligned with your destiny.

Moral Purpose App: What drives you to take action to achieve a specific outcome? How does that outcome influence the growth, development, or sustaining of mankind? It is not only essential to have a purpose-driven life; it is critical to align purpose with morality. Does your current career fulfill a moral objective or assist in helping others? Does it leave the world a better place for the next generation?

Each of us is born to achieve a specific mission, objective, and goal. It is my belief that our missions, objectives, and goals are strategically aligned with moral purpose. Discovering a new technology or drug that extends life, solving world hunger, and creating solutions that solve social problems are all examples of a purpose-driven life that also issues a moral challenge to others. It is my belief that humans are placed on this earth to solve problems. If that were not the case, how else would we occupy our time?

How are you anchored to a moral purpose in your life? Are you on the planet to make a difference, or are you only here to drink up all the water and eat up all the food along your journey? I would invite you to attach yourself to a moral purpose that is bigger than you are. It will give you satisfaction and gratification in pursuing a mission, goal, and objective. You will live a life of excitement and gratitude, and build a legacy for others to follow.

Intellect App: Intellect is the fuel for the mind. What you feed the mind resembles what you will get out of it. Have you ever listened to a catchy song for the first time and could not get it out of your head? The song would play over and over in your head as if you had downloaded it into your mind. Guess what? That is exactly what you did. When you listened to it, your brain downloaded it so that you could unconsciously recall the lyrics, beat, and voice as if it were playing.

How does this happen, you ask? Neurological brain waves—information or data you allow into your mind—will influence your actions, thoughts, and decisions. All actions in the past, present, and future will be based on data points, observations, and information you allow into your mind.

The Intellect App is the most important application, because your thoughts determine your actions, and your actions determine your future. Family members, friends, colleagues, and associates influence your thoughts and mindset. If they are negative people, you will have negative thoughts and actions by default. Conversely, if they are positive people, you will have positive thoughts and actions.

If you want to have an exceptional future, you have to center yourself around positive thoughts, information, and people. What you feed your mind today will determine your future tomorrow. Use this Intellect App to upgrade your thoughts so you can reach your maximum potential.

Self-Awareness App: What motivates, intrigues, and excites you? What frustrates, bores, and hinders you? How do others' behaviors and actions influence your thoughts and feelings? What events, actions, and activities make you happy or sad? How do you adjust or respond to a discouraging chain of events that may occur in your life? This all boils down to your complete understanding of you: how you respond to conflict; how you react to personal challenges; and how others' behaviors, actions, and agendas impact you, both mentally and physically.

Understanding what makes you tick can influence your understanding of why you exist. I believe there are four categories of self-aware people. There are those that:

- Category 1—Know their gifts, talents, and skills, but struggle to discover their purpose in life.
- Category 2—Have discovered their purpose in life but are trying to uncover their gifts, talents, and skills in order to accomplish their purpose.
- Category 3—Are lost in the journey of the discovery process with an undetermined purpose and unused gifts, talents, and skills.
- Category 4—Live a fully self-aware life with purpose and potential.

People can have a career that is not aligned with their potential or purpose in life—a very good career at that. For example, when you solve problems and challenges at work, do you get a sense of satisfaction? When you are at work, do you dream about things you aspire to do or be? If that is the case, chances are you have fallen into categories 1–3.

Most people fall within those categories. Very few people are fully aware of their purpose and potential, such as those in category 4. Here's a free downloadable app for you: It is not up to your family, friends, supervisor, or human resources department to put you in a position to discover your purpose and potential. It is up to you to become self-aware of your likes, dislikes, strengths, and weaknesses. Once determined, strategically place yourself in a position to realize your purpose and maximize your potential.

When was the last time you saw yourself as a financial report and read that report? How many assets have you created in your life? How many liabilities resulted from the decisions you made regarding your purpose and potential? How many hours a day have you allocated for discovering or living your purpose? How many days a week have you invested in discovering or building your potential talents, gifts, and skills? How many products have your actions produced that energized, excited, and engaged you? Evaluate your career, be self-aware of your purpose and potential, and become your own life strategist.

Relationships App (Family, Friends, and Associates): Family, friends, associates, colleagues, and even pets are all relationships that we have to simultaneously manage. You would think that these relationships could be ranked in order of importance. Do you know that there are some people who love their pet more than a sister, brother, mother, friend or child? Or someone who may love a best friend or colleague more than a family member? How much time do you spend showing any of these people how much you care about them? How often do you get together with them? Do you let your workload dictate how much time you spend nurturing relationships? The right relationships are critical; they are the lifeline that allows you to maxime your purpose and potential.

The key to setting relationship priority is in understanding how these relationships align with your purpose and potential. Those relationships that align, you continue to develop. Those that do not, you learn to let go. Many people do not maximize their purpose or potential in life because they do not have a Relationship App to help them distinguish between those people in their lives who are helping them reach their maximum potential and purpose, as opposed to those who are hindering their progress. The message is simple: you have to decide whom you save or delete from your application!

Wealth App (Spiritual, Health, and Financial): How are you doing financially and health-wise? Wealth is contingent on spiritual, health, and financial solvency. Solvent is defined as 1) something that solves and explains, and 2) a substance that dissolves another to form a solution. Simply put, the solution to achieving wealth is having spiritual health and financial solvency!

We are spirit beings. If you are not connected to the spiritual aspects of life, then you cannot connect to others. To honor and respect human beings is a critical component of wealth. Having spiritual wealth is the ability to value others and to recognize their differences and beliefs without devaluing them. Are you pleased with the accomplishments of others? Do you rejoice when they are victorious? Do you help them aspire to be more, do more, and achieve more? Are you joyfully pursuing your destiny? When people interact with you, do you brighten their day? How many people can come to you to recharge?

If you produce this type of energy, the universe will bend to you and re-project that same energy. But if you project negativity, confusion, and a spirit of dismay, that too will come to pass. Be spiritually wealthy and align your mind, hands, and feet with the purpose and potential in your heart.

How do you feel health-wise? Are you maintaining your body in a way that maximizes your potential? Your body is the vessel that stores your talents, gifts, and skills—your potential. Are you getting enough rest and exercise to overcome life's challenges? Have you stimulated your mind with books, articles, and theories to assist you in overcoming doubt, fear, and mindsets of impossibility?

I worked for a healthcare company for 10 years. One day I sat in my car in the parking lot and watched the professionals come and go from the building. By their appearance, you would not think these people worked in the healthcare industry. Most people in healthcare do not get regular checkups, do not exercise, and do not consume foods recommended by the American Heart Association. Why? Because they are normal Americans who just happen to work in healthcare. As a friend said, "We like pizza and junk food, too!"

The fact is that health must be your top priority. If it is not, you can forget about wealth because you won't have the health to acquire or enjoy it! I am so fortunate that I did a health risk assessment when I worked for this healthcare company. My assessment categorized me in the borderline danger zone in every category: blood pressure, cholesterol, obesity, etc. I had to take action if I wanted to have a strong life system. Today, I still struggle with healthy eating and portion control but am improving every day.

How about you? What is your health assessment? What health areas do you need to work on? How does your health hinder or assist you in realizing your potential? If you want to maximize your potential, start with your health. You will be amazed at what you can achieve both physically and mentally with a tune-up!

The love of money is the root to all evil. Notice that I didn't say money is the root of all evil. Money is the most likely answer to everything because little gets done without it. How is your financial situation? Do you have at your fingertips the financial ability to make optional decisions based on circumstances? Or do your decisions become actions as a result of your circumstances?

What are you doing to increase your wealth? How are you investing in your and others' potential? Do you support foundations and organizations that improve the life of others? Have you considered creating a foundation to raise money to create opportunities for others and to build a healthier economy?

If you don't have money, you can't give money. How are you getting what you need financially to reach your goals and aspirations? Do you have a college fund, retirement plan, multiple streams of income, side business, or special talents and gifts you can provide in exchange for building wealth?

Living life just by making ends meet is no fun. I encourage you to live a life acquiring means that never end. As the late Zig Ziglar said, "If you help enough people get what they want, they will help you get what you want." So go get it, starting now!

•••

When you have all six of these Life Applications installed within you, you reach life optimization. You will be able to respond in stride to any life-challenge virus, system crash, or attack.

We all have areas that need application upgrades. I call these "areas that need fixes." Like a computer application, if a program is not working, a programmer may have to create a fix to correct the programming error. It is the same in life. We are all given these applications, but sometimes they fail or catch viruses. You cannot expect an application to be optimal if there are bugs and errors in the program. In our lives, we have to make sure our Life Apps are running at their maximum potential.

As you review all six Life Apps, notice how you are doing in each category. Have you mastered one area but are well below your potential in others? Are there categories that have gone undeveloped or unmaintained? The Life App is a system that requires investment and sacrifice, but when you reach balance in each zone, you will begin achieving extraordinary results in your professional and personal life.

You can assess your Life Apps by answering the following:

- Describe the person, place, and/or thing that limits your progress in achieving universal balance with the Life Apps.

- What Life App do you need most to bring universal balance into your life?

- Which Life App have you mastered so that energies can be redirected to improve weaker Apps?

Life App Exercise

In order to maximize your life, you must maximize your potential. The following Life App test will upgrade your potential and help you uncover areas that require patching, fixes, and perhaps, life overhauls. I encourage you to view this assessment as a potential test. Assess your performance in each of the Apps, and, more importantly, identify what your potential is to achieve universal balance in the next six months. Based on your potential, what zone can you reach in the next six months? Rate your potential for each of the six according to this potential scale.

Life Apps	Limited Zone 0 1 2	Normal Zone 3 4 5	Optimal Zone 6 7 8	Maximum Zone 9 10
Universal Faith				
Moral Purpose				
Intellect				
Self-Awareness				
Relationships				
Wealth				

Now look at your results. These are not test scores; they are indicators of your future potential target zones. Regardless of the zone you selected for each category, I want to congratulate you on stepping up and into your potential. You are aware that you can do better in each of the Life Apps, regardless of where you are today. I am more interested and excited about your potential than where you see your performance today.

In order to determine your potential in the next six months, you had to assess where you stand today, correct? So let's discuss how you will reach your future performance in the Life Apps with your current potential.

For each area, reflect on what actions and behavior changes you will adopt to reach your target potential over the next six months. Then I want you to write an e-mail that discusses your goals, including target completion dates, for each area. Now, send them to two people: yourself and your accountability coach. For example, if you think in six months you have the potential to be in the Optimal Zone in the Wealth Life App, I want you to write down specific goals, actions, and outcomes you will realize to achieve growth in that area. Your accountability coach must be someone taking the same challenge you are. Your accountability coach will hold you accountable for achieving results and help you monitor your progress, as you will do for them. This is a great exercise for someone close to you, such as a significant other, relative, friend, or coworker. Copy me at Robert@robertcmcmillan.com. I want to send you and your accountability partner a special gift for stepping into your potential.

Now that we have covered the Circle of Life Apps, let's jump into the Six Leadership Senses that will guide your pathway in stepping into your leadership potential.

Stepping Into Leadership Shoes

● ● ● ● ● ● ● ● ● ● ● ● ● ● ● ●

The Six Leadership Senses

In 1991, I boarded a plane to Cleveland, Ohio. It was my first trip on a plane on my own. My mom and dad dropped me off at the airport and escorted me to the gate. As I walked onto the plane, I scanned the aisle, searching for seat 24C. After wandering around the plane, a flight attendant directed me to my seat.

I sat down and put on my seat belt. Little did I know I was about to take a journey to discover the six leadership senses: sight (ophthalmoception), hearing (audioception), taste (gustaoception), smell (olfacoception), touch (tactioception), and kinesthetic leadership (sixth sense—intuition and envisioning).

My uncle was the first member of my family to work as a professional in Corporate America. During his more than 30-year career, he was a leader of significance for Fortune 500 companies such as Dixie Cup, General Electric, and Rockwell Collins, in leadership development, recruiting, and training, to name a few. He was a member of the master leadership talent relied on by Jack Welch of General Electric. I didn't know how successful he was, I guess, because I was only 20 years old at the time. But I did know that he had reached a position and status I aspired to attain.

Before I flew to Shaker Heights to visit my uncle, I had been part of an organization called Inroads, a successful program designed to help college students gain access and experience in working in Corporate America. Inroads is still recognized today as a major contributor to creating opportunities for aspiring youth. Countless people owe Inroads for their success. For example, as a member of the Inroads organization, my older brother received several opportunities to work in Corporate America in both intern and professional positions. My Inroads experience didn't provide the benefits of corporate work experience as it did for others; it provided me the benefits of learning how to accept rejection.

Year after year, as I watched others, including my brother, receive internships and professional career opportunities, I experienced constant runner-up results. Simply put, after countless interviews, I was always among the top three candidates for the job but was never selected for the position. As I recall, after five separate interviews, I was second choice for each position. Disappointed and frustrated from the constant letdowns, my parents asked my uncle to work with me and also to see if there were any opportunities in his organization, General Electric.

As the plane took off, my mind replayed all those negative rejections over and over, but there was something in me that wouldn't let go of aspiring to be like my uncle. I didn't know what it was then, but I saw something that I liked.

As I exited the plane, my uncle was waiting for me. He gave me a big hug and asked about my travels. As we got into his 300Z to drive to his home, he asked if I had packed the black suit and tie, white shirt, and dress shoes he had asked me to bring. I said yes.

My uncle had arranged an interview for me for the next day to apply for an internship position with several divisions within GE: marketing, sales, and product development. From 7 p.m. to 2 a.m., we practiced responses to questions the interviewers might ask me.

Around 2 a.m., he asked to see my black suit, white shirt, and shoes. He inspected each item. "The suit," he said, "is good. The shirt...perfect." Then he got to the shoes. "What the hell are these?"

I'd packed my favorite dress shoes. They were my favorite because they were the only pair I owned. As a college student, funds were tight. The problem with the shoes was their color: light gray. He told me the shoes wouldn't work because how you dress is a big part of the interview process. GE professionals only wore black Bostonian wingtips. I didn't have any Bostonian wingtip money, I thought to myself. Besides, I was already living on a "wing and a prayer."

Because my interview was at 9 a.m., there was no time to go to the mall and buy a new pair of shoes. Plus, I didn't have the money. And I could not wear my bright, light gray Urkel shoes to the interview.

Then my uncle asked me, "What size shoe do you wear?"

At that time, my feet were smaller than they are now. I said, "9."

"I wear an 11. Perfect," he said.

I remember thinking, "How can a size 9 and 11 be perfect?" The answer was you stuff a balled-up sock in the back of the shoe.

He reached into his closet, handed me his Bostonian wingtips and said, "Wear these."

It was like Michael Jordan giving a fan his Air Jordans to wear, or Mean Joe Green giving his jersey to a fan in the stadium tunnel after the game. I didn't care if the shoes were too big or too small; I was excited because I had the opportunity to "walk in his shoes."

The next morning, I got dressed in my black suit and tie, white shirt, and borrowed shoes, and went on a series of interviews at GE that would change my life and awaken my inner leadership potential. That day I stepped into my leadership awareness. As a result of my experience at GE, I developed the "Six Senses of Leadership."

Seeing Leadership—Ophthalmoception (Sight)

That morning as I arrived on the grounds of General Electric at Nela Park in Cleveland, I saw people walking to and from buildings on the beautiful campus. As I pulled in, I saw a leader, my uncle, standing there, anticipating my arrival.

As I parked the car and we began to walk into the building where his office was, I noticed leadership everywhere. I didn't see names and titles, positions, or status; I just saw people in action. People were not introduced to me by title; they were introduced by their first names. They treated each other like family. From secretaries to vice presidents, everyone was working either individually or as a team toward common goals.

As I sat in my uncle's office, I got a glimpse of what leadership success looked like up close and in action for the first time. In his office were items highlighting GE's success in the marketplace: goals, strategic plans, awards, plaques, reports, and scorecards.

Here is what I learned that day about the seeing leadership sense: Great leaders have goals that they develop strategic plans to achieve them. Great leaders recognize the accomplishments of others before recognizing their own. Good leaders ignite performance and monitor success via reports and scorecards. True leaders include everyone on the team and provide leadership opportunities regardless of position, pay, or authority. For the first time, I saw leadership in action.

Hearing Leadership—Audioception (Hearing)

Around 8:55, we made our way to my first interview. I interviewed with each director and vice president of the products, marketing, and sales divisions. Throughout the interviews, I heard what leadership sounded like through conversations and questions: What are your goals? Where do you see yourself in 3 to 5 years? What excites you? How are you motivated? What are your weaknesses and strengths? Why should we hire you? These are questions they asked loud and clear.

I heard these questions from each person I interviewed with. I also heard their own personal answers to the same questions. They told me what their business and personal goals were. They shared where they envisioned themselves in 3 to 5 years. Each of them told me why their jobs excited them and how they motivated themselves to reach the next level of excellence. Surprisingly, they shared how they created opportunities for growing by setting stretch goals.

Here is what I learned about the hearing leadership sense: Great leaders send leadership messages in their communications with others. They are positive, motivating, and transparent. Each word echoes leadership values and principles. That day I heard what leadership sounds like.

Tasting Leadership—Gustaoception (Taste)

Great leaders provide opportunities for others to grow by giving leaders a taste of leadership, a chance to lead activities, tasks, and actions. One of the vice presidents I interviewed with extended an opportunity for me to sit in on a leadership meeting with him.

Of course I said yes. We got to the meeting location, a conference room full of people, and I sat next to him. Soon another person entered the room, opened the meeting, and went on to present. He did an outstanding job and I recall saying to myself, "I want to do that!"

After the presentation was complete, he received a round of applause from the attendees. Many went up to him with congratulations on the successful meeting outcome. He walked over to me and the vice president, who brought me to the meeting. I thought to myself that he was probably a vice president, so I gave him my vice presidential firm handshake. The person I interviewed with introduced him to me as an intern from last year who became an employee several months ago. I was amazed!

Here is what I discovered that day about the tasting leadership sense: Great leaders give others a taste of leadership. I later learned that the person I interviewed with gave the new employee an opportunity to present in front of leadership. Clearly the vice president was capable of presenting, but he wanted to give a taste of leadership to others.

You can literally taste leadership in an organization that has a strong leadership presence. But in order to seize the moment, you also have to have a hunger and desire so strong that you can taste the leadership opportunities.

Smelling Leadership—Olfacoception (Smell)

Good leadership produces a rosy smell; bad leadership just flat out stinks—it's foul. Have you ever heard someone say, "The leadership stinks"? Well, they are talking about a performance of leadership so poor that it stinks. A culture that distrusts, misleads, and miscommunicates is a leadership system that does not breed leadership; it breeds a leaderless environment.

As I interviewed and walked the hallways of GE, I could smell the leadership in the fabric of the organization: people being open, honest, supportive, engaging, and respectful of others. In the meeting I attended with the vice president, you could close your eyes and smell the degree of support, enjoyment, and leadership in the air.

Here is what I discovered that day about the smelling leadership sense: Great leaders create an environment that people like to operate in. That day left me with a leadership fragrance that reminds me each time I enter a new organization—whether there to speak, consult, coach, train, or facilitate a session—what leadership should smell like. I discovered that, from day one, you can smell bad leadership a mile away.

Simply put, if people have smiles on their faces and are excited about what they are doing for the organization and themselves, leadership probably smells good. On the other hand, if people have a frown on their faces and are gasping for air, leadership usually stinks.

Touching Leadership—Tactioception (Touch)

A good leadership system should be something that you can reach out and touch. Good leaders are in touch with their teams. Good leaders are in touch with everyone, not only with a certain group.

As I changed rooms to interview with the GE leaders, I noticed that leaders were present on the floor, and in the departments and units within the organization, speaking with and engaging people. Leaders were not closed off in their offices with deadbolt locks and security outside the door. Professionals were not in line trying to get an appointment with a leader's secretary whose major job function was to block access.

Here is what I discovered that day about the touching leadership sense: The people I saw were "touching leaders." They operated in a way so that you could reach out and touch them, and they could reach out and touch you. You had the opportunity to touch and feel the shape, structure, and solidness of a leader. To be a good leader, it is obvious that you must be able to see leadership in action, but it is just as important to be able to touch it and it touch you.

Kinesthetic Leadership—Sixth Sense (Intuition and Envisioning)

Kinesthetic is having complete awareness. As I interviewed with each vice president and the directors of marketing, product development and sales, many of the same questions and answers that my uncle practiced with me the previous night were asked.

As my uncle and I role-played the night before, I envisioned how leadership would look, smell, feel, taste, and sound. As frustrating and tiresome as it was, that night I built what I call "kinesthetic leadership skills." I could mentally see, hear, touch, smell, and taste leadership.

Here is what I discovered that day about the kinesthetic leadership sense: The most interesting thing about the interview process was that, as each interview progressed, I got better and stronger in answering and asking questions, and engaging in conversation with the leaders, all while using kinesthetic leadership sense. Kinesthetics pulls from all of the other five senses through intuition and envisioning.

I did not know this was kinesthetic leadership until I experienced it with the GE leaders interviewing me that day. They talked about their ability to lead others into new areas, into unchartered ground with unforeseen obstacles. They were good leaders because they were able to lead with their eyes closed and touch their nose at the same time.

•••

That day, I learned that the Six Senses of Leadership—seeing, hearing, tasting, smelling, touching, and kinesthetic—are critical senses that every aspiring leader needs to fully understand in order to be a leader of significance. The Six Senses of Leadership allowed me to come into the awareness of my leadership potential.

As I hit each of the interviewer's questions out of the park, my confidence grew. It felt great! I didn't know if it was me or something magical in those Bostonian wingtips.

A few days after the interviews, I was packing for my return flight. I turned to my uncle, who was helping me pack, and thanked him again.

Smiling and lifting up the shoes, I asked him, "Can I have these? I'll grow into them."

"My Bostonian wingtips? Hell no! Are you crazy? These damn shoes cost me $175," he responded in his comedic way. Those shoes were worth more than gold. I am forever grateful to my uncle for the valuable lesson.

If you are still wondering if I got the job, I won't torment you any longer. The answer is no. No, I didn't get the job, but I did get something a million times more valuable that I will share with you. What I got was the first secret to leadership success: discovering the awareness that one is a leader regardless of position, pay, or power. It was that awareness of my leadership potential that convinced me from that day forward that I was a leader, not a follower.

As you read the next chapters, remember the Six Senses of Leadership. Apply them as you discover where you align in the leadership system and how you can maximize your true leadership potential.

In the 6G Leadership System described in earlier chapters, the first network is 1G–Genetic Leader. My GE experience was my entry-point into this network. I invite you to explore in the next chapter the traits, features, limitations, and applications associated with the Genetic Leader Network that will enable you to maximize and upgrade your leadership potential.

Before we go on to Part III, let me tell you that I did get those shoes from my uncle. He placed them in my bag when I wasn't looking. After close to 20 years, I am still growing into those Bostonian wingtip leadership shoes. Let me ask you: What shoes are you growing into?

Part III of this book, Six Generations of Leadership, contains the complete 6G Leadership System, which is the solution to maximizing individual, team, and organizational leadership potential in your personal and professional life. Whether your assessment in Part I of the book identifies your dominant Leadership Network as 1G–Genetic Leader, 2G–Generic Leader, 3G–Go-To Leader, 4G–Growth Leader, 5G–Gateway Leader, or 6G–Genius Leader, the remaining chapters will provide you with a system to maximize potential on each of the networks. Remember that leadership is circular, not hierarchical. The goal is not to reach the highest level but rather to rotate between all leadership networks on the system to maximize potential.

I invite you to harness everything you have learned in the prior chapters to now begin upgrading your mind, heart, and hands to become the next generation leader in you!

Part 3

The Six Generations
of Leadership

1G–Genetic Leader and the Awareness App

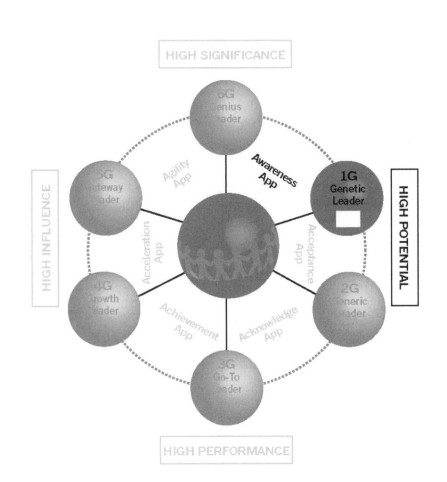

Innovation distinguishes between a leader and a follower.
—Steve Jobs, late CEO of Apple

Born in Leader Genes

There are those who would like you to believe that leadership begins with being given the position or permission to lead—it doesn't. You were born with all the leadership potential you will ever need and given the gift of leadership. You were born with leadership in your heart, mind, and soul. The script of life says, "Let us make man in our own image." The Creator exemplifies leadership, and you were made in His image. Leadership does not start with position or permission; it starts with the awareness that you were born to be a leader.

Have you ever wondered why some people step into leadership opportunities and others run away from them? As a leader, individual contributor, speaker, consultant, trainer, and coach for Fortune 500 companies, I have met professionals from all walks of life. When first meeting someone, I will often ask a basic question, such as "What is it that you lead and how do you like being a part of the leadership team?"

The response I receive from management personnel most of the time is "Oh, I'm not the leader. I just make sure the work gets done. The leaders are at the home office!"

Non-management personnel respond similarly. "Oh, I'm not the leader. I just work here. The real leaders are over there," they say, pointing to the management personnel who said the leaders were at the home office.

But more often than not, I see examples of leadership action in organizations that support my belief that there are basically two types of professionals: those who choose to lead and those who choose not to lead.

I was consulting on a project for a billion-dollar company, and as I was scheduling the next decision-making meeting, I had the pleasure of meeting an administrative assistant named Paula, the assistant to one of the officers of the company that was sponsoring the meeting. The first challenge we had before us was scheduling: getting all 10 high-profile officers together at the same time. To do that, we had to coordinate with each of the officer's administrative assistants. During my first time meeting with Paula, I asked my basic question, the same question I ask everyone I meet for the first time. "What is it that you lead and how do you like being a part of the leadership team?"

Her response was astounding. She said with confidence and slight attitude, "I lead these officers and secretaries every day by directing them and scheduling meetings so that everybody is where they are supposed to be. These people would be walking in circles without me."

Pausing to take a sip of coffee, she said, "In terms of your second question, I like my leadership role. But do you know something? Good help is hard to find!"

Laughing, I asked a follow-up question. "Do the administrative assistants report to you?"

"No, they don't. I have my hands full trying to lead these officers!"

So what is the difference between Paula's responses to the leadership question and the answers of those who declared they were not leaders?

The answer is simply *awareness*. Paula had an attitude of awareness. She made a choice to be a leader without position, appointment, or permission. It was all in her mindset. In fact, I saw her literally directing the officers she supported to their meetings, telling them what was on the agenda, giving them advice on how to prepare for the meeting, and communicating what they should bring. What I saw in her was a leader. It was as if in some way they reported to her, though technically, they didn't. It was not about title and position; it was about the value she provided to them.

The first point I want to get across to you in this chapter is that adding value to others is leadership. How many professionals do you know who are in appointed leadership positions that add little to no value to others? How many people do you know who only produce work products at the expense of others? Well, that is not leadership—a key component to leadership is adding value to others.

Paula stepped into her awareness and added value to others. Leadership awareness is when a person recognizes his or her leadership potential regardless of others' opinions or actions.

You Are in Good Company

The first network on the 6G Leadership System is 1G–Genetic Leader. The Genetic Leader operates on what I call the Awareness App. If you scored the majority of your points on the Leadership Aptitude or have scores in this network, this chapter is for you. This chapter is the cornerstone of the 6G Leadership System, and understanding the elements of this network is critical to understanding how to navigate on all of the other networks, which will be discussed in the coming chapters.

Being a 1G–Genetic Leader puts you in good company. You are in the company of those in the beginning stage of leadership who have high aspirations to be leaders of significance. In many ways, you are leading without a "badge." You have heart, desire, and raw potential. You have broken the traditional mindset and philosophy that leadership is a position, and you have proven that leadership is awareness. How did you do this, you may ask? With the genetic makeup you were given by the Creator!

Everyone, at some point in time, operates on the 1G–Genetic Network. Some operate on this network less than others, and for some, this is their dominant network. The fact of the matter is, every leader (even the great ones) have spent time on this network at some point in their professional and personal lives. If you really think about where you are in your leadership journey, you might recognize a few leaders who started out like you did: Martin Luther King, Nelson Mandela, Mother Teresa, and Mahatma Gandhi. How could you be compared to them, you may ask?

Each of these leaders started by simply being aware that they had the potential to lead. Each of them relied on their Genetic Leadership gifts to get started on their leadership journey. You have discovered the same potential in yourself. The only difference between you and those exceptional leaders are your unique results and outcomes. The starting point is the same.

For example, Nelson Mandela was not appointed by the government or given a title or position, yet he transformed South Africa from its embarrassing apartheid state to the democracy it is today. Martin Luther King was not given a seat at the table, let alone a government position, but he had great influence on Presidents Eisenhower, Kennedy, and Johnson to pass civil rights laws for equality in America. Mother Teresa did not sit idle and wait for someone to direct her to begin ministering to the poor, sick, orphaned, and dying. And Mahatma Gandhi did not wait for a title before he began advocating a policy of non-violence and cooperation that led to the independence of India.

All of these great leaders acted without a formal title, position, or status. They used their Genetic Leadership abilities to ignite their potential. Each of these heroic leaders started out on the 1G–Genetic Leadership Network and ultimately expanded to the 6G–Genius Leadership Network. You have the same potential for professional achievement. You are in good company!

1G-Genetic Leader Profile and Traits

It takes a lot of courage to be on this network. Think of all of the people you know who are not aware of their leadership potential. How about those professionals who do not realize they have the genetic gift of leadership? Being on the 1G Network is better than not being on any network at all! So don't think that being at this network is a negative; think of it as a positive. You are on the network! Diagram 1 summarizes the Profile of a 1G–Genetic Leader and the Awareness App.

• •

Diagram 1

High Potential Leader, with awareness of ability to lead tasks and others. Leaders allow you to influence them because they see potential.

Awareness App—*Awareness* is an individual state of knowledge of leadership potential.

Overview of the Genetic Leader

- Genetic Leaders have the potential to be good leaders. They have a natural tendency to lead with structure but may lack the awareness of their potential. If they become pressured to lead, they may become nervous and stressed, drifting off course.
- Genetic Leaders limit risk-taking and refrain from challenging directions. This can be a good thing in highly complicated environments. However, their lack of inquisitiveness can be detrimental in situations requiring root cause analysis for solving business issues.
- Genetic Leaders are task-natured and shine when working in tight timeframes. But complexity, change, and dealing with chaos can be their worst enemy.

Maximum Potential—realized in a scenario with tight timeframes, structure, and predefined tasks.

Least Potential—an environment that requires risk-taking and working with large teams.

Core Leadership Value to Teams and Professionals

Professionals value you because they see potential. Professionals allow you to lead because their actions demonstrate their innate abilities to lead.

- Leads without permission or position.
- Focuses on predetermined goals.
- Limits taking risks on complicated tasks, assignments, and initiatives.
- Demands work completeness and accuracy.

• •

Just as an iPhone and iPad have features, so do the networks within the 6G Leadership System. If you are an aspiring leader or if your aptitude results indicate you are operating on the 1G Network, here are the profiles, features, limitations, and applications of the network you will need to understand as you expand to the next network. As you review this network, celebrate its value and get excited about overcoming any visible limitations you might have as you introspectively and independently (or with a coach) complete the G1 exercises and self-assessment.

First, let's review the profile and traits. Genetic Leaders have traits and behaviors that are easily identifiable. In many instances, Genetic Leaders are often considered High Potential because of their aggressive nature and ability to execute complicated and challenging assignments. In Diagram 2 is a limited set of traits to help you understand the Genetic Leader Network.

· ·

Diagram 2

Review each of these traits and indicate on each trait those that resonate with your actions, behaviors and habits by providing a score in the box between 5 (often), 3 (sometimes), or 1 (rarely).

Genetic Leader:

- _ Usually are not in a management function.
- _ Can be new to leading teams or be seasoned individual contributors.
- _ Are often considered High Potentials.
- _ Constantly deliver work completeness and accuracy.
- _ Have the courage to lead without authority.
- _ Have the instinctive tendency to drive tasks and lead others, but lack full awareness of their potential.
- _ Act and ask questions later.
- _ May often become stressed and frustrated in highly political organizations.
- _ Like challenges.
- _ Limit risk-taking and refrain from challenging leadership direction.
- _ Aspire to be good leaders.
- _ Lack of resistance can be detrimental in situations requiring root cause analysis for solving business issues.
- _ Are task-natured executors.
- _ Strive on complexity, but constant change and chaos can be their worst enemy.

· ·

Features of the Genetic Leader

The Genetic Leader Network has features that add significant value to those who operate on the 6G Leadership System. Each of the networks from 1G to 6G works together to produce leadership. Each network has specific features that add value to the leadership system. 1G–Genetic Leader is the base infrastructure and critical to the overall success of the system.

Here are several key features that each user of the leadership system needs to be able to fully comprehend, optimize, and leverage. These features apply to both those whose dominant network is 1G, as well as those who may extend onto other bands.

Genetic Leaders Believe They Can Lead Others Without Titles

Genetic Leaders do not allow the lack of a formal title, position, or appointment to limit their abilities to influence outcomes or demonstrate leadership behaviors. This is contrary to how most people view leadership. Most of the time, people display leadership behaviors only if appointed, authorized, or given permission to lead—but not Genetic Leaders. Genetic Leaders have raw leadership potential and often don't even realize they are leading. They have a well of potential that is yet to be discovered.

On the other hand, there are some Genetic Leaders who are babes in the process and have only recently become aware of their potential to lead. They refrain from challenging direction and can feel pressured when faced with solving complicated problems. Typical Genetic Leaders love to operate in tight timeframes, but complexity, change, and chaos can be a developmental nightmare for them.

I remember when I stepped out of fear and into my genetic ability to lead others. I was a staff auditor working for an accounting firm in Washington, D.C. After getting several audits under my belt, I discovered that the audit program written by the audit supervisor was ineffective; as many as 95 percent of the procedures identified were not uncovering significant financial findings. Rather than spending a lot of time and effort on the non-valued audit steps, I began to focus more on the remaining 5 percent of the procedures where most of the findings typically were identified. With that approach, I completed more audits than the other staff members and had more findings than any other auditor in the entire firm.

Other auditors started asking me how I finished my audits so quickly and how I had so many financial findings. I shared my approach with them; their productivity doubled and their findings quadrupled.

I had no permission, power, or authority to direct others. I just engaged my genetic gift to lead others. A year later, my supervisor discovered I had influenced the entire audit department with my approach and was asked to be a team lead. I did not become a leader that day. I had become a leader a year before. It just took her a year to figure it out. Many of you reading this book have been leading for years, and sometimes it takes others more time to figure that out, but I encourage you to continue leading.

If you are already leading and using your innate leadership skills, gifts, and talents without permission, pay, or power, I congratulate you. Organizations need more professionals like you. If you have not begun to step into your leadership awareness, I invite you to discover what I know is within you.

Genetic Leaders Are Individual Contributors

Professionals who fall within this category are not in formal leadership positions. They do not possess a title, position, or placement on an organizational chart with any responsibility over a function. They are not on the intranet or directory; they do, however, exist on an execution chart for the completion of assignments, tasks, and initiatives that are critical to the organization's success. They are not in the spotlight, but they are on others' radar because they are valuable. These are professionals whom I call leadership's individual contributors.

Individual contributors are Genetic Leaders who help achieve goals, objectives, and initiatives that otherwise would be failures rather than successes. They are professionals who focus their time and efforts on predetermined goals. They identify problems and interact well with both small and large teams.

When I played football in college, I started out as a walk-on freshman. I was not fortunate enough to have a scholarship like many of the other players who had secured at least a one-year scholarship. But I was given an opportunity to prove myself among the players who were awarded scholarships in advance of tryouts.

During the practice tryouts, I overshadowed some players who were awarded scholarships. When the roster was posted at the end of the tryout period, my name appeared—not on the cut list, but on the "A" team list. I was named second-string defensive back, beating out a few players who received scholarships for that position. In the games and during practices, I went up against the fastest running backs and receivers; I stuck to them like glue and stopped them dead in their tracks during tackles. Although I was not named a team lead, captain, or group leader, many of the second-, third- and fourth-string players looked up to me as a leader. I was leading without a first-string position. They asked me to help them improve their skills because they recognized my value and accomplishments. In their eyes, I was a leader and an individual contributor.

As a Genetic Leader, you must recognize that you are always in a leadership position. People are always watching and looking out for leadership. It is a shame that people have been misled into believing the traditionalist view that leadership can only begin with the acquisition of a formal position or title. That is the furthest from the truth. The truth is that individual contributors can add just as much and sometimes more value than those in formal leadership roles. They lead through the awareness of their potential and use their natural leadership gifts, talents, and skills.

Genetic Leaders Are Growth Engines

Genetic Leaders aspire to be the best leaders they can be. They have an extraordinary capacity to grow given the complexity and challenges of tasks and assignments. Genetic Leaders have a growth engine that has to be fed with stretch goals and assignments. The more challenging the assignment, the more energy and excitement unleashed.

The 6G Leadership System is networked on the concept of professional development and growth. To operate on the 1G Network, your desire to maximize your potential has to be in line with maximizing leadership opportunities. Genetic Leaders unconsciously take every opportunity to lead. They have a desire to develop and grow and, therefore, will lead without permission. As my grandfather used to say, "The early bird catches the worm." Genetic Leaders act first and ask for forgiveness later. Their desire to lead is so great that their innate genetic abilities overpower hierarchy leadership.

If you were to ask a Genetic Leader, "Who put you in charge?" they would reply, "I did!" What a proactive attitude! Genetic Leaders are self-empowered and self-motivated. They are the type of professionals who solve the problem first and report the solution later.

Working With Appointed Leaders

Often, Genetic Leaders compete with leaders who have been "appointed" because of their expertise in a particular area. Appointed leaders with self-esteem issues sometimes see Genetic Leaders as rebel rousers because of their raw leadership skills. Confident leaders provide them with more opportunity because they recognize their leadership potential.

If you are a Genetic Leader, be a growth engine. Pursue developmental opportunities to transform your raw talent into sculpted talent. This is the perfect opportunity to determine what steps you can take to expand your leadership capabilities to the next network. If you are an influential leader now, even without a formal position, just think how influential you can be when you are in a formal leadership position.

Genetic Leader Limitations

If you are a Genetic Leader, know professionals who fit this profile, or perhaps have people in this category report to you, you should be aware that every system and network has its features and limitations. The 1G–Genetic Leadership Network is no different than a new product or software. It, too, has its limitations. However, if the right environment exists, those limitations can be turned into benefits.

With limitations come opportunities. As you explore your leadership applications, behaviors, and skills, you will uncover some weaknesses, organizational gaps, and blind spots that may limit your ability to maximize your potential. These limitations can become your opportunity to improve your aptitude and expand to broader networks, enabling you to become a leader of significance.

As the foundation leadership network, the 1G–Genetic Leader is where many new and aspiring leaders exist. It is important that everyone understand this network's limitations—not to devalue those on this network, but to help them grow along their leadership journey.

For those who are within this category, this is a great place to be. But you should be aware of several limitations that exist on this network and a few potential solutions to help alleviate those limitations and optimize leadership performance.

1G-Genetic Leaders Do Not Have Management Authority

Leaders in this category can, to some degree, effect change but cannot dictate change. They contribute to results but do not have authority over functions, personnel, or direction. Genetic Leaders influence results individually, as part of a team or as a team leader, executing assignments, activities, and tasks.

Genetic Leaders have the natural gift of leadership, but many lack the awareness of their full potential. Genetic Leaders who are aware of their potential often become frustrated because of their inability to change the course of direction. Those who are not fully aware of their potential become stressed, pressured, and nervous when they are presented with a leadership opportunity.

Genetic Leaders operating on the 1G Network are not equipped with the necessary features to direct change or set goals. They execute existing protocols, processes, and procedures and ignite subtle change with their raw leadership skills.

Because of their natural tendency to lead tasks and assignments and complete specific requests, supervisors and management often have false expectations. They might expect Genetic Leaders to become decision-makers without the appropriate "badge" or approval from a manager. The 1G professional can be put in awkward and career-challenging situations because management has been unclear to others, thus creating confusion, infighting, and role conflict.

To maximize the potential of the 1G Genetic Leader, it is critical that goals, objectives, and expectations be successfully met so that burnout and frustration do not set in while the raw leadership talent within the 1G Leader is being explored, developed, and sculpted.

Genetic Leaders Are Natural Explorers

Genetic Leaders are in a phase of exploring their natural leadership gifts, talents, and skills. They reject the notion that their value is limited only to their job description. They need to be in a safe environment that gives them the flexibility to act without being penalized for their actions. They are, in fact, explorers of themselves and, therefore, might not perform well in a command-and-control environment that limits their assertiveness and creativity.

Job descriptions are the biggest challenge for Genetic Leaders. Here is what I know about job descriptions: they are outdated; they unnecessarily duplicate other roles; and they are, in many instances, written by people who have never performed the job. In short, job descriptions are like driving directions: they get you from Point A to Point B, but leave out the scenery and landmarks along the way.

Genetic Leaders are most effective in a safe and flexible operating environment. They need the ability to explore assignments, activities, and projects outside of their job description. Organizations that have a command-and-control operating model and "do as you are told" management system will not be effective for this developing leader. Typecasting these leaders as defined by a job description stunts their growth and development. They must be given challenging and character-building assignments that stretch their abilities without sustaining career injuries.

To be most effective, Genetic Leaders should view the job description as a guardrail on a six-lane highway. You can ride in any lane, enjoy the scenery, and go as fast as you please, but avoid hitting the guardrails.

Genetic Leaders Are Competitive

There is a song that says, "All I do is win, win, win, no matter what!" That, in essence, defines Genetic Leaders: they like to win. For a Genetic Leader, a non-competitive environment introduces boredom and complacency. These leaders are innately competitive and are often misdiagnosed as being overly confident and aggressive. The bottom line is that this particular category of leader is driven to compete at their optimal level. To those who are satisfied with mediocrity, this behavior might appear intimidating and controversial, especially if this type of leader is operating in another person's space. Because of their competitive behavior, Genetic Leaders can create an environment of one-up-man-ship in their desire to maximize their potential.

I recall a new employee who was so competitive she would attempt to outperform a team lead, who was the best claims processor. By reviewing the claims processing report, this new employee found out how many claims the team lead processed a day. She then set her goal to exceed that number. Not only did she exceed it, she doubled it. The team lead was taken aback and felt that the new employee was a condescending "showoff."

The new employee was a Genetic Leader, and she was being naturally competitive. Others did not see it that way, however. Genetic Leaders who have decided to fully step into their potential and recognize their ability to lead are very competitive. This can result in infighting if the culture of the organization is not primed for healthy competition or if professionals are not conditioned to maximize their potential.

Genetic Leaders need to be in an environment that embraces and rewards competitiveness. They must have competition or they will not perform optimally. They are the professionals who push the bar and challenge others to tap into their well of potential. Without this, Genetic Leaders will quickly fall into the acceptance of mediocrity.

The Awareness App

What is necessary to change a person is to change his awareness of himself.
—Abraham Maslow, psychologist

Understanding the Awareness App

The Awareness App is "mindware" and can be your best friend. Just as any computer, cell phone, or iPad runs on an operating system, our operating system is the brain. Remember the saying "Garbage in, garbage out"? Well, that is true for the brain as well.

The Awareness App within the 1G–Genetic Leader is an upgradeable application that runs unconsciously in your mind, constantly fighting off internal and external negative beliefs that stunt your potential. Actions or words expressed by family, friends, or coworkers can defuse your energy, confidence, or belief in your potential. This App stores both positive and negative information—past, present, and future—that can be overwritten based on what you code into your App. If you code negative thoughts into your App, you will have negative thoughts. If you code positive thoughts about your potential, then you will have positive thoughts.

The Awareness App consists of neurological networks in the brain that regulate predefined beliefs regarding your potential. You want those beliefs about your potential to be optimized in this App; it all starts with your state of "mindware."

The App has a virus-resistant feature as well. The stronger your state of "mindware," the more resistance you have to negative comments from internal and external parties. Have you ever told yourself, "You can't do that. It's too difficult"? Have you ever talked yourself out of doing something? This Awareness App defends neurological breakdown by rejecting criticism, defamation, and attacks against your potential. The bottom line is that you can control your awareness or you can let others control it and pilot your course.

In addition to being virus resistant, the App also is a change agent. The Awareness App allows you to transform desired actions into habits. The mind is so powerful that if the temperature is 95 degrees, and you tell your body you are cold, your body temperature will drop because your mind can control your body's temperature. The same is true if you tell your mind to import a positive behavior; your mind will import that behavior as a conscious action. Through time, it will become a habit. The trick is becoming aware of your potential in congruence with who you want to become and acting on it.

Now that you know a little about the Awareness App, answer these questions:

- Who do others say you are?
- Who do you say you are?
- What defines who you are?
- What do you envision yourself to be?
- What is your potential?

Awareness to Change

Some time ago, I came across a piece by Oprah Winfrey recalling an experience she had with her grandmother as a child. She said, "I remember a specific moment, watching my grandmother hang clothes on the line, and her saying to me, 'You are going to have to learn to do this,' and me being in that space of awareness and knowing that my life would not be the same as my grandmother's life." ("Sheryl Sandberg, Facebook COO, Interviews Oprah Winfrey Live Online," HuffingtonPost.com, 9/9/2011)

Awareness is not only a key professional app but also a Life App. Awareness is the deciding factor for living a life consistent with your destiny or living a life defined by others. I want you to live a life defined by destiny.

Oprah was born in Mississippi in 1954. She made a conscious decision to follow her destiny rather than live a limited life only slightly better than her predecessors. I am sure there were those who had no idea Oprah would become a media icon several decades later. She was able to reach such a high level of success by coming into awareness and following her destiny rather than living her life based on others' visions.

This is a dilemma many people struggle with. In order to gain awareness of how great a leader you can be and the awareness of the leader within you, the key question you must answer first is "Where are you in your journey?" Are you following your destiny, or are you following someone else's vision for your life?

Without awareness, life can be very confusing. Without awareness, careers can be frustrating and uninspiring. We can find ourselves assuming titles, positions, and roles that do not provide an opportunity to unleash our true potential. Much of awareness has to do with recognizing our individual potential, knowing that we have the potential to achieve things that others only think of, but never act on.

The good news is that once you step into your awareness, you have stepped into the leadership zone, regardless of how others see you. Make no mistake: others may see you not as a leader but as an accountant, sales rep, engineer, secretary, customer service representative, associate, programmer, anchor, writer, actor, educator, speaker, activist, analyst, or janitor. In their minds, you have not been formally placed in a leadership position. But as I have said before, leadership is not a position; it is an action.

Abraham Maslow said, "What is necessary to change a person is to change his awareness of himself." Coming into awareness means understanding one's abilities, talents, and potential, regardless of what others see in you.

In 1995, I was faced with a situation that changed my life forever. I was a staff auditor working for an organization that was going through significant change. As a result of a divisional reorganization, my supervisor and I were moved to the internal audit division. The organization had just hired a new vice president of internal audit, and he made the decision that all 50-plus employees in his division had to interview for their positions. His rationale was that he had not hired any of the employees, and he wanted to validate their competencies to do the job without the influence of management's opinion. The average employee had been with the division for more than 15 years.

He decided to interview all of the employees himself, with limited support from human resources. The employees' options and outcomes were the following: an employee could interview for a higher-level position and possibly be selected, an employee could interview for his current position and be selected as the candidate of choice, or an employee could not be selected for any position interviewed for, resulting in displacement.

As a result of reviewing the job postings for open positions, I came across a team lead position that I thought I was qualified for. To better my chances, my plan was to interview for two positions: my current position and a team lead position one level above my current staff auditor position. I applied formally for both position openings.

The human resources recruiter contacted me and scheduled an interview the next day with the new vice president. Upon entering the conference room, I was told I had to choose only one position to interview for and that I could not be considered for both. I asked him what would happen if I were not selected for the position. He told me that would result in a displacement. What a way to start an interview!

As I thought for a second, he said, "You should play it safe and interview for the job you are already in. You will never be a team lead. In my opinion, you just don't have the skills."

At that point, I felt like Oprah. I wasn't going to let someone define my destiny. I looked at him and told him I was interviewing for the team lead position! He looked at me in disgust then proceeded with the interview.

After the interview, with my newfound belief in my leadership awareness, I also responded to an external job posting for a management consultant with PriceWaterhouse (now PriceWaterhouseCoopers).

A few weeks later, I interviewed with the PriceWaterhouse recruiter and partner for the management consultant position. I was determined to show my potential to meet and perform demands of the job. I was overexcited, and thought that I had done poorly and didn't have a shot at the position.

The day after the interview with PriceWaterhouse, I decided to check with the vice president who re-interviewed me at my current company, to see if he had made a decision about the position I had applied for. I mentioned to him that I was interested in a management consulting position with PriceWaterhouse that would give me leadership experience, and because he had a consulting background, I wanted to know his thoughts about the company and consulting.

"You will never make it there as a consultant. They won't be interested in you. You don't have what it takes," he looked at me and said.

Then I asked him about the team lead position I had applied for. He said, "You don't have what it takes for that, either."

He had a plan for me that was different than my destiny—but destiny had more power than his opinion. I politely got up out of the chair, walked out of his office back to my cubicle, and never mentioned this to anyone in the office that day. I went home feeling bad about myself. I had interviewed my way out of my own job by believing I could be a leader. I thought that stepping into my awareness had caused me to lose my job.

The next day while I was sitting in my cubicle, I received a phone call from PriceWaterhouse offering me the management consulting position I applied for. I immediately accepted. I had no doubt that I was destined for leadership. Stepping into my awareness created challenges, but it also delivered opportunities!

Three years later, I was in Hoboken, N.J., running a project for Paine Webber. As I exited the building to catch the ferry over to New York, guess whom I bumped into? It was that vice president who refused to see my leadership potential. He looked at me like he had seen a ghost.

I asked him how he was doing. He said he was interviewing for a leadership position at Paine Webber to join the team engaged to run the consulting team implementing Oracle. He asked me, "What are you doing now?"

"Still consulting," I replied. With an expression of disbelief on his face, he turned and walked away. I guess he didn't think my career in consulting would last that long, and he certainly never thought he would be interviewing for a position on my consulting project.

I would never see him again, but I will never forget the look of disbelief on his face, even 20 years later. I am thankful for that look of disbelief, for it was at that moment I truly understood this concept that I now call the Awareness App.

Summary

The Awareness App is having the mindware to believe in your potential when others doubt it. Others may operate in disbelief, but you operate within your belief! That is the essence of awareness. This Awareness App spans each of the networks. In other words, whether you are on the 1G–Genetic Leader Network or the 6G–Genius Leader Network, the Awareness App is your best friend and is the software for maintaining the awareness of your well of potential, and limiting the negative internal and external viruses that can infect your destiny.

Awareness is universal. When you apply this App, your mind, body, and soul will bend to your destiny and unleash change, opportunities, and action into your life:

- When you change your awareness, you change your expectations.
- When you change your expectations, you change your actions.
- When you change your actions, outcomes change for the better in your life.

6G Leadership Coaching is the art and science of retraining your brain through meditation, thought, action, and repetition. In this chapter, as well as others, you will complete the exercise and immediately grasp and put into action the concepts we have discussed.

Here are 10 ways to use the Awareness App, including affirmations, action steps, and applications each day on your journey to becoming a leader of significance. Remember, the stronger your Awareness App, the greater your potential!

6G Leadership Coaching Exercise

The 1G–Genetic Leader chapter ends with a lot of writing. One of my favorite scripts of life says, "Write the vision down and make it plain on tablets so that others can run with it." In this case, "others" is you, and the "tablet" is your iPhone or iPad!

To be a good leader, you must first be able to lead yourself. The 6G Leadership Coaching exercises are designed to help you create an action place for achieving full awareness of your leadership potential. If you haven't already completed the exercise, I would encourage you to take the time to do so before proceeding to the next chapter.

• •

1G–Leadership Coaching Exercise:
Awareness Affirmations, Action Steps, and Applications

1. Each morning when you rise, repeat three times, "Today I will step into a new awareness of my potential!" Write down the areas of your infinite potential. *This will open your mind to seeing those things that are opportunities but look like work.*

2. Identify three leadership traits to work on and improve on each day. Identify an accountability partner to provide FeedForward observations on progress. This will help exercise your awareness of potential. *Remember, no feedback. We are going forward, so we want FeedForward only.*

3. When leadership haters enter your presence, respond mentally by repeating three times: "I am made in God's image. I am a leader!" This will build your confidence to expand on the leadership network system. Write down: *"I am a leader." Look at it during your lunch break each day for 90 days until it becomes an unconscious thought.*

4. As negative people try to decree their plan for your life, state affirmatively: "I choose a life of destiny over a life of desecration." Identify the friends, family, and coworkers who negatively impact your thinking, and to the extent possible, stay away from them. *Doing this will bring life purpose to clarity.*

5. During breaks and lunchtime, reflect on what actions you can take for the remainder of the day to force into habit your conscious leadership behaviors. Write down three things you can start doing today. *Following this action will transform conscious acts into unconscious behavior.*

6. Repeat daily: "I have an open well of potential. To access it, I have to pump it and prime it with positive information." Write here how you will pour positive information into your well of potential. *This will ignite a positive attitude and mindset throughout the day.*

7. During your commute home, reflect introspectively on leadership weaknesses you demonstrated throughout the day, which you need to upgrade. Define leadership failure points that can

be turned into success points. *This will introduce into your psyche the concept of operating and striving for excellence.*

8. Repeat daily: "Leadership is not position, it is action!" List three leadership behaviors that are stretch actions, which you will try to demonstrate each day. *This daily regimen will shake loose the traditional command-and-control hierarchical leadership structure that confines you.*

9. Don't let career haters be mind-regulators. Assess daily your reaction to negative influences to ensure they are not impacting your potential. Identify things that haters say that annoy you then define a method to eliminate their impact. *This will create a shift in not allowing others to dictate your state of mind using emotional intelligence.*

10. Before you leave the office each day, write down one thing you could have done differently and redo it tomorrow. What is the one thing you can do differently, starting today? Write it down. *This turns desires into habits and creates a self-coaching environment.*

• •

In the next chapter, we will explore the 2G–Generic Leadership Network's profile, features, limitations, and Acceptance App. Let's upgrade to the next network.

2G–Generic Leader and the Acceptance App

• • • • • • • • • • • • • • • •

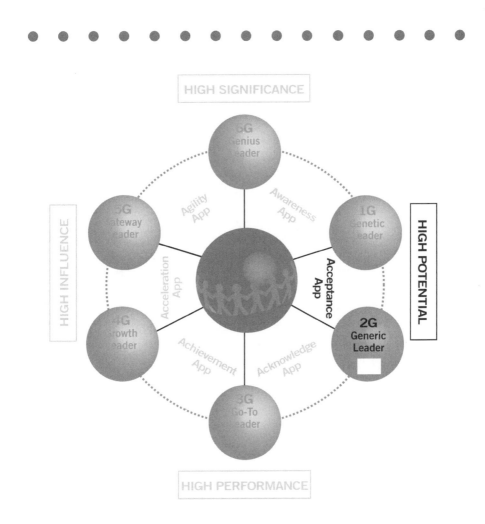

When I let go of what I am, I become what I might be.
—Benjamin E. Mays, scholar

Accept Your Potential

Accepting potential and being aware of potential are two completely different things. You may not know this, but before my career in business and as a thought leader, coach, and author, I had another career. I was a professional entertainer and comedian. My nickname Rob Mac followed me as my stage name.

That career taught me that acceptance of your potential will not automatically open doors for you but will allow you to see doors of opportunity that stand before you. You often will have to open those doors yourself and, sometimes—to be blunt—just flat out knock them down. I have had the opportunity to be in the presence of some iconic comedians—before and after their celebrity status—by sharing their stage: Sinbad, Martin Lawrence, Eddie Griffin, Dave Chappelle, Bill Cosby, and Dick Gregory. (I recently attended Dick Gregory's 80th birthday party; he grows funnier with age.)

One of my most memorable performances was in 1991 at the Landmark Theatre in front of about 4,000 people. I had the honor of sharing the stage with one of the greatest comedians of all time, Sinbad. He was the headliner and I was his opening act. It was acceptance of my potential that led to that doorway of opportunity. But, like all the great comedians I've had the pleasure of meeting, I had to kick down many doors before reaching my doorway of opportunity. What I learned in the entertainment world is also true in the business world: the greater the opportunity, the more challenging the door.

Throughout my life, from early childhood to college, I had the gift of making people laugh through storytelling, impersonating famous people, and turning neighborhood legends into funny characters. As a young kid, I was aware of my potential but did not fully accept my personal responsibility to act on it as a professional (getting paid for my gift). I had done plays, performed skits and appeared in shows, entertained at family dinners and gatherings, but never performed in front of an audience who paid me money to make them laugh. Performing for family and friends is totally different than performing before strangers who have paid to be entertained by you. People would tell me all the time, "You should be a comedian. Why don't you perform on stage at the local comedy club in Baltimore?" I was aware of my potential but did not fully accept it.

Sometimes life's surprises and challenges force you to accept your potential and put it into action. There are a lot of great people who are successful because of adversities in life. Some had no food to eat and were forced to find their potential and release it on the world in order to survive. There are others who grew up in single-parent homes or lost their parents at a young age, who had to find a way out of no way, and through their journey, a star was born. That is the story behind many great entertainers and comedians.

I am grateful that I did not have to discover what accepting your potential can do in your life under those dire circumstances. My experience was somewhat different. I experienced my epic moment during the spring of 1991. My parents were not rich or poor; they were in the middle, I guess you could say. They didn't always have enough money to get what they wanted, but they had enough to get what they needed.

Just as with any American family, college was a priority. There was no doubt that you had to go to college, but the question was, how would you pay the bill? Throughout college, I took on odd jobs as a resident assistant and a security guard for a hotel, and played both football and wrestling to earn some money. But there always seemed to be a tuition imbalance.

During the winter of 1991, I received a bill from the university stating that I would be kicked out of school if my outstanding tuition was not paid by the end of the month. It is amazing how circumstances can make you tap into your potential. There was no job where I could raise $5,000 in 30 days, and everybody I knew owed money to the university. There was no one I could borrow from, and the college wouldn't forgive the debt. I had to think of something.

I lay on my dorm-room bed and thought of things I could do that wouldn't land me in jail. It hit me like a ton of bricks. A positive voice said to me, "You have everything within you to make $5,000 in 30 days!"

My negative voice asked that voice, "And what possibly could that be?"

"Use your potential. Entertain and make people laugh."

I immediately signed up to compete in the university talent show, headlining as Rob Mac, scheduled for the following week. I showed up and performed the standup act I had done at family events, and won, receiving a standing ovation! As a result of winning that contest, a week later I was asked to perform during our homecoming event as the opening act for Doug E. Fresh, a famous rapper, the main attraction. Of course I said yes. I received a standing ovation for my performance there as well. I had accepted my potential and put it into action but had not earned much money for my efforts. My tuition was still due, but now within two weeks.

While performing on stage at the homecoming event, I had an epiphany. I saw people laughing as I performed, seats filled with 2,000 students, all who paid $20 each for a ticket. That night after the homecoming event, I had the amazing idea to produce my own one-night comedy show called *Rob Mac Live!*

Right away, I went to the Director of Student Events, Mr. Frank, and told him my vision. He offered to rent out Virginia Hall for the following weekend at a discounted price of $500 but required an upfront deposit of $100. The remaining amount was due 24 hours before the show. I reached in my pocket and gave him the $100 I had been paid for the homecoming show the previous night.

My potential began to work on its own and led me to doorways that were already open. During the next week, I passed out fliers I had made and had tickets printed for sale. The night of the event, more than 1,500 people bought tickets for $5 each. I earned more than $5,000 in one night, more money than I had ever seen! I would continue to produce and perform my own shows throughout my remaining year in college.

One of the people who bought a ticket that night wasn't a student. He was a talent agent. After my show, he asked if I wanted to enter his comedy show competition at a comedy club in Richmond, Virginia. He went on to say that the winner would perform with Sinbad at the Landmark Theatre. It was a no-brainer. I entered the contest and won. The rest is history.

After performing with Sinbad and graduating from college, I continued to do standup comedy for five years to pay the bills while working as a professional in Corporate America—performing and sharing the stage with Chris Tucker, Monique, Martin Lawrence, Steve Harvey, and Dave Chappelle, to name a few. More than 20 years ago, they were accepting their true potential as fans accepted them, and today they are comedic icons. They are not icons because doors were opened for them and they simply decided to walk through them. They are icons because they accepted their potential with passion, and when doors were not open, they kicked them down!

For me, my short-lived success as a comedian was a result of deciding to go beyond being aware of my potential and accepting it and putting it into action. I have had experiences that I would have never been able to realize if it were not for the acceptance of potential. I am ever so grateful for that experience. The same can be said about accepting leadership potential. What leadership potential are you aware of that perhaps you have not fully accepted and placed into full action? What behaviors, skills, and talents are you ignoring? How and what is limiting the awareness of your potential to take action through the Acceptance Application?

We all have the responsibility for accepting our potential, and too many times we allow circumstances to bury it rather than release it. I want you to release your potential by accepting it and allowing it to show you the doors that are already open to you. Accept it to such a great degree that if those doors are not open at your arrival or won't open when you knock, you will have the courage to kick them down!

Acceptance Is the Key to the 2G Network

There is a lot that leaders can learn from comedians. Similar to leaders, comedians provide leadership on several levels. First, they gain an audience's attention on a specific topic. Second, they direct the actions, emotions, and moods of audiences. And finally, comedians direct the thoughts and observations of audience members.

If you think about it, great entertainers and comedians such as Charlie Chaplin, Bill Cosby, Johnny Carson, Robin Williams, Richard Pryor, Gene Wilder, and many others, all have or had a unique gift and talent to lead the minds of their audiences on a journey with an end goal in sight, a thought that triggers an action: a laugh.

Professional entertainers/comedians need to accept their gift to lead people to laugh, and the audience needs to accept the comedian's ability to lead them to laughter. It is a mutual exchange that benefits both parties. The same is true for leaders. Leaders need to accept their gift to lead others, and others must accept the professional's ability to lead. Otherwise, there will be no laugh for the comedian and there will be no leadership for professionals.

Acceptance is the key to accessing the 2G–Generic Leader Network. Leadership acceptance is different than leadership awareness. Leadership awareness is a result of recognizing one's ability to lead others. Leadership acceptance is embracing one's leadership potential and releasing it into action. As a leader, others accept your ability to lead them.

Those who attend my leadership conferences and events still refer to me as Rob Mac, the entertainer and comedian. That's because, unlike others in the professional development profession, I have a unique ability to make people laugh while motivating, inspiring, and teaching them how to maximize their potential in their professional and personal lives. I connect with people through laughter in an effort to lead them to the genius leader within them. Leaders have to connect in order to lead others. I want to teach you how you can develop your own unique brand of leadership as a Generic Leader and how you can create opportunities to stand out from the rest simply by accepting your potential, as others accept your leadership.

2G–Generic Leader Profile and Traits

The 2G–Generic Leader is the second network in the 6G Leadership System. Expanding from the 1G to 2G Leadership Network requires two simple but challenging things: First, you must be in a state of full acceptance of your leadership potential by releasing it into demonstrable leadership actions. Second, others must accept your leadership role. Acceptance of your leadership role by others can come from a promotion into a formal supervisory or management role, or through an informal role such as a team lead, area lead, floor lead, department lead, project lead, or lead position in a non-management title.

If scores from your leadership aptitude identify your dominant network as 2G–Generic Leader, then congratulations are in order. That means that your coworkers, peers, and supervisors/managers, through the acceptance of your leadership behaviors, have given you some degree of leadership responsibility over people, functions, projects, and tasks.

To help you better understand your profile, Diagram 1 summarizes the profile of the 2G–Generic Leader and the Acceptance App.

- -

Diagram 1

High Potential Leader, with acceptance of ability and responsibility to lead. Leaders allow you to influence them because you accept leadership.

Acceptance App—*Acceptance* is embracing leadership as others embrace you.

Overview of the Generic Leader

- Generic Leaders are general leaders who have accepted their accountability to lead. They direct activities and assignments very well, and monitor progress. However, they struggle with identifying process challenges and issues given their commitment to timelines.

- Generic Leaders like to control the decision-making process. But when it comes to group thinking and collaborating to solve cross-boundary issues, they may become inflexible given their emotional ties to the process.

- Generic Leaders enjoy working in small teams and environments, but their need to be in charge may limit the growth of others.

Maximum Potential—realized in routine complex situations requiring specialized knowledge or skill.

Least Potential—created in an environment that requires creativity, collaboration, and diverse teams.

Core Leadership Value to Teams and Professionals

Professionals value you because you accept leadership. Professionals allow you to lead because you are accepted by others as leaders:

- Directs activities, tasks, functions, and/or assignments.
- Prefers to control decision-making.
- Solicits feedback before taking significant action.
- Team player and High Potential professional.

- -

If you are an aspiring leader or if your aptitude results indicate you are operating on the 2G Network, I'm going to share with you the profile, features, limitations, and applications of the 2G–Generic Leader. As you review this network, celebrate your value and get excited about expanding to the next network to overcome any visible limitations. Introspectively complete exercises and conduct a self-assessment in areas you can improve.

First, let's review the profile and traits. Generic Leaders have traits and behaviors that are easily identifiable compared to those without these behaviors. In many instances, Generic Leaders are considered High Potentials because of others' acceptance of their ability to lead.

Next, in Diagram 2, is a limited set of traits to help you understand the Generic Leader Network.

• •

Diagram 2

Review each of these traits and indicate those that resonate with your actions, behaviors, and habits by providing a score between 5 (often), 3 (sometimes), or 1 (rarely) on each trait.

Generic Leaders:

_ Usually are in a management function or lead role.

_ Are proven in leading teams and are seasoned individual contributors.

_ Are often High Potentials.

_ Typically answer to intermediate leaders who use general, common, and traditional leadership principles and styles.

_ May rely on authority, title, and rank to accomplish goals and objectives.

_ Constantly deliver work completeness and accuracy through teams.

_ Have been given authority to lead others.

_ Have fully accepted demonstrating their potential.

_ Resemble the management styles of their boss or operating leadership culture.

_ Take action but solicit feedback on matters of significance.

– May often become slightly stressed and frustrated in highly political organizations.

– Like challenges.

– Limit risk-taking and may question leadership direction.

– Aspire to be good leaders.

– Conduct causal analysis to solve business issues.

– Are highly structured.

– Shine when working in tight timeframes and have independent autonomy.

– Use common and general approaches to leadership. Change and chaos can be their worst enemy.

• •

What's Generic About Leadership?

To summarize the profiles in both Diagrams 1 and 2, Generic Leaders are critical of the leadership system because they are general and Generic Leaders in nature. There are several key benefits and features about them: others have accepted their leadership, they lead while doing, and they consistently deliver results. In short, they are driven, systematic, and highly influential to their peers and coworkers. In many instances, they are High Potentials.

As with any system, they also come with limitations. Limitations in this network have to do with user expectations, to a large extent. In leadership, leaders often have placed on themselves false expectations, in that they are expected to play all leadership roles and positions simultaneously. For example, in the entertainment business, an entertainer/comedian can't be a punch-line comic, a storytelling comic, a joke-driven comic, or a shock-and-awe comic all in one set. He or she, as well as the audience, would be confused; so is it true with leadership.

2G–Generic Network leaders have several limitations, and each can be transformed into benefits if appropriately developed. Generic Leaders are appointed, which is challenging in organizations that require leadership acceptance prior to appointment. They are largely transactional but not transformational leaders, and they often mirror the leadership style of a boss, mentor, or the existing culture of the organization's leadership.

Features of the Generic Leader

Just as in the 1G–Genetic Leader Network, the 2G–Generic Leader Network has features that add significant value to those who operate on the 6G Leadership System. Each of the networks from 1G–6G works together to produce leadership.

Each network has specific features that add value to the output of the leadership system itself.

2G–Generic Leader, in many instances, is the dominant network that most professionals who are given leadership responsibility reside on. Most Generic Leaders are in management positions; however, CEOs and officers operate on this network as well and, in many instances, it is their primary residence because they lead based on position, title, and rank.

Here are several of the key features for each user of the leadership system: those whose dominating network is 2G, and those who may expand into other networks. Each needs to be able to fully comprehend, optimize, and leverage the network.

Remember, if this is not your dominant leadership network, it is critical that you still understand how the network operates so that when you interact with others who are predominately Generic Leaders, you will be able to develop skills to better connect with them. Also, factor in that they could be your boss or work for you, now or in the future.

Generic Leaders Are Accepted by Others to Lead

The 6G Leadership System is structured so that nobody is placed in a leadership position or role until several things occur: they demonstrate acceptance of their potential to lead others through action, they fully accept leadership responsibility, and they consistently demonstrate leadership behaviors.

The 6G Leadership System is designed to produce Generic Leaders who operate on the 2G Network because, through time, they have demonstrated through their behaviors that they have accepted their leadership potential, and their actions have influenced others to accept them as leaders. More often than not, Generic Leaders have been observed by peers, supervisors, and management as professionals with the ability to lead a task, assignment, function, process, or project well before they are considered for a formal leadership position. They consistently demonstrate their ability to connect, build relationships, and oversee professionals. 2G–Generic Leaders have more than just the potential to be leaders; they have the skills and competencies. They have experienced leadership before being promoted into a position, power, or authority over others.

If you are a 2G–Generic Leader, welcome to the formal leadership network. The best leaders on this network are not successful because they use their appointment or title to accomplish goals and objectives through others. This transactional leadership model—lead for the transaction first, (i.e. results, goals, objective, scorecard) and worry about the people second—goes against the abilities of the Generic Leader. The best leaders use a transformational leadership concept—the acceptance of others to achieve extraordinary results (i.e. people first, and goals, objectives, and results will follow).

Operating on the 2G Leadership Network requires the following personal oath and pledge: *Accept your leadership potential; accept your leadership responsibility; and accept the fact that others must accept you as a leader.*

If you are willing to do these three things, and put into action the right behaviors as identified in the Leadership Aptitude Assessment, you are on your way to becoming a great leader!

Choose the path of acceptance from others. It is the way to expand to the 3G Network and to become a Go-To Leader while achieving significance in professional development, business growth, relationship management, and acceptance.

Generic Leaders Lead While Doing

Generic Leaders are consistent in delivering results by establishing predefined goals and using teams. When professionals are placed in leadership positions, whether in a formal management position or a position informally created for them, they are usually selected because they make sure things get done. If we truly think about a Generic Leader, they are in the strategic position of making sure work products are delivered based on predefined processes and objectives, and limiting deviation to the greatest extent possible. Generic Leaders are the captains of the ship and oversee generic processes.

In order to be effective on the 2G–Generic Leader Network, leaders must follow processes, procedures, and business rules to the tee. On this network, there is not a lot of flexibility to creatively change, alter, or modify set processes on the fly. Therefore, Generic Leaders are the referees who ensure professionals are executing assignments within the rules. To this extent, they are designed to limit changes, risks, and errors. To achieve this, Generic Leaders rely heavily on structure and teams.

Generic Leaders manage activities and assignments very well and monitor progress along the way. The best Generic Leaders also are individual contributors working with the team as they manage the overall activities and progress as necessary. They have a good working relationship with the teams because not only are they leading, but they are doing while leading.

Several years ago, a friend of mine, who is a manager for a Fortune 500 company and a Generic Leader at heart, called with a story about his newly appointed boss, who also has traits of a Generic Leader. My friend went on to tell me that, on occasion, this leader would call employees during and after work hours, asking for the status on certain assignments, then begin to dictate step by step how he wanted the assignment completed. As a result of those phone calls, almost everyone on his team began to operate in fear and to question their own judgment, ultimately losing self- and team-confidence. The leader never visited the employees during the day or stopped by on the floor to motivate or inspire the team; the majority of his communications occurred during the workday when phone calls were made from his office, two floors above, to inquire on the status of assignments.

This is an example of how a leader could reside on the 2G–Generic Leader Network, solely by authority or appointment, and at the same time be completely ineffective in connecting with, relating to, and positively influencing other aspiring leaders. Second, this is a good example of what not to do if you are a newly promoted or transitioned leader. In this example, the leader made the choice to use authority to influence action rather than being present to help the team achieve the desired outcome—leading by doing. As a result of the leader's actions, fear and anxiety spread throughout the organization. Needless to say, the leader did not stay connected to the leadership network for long. Ultimately, employee morale and business results plummeted.

The best Generic Leaders maximize leadership potential using the concept of leading by doing. Generic Leaders establish positive relationships with professionals, teams, and individual contributors. Generic Leaders recognize that everyone is a leader, and their actions reflect mutual respect. Generic Leaders who optimize the 2G Network make time to visit the floor, engage with aspiring leaders, and insert themselves into the process without controlling decisions and the actions of others by using their authority. They don't have to check in because they never check out.

To become a High Potential and establish recognition as an effective Generic Leader, simply lead while doing.

Generic Leaders Are Generalists and Good Communicators

Generic Leaders are generalists in the sense that they have broad general knowledge and skills in several areas, which is often why they are placed in leadership positions with responsibilities over tasks, functions, processes, or projects. The value that Generic Leaders provide to the leadership system is their ability to ensure the accuracy, completeness, and timeliness of critical work products that are required for organizational success. They have the unique ability to exemplify a broad knowledge of technical roles, and they are able to provide direction and support to teams and individual contributors who do not see the "big picture." Generic Leaders have the ability to conduct causal analysis of business issues and develop executable solutions.

In addition to being great generic generalists, Generic Leaders are also good communicators. They have the ability to communicate in both visual and auditory mediums. Professionals are either visual or auditory learners, and leaders must have the ability to determine which medium is most effective for their teams and individual contributors. Generic Leaders must also use skills to connect with professionals who may be categorized as introverts or extroverts. The ability to be a leader who is a good communicator creates strategic opportunities for leaders to create an environment of ideas and suggestions on how products or services can be delivered more effectively, ultimately improving customer satisfaction, both internally and externally.

The Generic Leader is the key leadership role that impacts quality, performance, productivity, and profitability. 2G–Generic Network Leaders are a great resource and critical to any organization and team.

Generic Leader Limitations

Generic Leaders Are Often Appointed as Leaders Before Being Accepted by Others to Lead

Unfortunately, being accepted as a leader by others is not standard protocol in Corporate America, but it should be a part of every organization's leadership system. We all know people who are in leadership positions, and as we observe their behavior, we ask, "How the hell did they get in that position? Who hired them?" Within organizations and, for that matter, in the 2G–Generic Leader Network, there exist leaders who have not necessarily accepted their leadership potential, have not taken the oath of responsibility, or have not been accepted by professionals as a leader. In that sense, they are leaders solely by a hierarchical structure or appointment—not by the approval of people or by professionals. Although it is not unethical to be appointed into a position without acceptance from others, it is not the best way to maximize the potential of the leader, the professionals, or an organization.

In many instances, this unfortunate situation occurs because of the lack of an effective organizational leadership system, resulting in professionals being promoted and advanced into formal leadership positions such as team leads, managers, directors, etc., without the development of their potential. This negates their conscious acceptance and acknowledgement of their internal abilities to lead by other professionals. This may occur because a business requires that a leader vacancy be filled immediately, by the external recruitment of an untested talent, a lack of succession planning, errors in judgment, and, in some instances, just plain old favoritism—people advance based on who they know, a concept that more often than not backfires.

Generally, these events place the leader and the organization at a huge disadvantage because professionals are clueless about the leader's abilities, potential, and capabilities, and often are resistant to that leader. This also creates a scenario where the leader is not sure of his or her potential, and has not fully accepted his/her leadership role.

If you are one or know of a leader who chooses to take the easier, appointed route, rather than working for advancement and acceptance, you have probably observed that the results of this approach produce little to no effectiveness, professional growth, business results, or acceptance by others. Many people who flash the "leadership by appointment card" often reside until retirement on the 2G Network, never expanding to networks 3G–6G, or in some instances become obsolete, like an old cell phone losing its connection to the network, never to reconnect again.

The key to success for the Generic Network Leader is to reach leadership acceptance from others first and limit flashing the "leadership by appointment card."

Generic Leaders Are Not Yet Branded Leaders

As with professional comedians and entertainers, the icons stand out from the rest of the performers in their industry because they are uniquely branded. On the contrary, comedians who blend together, similar to my career as a comedian, are unknown because they are too generic—many of them have the same style, tell the same types of jokes, and have the same appearance. Yes, they are funny, talented, and gifted, but because they are generic, they simply don't get the spotlight. The same is true with leadership; there are Generic Leaders and brand leaders. Brand leaders always stand out from the rest.

In some instances, Generic Leaders are new to the leadership "marketplace" while others have spent their entire careers there. But it is important to understand that in both scenarios, Generic Leaders have not developed their own unique brand of leadership. They operate generically.

As a C-level executive for one of the world's largest healthcare conglomerations, we spent a significant amount of time managing pharmaceuticals (pharma)—drug benefits to members. In the pharma industry, generic is defined as a drug sold without a brand name or trademark. Generic Leaders are just that—generic in nature when it comes to leadership. They have not yet developed their unique leadership brand. They are generic oftentimes because they have adopted someone else's leadership brand.

Have you ever been in the presence of two or more leaders in a hierarchical relationship and noticed that the subordinate leader mirrored the style, approach, or behaviors of the dominant leader? That is a good example of a Generic Leader. The Generic Leader is packaging and marketing his or her leadership style from that of a mentor, supervisor, or brand that already exists in the culture.

A major limitation to 2G–Generic Leaders is their inability to separate their approach, style, and behaviors from the culture in which they operate. In terms of tenure, some Generic Leaders are new leaders and many are intermediate leaders; in both instances, their leadership style is most often a carbon copy of other leaders. Often, other professionals will make statements such as "He is trying to be like so and so." Or perhaps you may have heard professionals say, "That's her protégé." Some of this might be attributable to envy. But the majority, I believe, has to do with professionals becoming confused with who a person truly is, because Generic Leaders tend to copy someone else's brand while trying to create or discover their own.

It is critical for 2G–Generic Leaders to spend time self-reflecting and developing their own unique approach to leadership that will separate them from the perception that they are leadership clones by those who accept but have not fully embraced their leadership.

As a result of developing your own brand as a leader, more professionals will accept your leadership, and it will also position you as a unique and authentic leader.

Generic Leaders Are Transactional Leaders, Not Transformational Leaders

The biggest mistake you could make with a Generic Leader is to place them in the role of being a transformational leader. Generic Leaders are the complete opposite of transformational leaders. It is not that they cannot be or do not have the potential to be transformational. Instead, their position requires transactional thinking and processing. Generic Leaders are in a leadership position to ensure that tasks, workflow, and work products are completed on time, effectively, efficiently, and within budgeted guidelines. In order to accomplish that huge objective, they must be narrowly focused, disciplined, and attentive to every process and procedure associated with the activity they are responsible for leading.

There is an old saying, "You can't see the forest for the trees." If a Generic Leader is responsible for making honey and you place them in a forest full of trees, they won't see the forest or even the trees in this scenario. Their attention won't be on anything other than following bees to their honeycombs. They are transactional, zeroed in on the short-term, which is what makes them valuable!

Transactional leaders are focused on the short-term processes and procedures that result in the transaction of a product or service. That generalist focus is the reason they were put into their roles as transactional leaders. In turn, transformational leaders are focused on the long-term, identifying value-based outcomes that in the future will require changes to transactional processes and procedures in order to be obtained.

More often than not, because of complex business issues and challenges, Generic Leaders' expectations can at times become blurred, because they are also expected to be transformational.

For Generic Leaders to achieve their maximum potential, they must focus their energy on the short-term of transactional leadership and be able to collaborate with other transformational leaders to improve overall business goals and objective outcomes.

If you are a Generic Leader, this is the pathway to expand beyond the 2G–Generic Leader Network to the 3G–Go-To Leader Network.

The Acceptance App

The Acceptance App, the second "mindware" application, optimizes your ability to perform on the 2G–Generic Leadership Network and also prepares you for expansion to the 3G–Go-To Leader Network.

When you are appointed into leadership as a floor lead, department lead, team lead, individual contributor lead, supervisor, director, or perhaps as an officer, you initially operate on a Generic Network—regardless of your level of experience—because of your connection to others. Many leaders on this network are new to leadership, while others are veterans. The growth to expand to the other networks is largely contingent on one's ability to come into full acceptance.

As a 2G–Generic Leader, you require a mindware application that will operate as virus protection software to protect your self-esteem and confidence and, at the same time, help you process and accept the reality of your leadership situation in your professional and personal life. To maximize your potential as a 2G–Generic Leader, you must have an application that accepts the following leadership realities:

- Your leadership role will have its difficulties.
- You are a minority among many.
- There are professional haters who will envy you.

Now that you get the gist of the Acceptance App, please answer several questions about where you are in your professional and personal life with regards to acceptance.

- What is it that you have difficulty accepting in your leadership role?
- Why were you chosen as a leader?
- What perceptions would you change about you?
- What things do you have control to change?
- How do you deal with conflict?

Accepting Your Leadership Situation and Role

When I was a child, The Serenity Prayer hung on the wall in my parents' home. It was written by a man whom I learned later was Reinhold Niebuhr, a famous theologian and commentator. Reinhold Niebuhr was the recipient of the Presidential Medal of Freedom in 1964 and a significant influence on many public officials and U.S. presidents, including Jimmy Carter and Barack Obama, as well as Madeleine Albright, Hillary Clinton, and John McCain.

The prayer reads: *God, grant me the serenity to accept the things I cannot change; the courage to change the things I can; and the wisdom to know the difference.*

Through the years, I have reflected on this prayer. As a result of more than 20 years as a leader and observing other leaders, I have discovered that the first step to leadership is simply accepting the things you cannot change, accepting the challenge to change the things you can, and the wisdom to know the difference. Leadership is about acceptance! As a 2G–Generic Leader, understanding what you can and cannot change and knowing the difference is one of the keys to success.

You may be in a situation where you are pressured to be more effective and efficient with the delivery of products, service, functions, or resources that you manage. Or perhaps you have customers demanding more value; the business demanding you do more with less; or a professional screaming, "I can't do anymore." These are constant struggles in leadership.

Accepting the environment you are operating in is critical to assessing your situation, defining your role and determining your approach. Here are some things you cannot change about expectation leadership: you cannot change customer demands; you cannot change business demands; you cannot change professionals from saying, "I can't do anymore!" But you also have to accept the things you can change: you can change results!

Generic Leaders accept what they can't change and accept what they can, and know the difference between them. The best Generic Leaders take expectations and develop specific outcomes with measurable steps to achieve the desired results. You may not be able to change the demand for more value, but you can positively change the outcome of customer satisfaction scores. A leader may not be able to change a business directive to do more with less, but he can influence what more and less is.

Successful Generic Leaders do not have the luxury of picking and choosing which goals and objectives they will play a role in. Successful Generic Leaders have a leadership Acceptance App that guides them to acceptance of their leadership situation and role and helps them decipher those things they can change and those they cannot.

Accept That You Are a Minority Among Many

Did you know that you are diverse? Did you know you are a minority among many? I'm not talking about race, social class, or ethnicity; I am talking about you as a unique person. There is nobody like you on the planet.

In the 2G–Generic Leader Network, you will be faced with people who do not think like you do. Some professionals will not see things as you see them; some leaders will not interpret or read things as you interpret them. To be successful as a Generic Leader, you must face that fact and fully accept that you are among the minority. In your leadership position, you need an Acceptance App in your head that produces an auto response so that when others disagree with your thoughts, ideas, or suggestions, it responds like an auto-voice recognition in your mind saying, "There is nothing wrong with you. You are a minority among many."

So many times on the 2G–Generic Leader Network, new and veteran leaders are crushed because of varying opinions, approaches and decisions—so much so, that their opinions can be swayed by others in an effort to appear consistent with their points of view.

Have you ever wondered why, if you ask a question privately about a business matter and then you ask the same question to the same person again later in a public setting, you will often get a different answer, usually similar to the answers others have given to the same question?

Why does that happen, you ask? It is not that people can be influenced by others; it is because, when it comes to decisions, actions, and thoughts, people prefer to be in the majority rather than in the minority. If you think about it, that is the essence of peer pressure. In business, I refer to it as "leadership peer pressure."

The best 2G–Generic Leaders are not swayed by the majority. They don't base their answers on popularity or the potential for promotion. They accept that they are in the minority and make suggestions, recommendations, and decisions based on their experiences, observations, and thoughts. It is critical that Generic Leaders accept their ideas, thoughts, and suggestions and not subject them to the filter of "leadership peer pressure." Using the Acceptance App will provide you with confidence and with the assurance that there is nothing wrong with being diverse or different. There is value being the minority among many.

There Are Professional Haters Who Envy You

Getting to the 2G–Generic Leader Network is no small task. Those who succeed in being on this network spent considerable time in developing themselves, releasing their potential, influencing others, and assuming risks, with the reward of gaining access to the 2G gateway of leadership. Congratulations on your success, but you must also accept the challenges that come along with the appointment into leadership.

2G–Generic Leaders must accept early on in their leadership role that there will be times when they experience interaction with professionals at all levels who may have false perceptions of you, who question your leadership ability, and just flat out make your leadership experience miserable. If you are new to leadership or an old-school leader and haven't yet figured out who these people are, let me help you: they are Professional Haters! There, I said it—Professional Haters. As the late hip-hop rapper Biggie Smalls (The Notorious B.I.G.) said, "If you don't know, now you know!"

When speaking at conferences and events, I refer to them as "Professional Haters" because they spend company time, money, and resources hating and envying you. Unfortunately, they get paid for hating you and others!

They can be disguised as leaders, supervisors, officers, friends, or relatives, but their mental job description has "hater" in it somewhere.

This may come as a surprise for many new leaders and can, quite frankly, create such low confidence that some leadership careers may end prematurely. It is also the reason why many Generic Leaders don't expand to the other networks in the 6G Leadership System. They have not learned how to deal with Professional Haters. Their confidence weakens. They fall prey to devaluing themselves and become doubtful of their own abilities because of this unfortunate experience. Trust me, as painful as it was to recognize, the person who recruited me for an executive position was a hater, while in disguise as a leader, who attempted to sabotage my career for several years straight. It was only after I left the company that my former boss fell into the hole she dug for me.

As 2G–Generic Leaders, I want you to know and accept that Professional Haters will try to impact your thinking and actions, and sabotage your career. The Acceptance App is critical and applies to every network on the 6G Leadership System. It will give you the necessary defenses to identify the haters and adjust your emotional intelligence to conquer them. In each network, there will be experiences that can impact leaders negatively if they don't accept the fact that there are Professional Haters lurking. Use the Acceptance App to counteract their attacks. I used this app for five years.

You cannot change Professional Haters, but you can change how you allow them to impact you. When Professional Haters attack, use your Awareness App to produce an anti-negative virus protector as a part of your "mindware" that:

- Won't allow the penetration of their words or actions to impact your state of mind.
- Will quarantine your environment from all negative energy.
- Won't allow their negative words to cause you to act negatively toward others.
- Will reject all negative attacks on your confidence, empowerment, and self-esteem.

Summary

Leadership comes at a cost, and that cost is Acceptance of leadership challenges. The 2G–Generic Leader Network requires a mindware that keeps you connected to the network and creates the potential to connect to the 3G–Go-To Leader Network, if optimized effectively. Accept your leadership situation and role, accept that you are a minority among many, and accept the fact that there are Professional Haters who will envy you. In all your accepting, remember to accept the things you cannot change, change the things you can, and have the wisdom to know the difference.

6G Leadership Coaching is the art and science of retraining your brain through meditation, thought, action, and repetition. In this chapter, you will complete the exercise so you can immediately grasp and put into action the concepts we have discussed.

Here are 10 ways to use the Acceptance App, including affirmations, action steps, and applications daily on your journey to becoming a Leader of Significance. Remember, the stronger your Acceptance App, the greater the potential!

• •

2G–Leadership Coaching Exercise:
Acceptance Affirmations, Action Steps, and Applications

1. Each morning when you rise, repeat three times, "Today I will accept those things I cannot change and have the courage to change the things I can!" Write down three things you will begin changing today (outcomes, behaviors, and mindset). *This will open your mind to begin the acceptance of change process.*

2. Identify three areas in your life that impact your emotional thoughts at work that you need to accept in order to be a more effective leader. *This will help to exercise your acceptance of circumstances you may not be able to control.*

3. When professionals question your ideas and thoughts, repeat in your mind three times: "I am a minority among many, which makes my opinion just as valuable as any!" *This will build your confidence. Write down areas where you have unique ideas and opinions and discuss them with other leaders.*

4. As Professional Haters attempt to negatively influence your thoughts and confidence, state affirmatively, "Don't hate the player; hate the leadership game." Identify three professionals who are Professional Haters and determine steps you can take to make them allies. *Doing this reverses negativity into positive energy.*

5. During lunch and after the day is over, think about how you may be able to demonstrate the behaviors of a transformational leader. Write down three things you can start doing today. *Following this action will transform conscious acts into unconscious behavior.*

6. Repeat daily: "Lead by doing!" This is a reminder to visit the floor and be present so others can see you are not an ivory-tower leader. Write down ways in which you can participate in activities and projects to maximize engagement levels. *This will ignite morale and positive energy in the team.*

7. During your commute home, introspectively reflect on your leadership communication. What areas can you improve on? *This will introduce to your psyche the concept of operating and striving for excellence.*

8. Repeat daily: "I may not be able to change others' perceptions of me, but I can change my perceptions of others!" List three perceptions you have of others that require changing in order to build a stronger relationship. *This daily regimen will force you to take your attention off others and work on you.*

9. Don't let Professional Haters be mind-regulators. Assess daily your reaction to negative influences to ensure they are not impacting your potential and thoughts. Identify things that haters say that annoy you, and define a method to eliminate the impact. *This will create a shift in not allowing others, by using emotional intelligence, to dictate your state of mind.*

10. Before you leave the office each day, write down one thing you could have done differently and redo it tomorrow. What is the one thing you can do differently starting today? Write it down. *This turns desires into habits and creates a self-coaching environment.*

Now that you have completed this exercise, review each week and assess your progress. In the next chapter, we will explore the 3G–Go-To Leadership Network, its profile, features, limitations, and Acknowledgement App. Let's upgrade to the next network.

3G–Go-To Leader and the Acknowledgment App

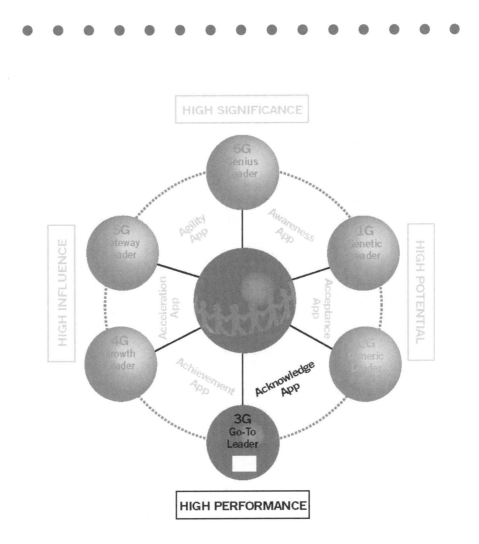

*The most important quality in a leader is that of
being acknowledged as such.*
—Andre Maurois, novelist

*If you wish your merit to be known,
acknowledge that of other people.*
—Proverb

Acknowledge Others and
They Will Acknowledge Your Leadership

One of the most gratifying feelings for a professional is when they are acknowledged for their actions. But what is even more gratifying is when a team acknowledges their leader for their results.

Go-To Leaders are acknowledged high-performing leaders because they have the unique ability to lead others and individually produce results. Go-To Leaders are three-dimensional in that they perform many roles, like a multi-position athlete does.

Magic Johnson has been acknowledged as one of the greatest basketball players of all time. Hands down, he is the best multi-position athlete who ever played the game. Magic played shooting guard, forward, and center often in his NBA career. He earned the nickname "Magic" because he was the Go-To Leader on the team. If the team was desperate for a shot, who would they "go to"? Magic. And that is exactly what occurred every time he touched the ball: magic.

The most memorable moment when Magic was the ultimate Go-To Leader for the Lakers was on May 16, 1980, at the Philadelphia Spectrum, Game 6, NBA Finals, Los Angeles vs. Philadelphia. Kareem Abdul-Jabbar had severely injured his left ankle in the Lakers' NBA Finals Game 5 victory over the Philadelphia 76ers. Many Lakers fans were sure that Kareem would walk out on the court to take his position at center stage to beat the Sixers. But it was not Kareem who would play center that night; it would be the youngest Laker, 20-year-old rookie point guard Magic Johnson.

As the Lakers and Sixers walked onto the court and prepared for tipoff, 6-foot-9 Magic Johnson stepped into the center of the court, taking Kareem's spot. The opposing player on the Sixers, center Caldwell Jones, looked at Magic, smirked and said, "This is a joke, right?"

The rest of the night would not be a joke. If it was, the joke was on the Sixers. On offense, Magic became the Go-To Leader, moving into the low post, catching passes, and launching hook shots, Abdul-Jabbar style, all night long!

Throughout the night, Magic magically transformed himself into three players: center, forward, and guard. He crashed the boards, created assists, set up the offense, and guarded literally everyone on the floor, including Dr. Julius Erving.

Fast forward to the scoreboard. Magic Johnson authored the greatest individual rookie performance in NBA history: 42 points, 14 of 14 from the free-throw line, 15 rebounds, 7 assists, and 3 steals. The Lakers beat the Sixers that night. Throughout Magic's career, he would have many extraordinary accomplishments, making him the Go-To Leader for the Lakers for many years. Kobe and Shaq are still trying to match his accomplishments. (If you don't know who they are, Google them and you will be impressed by their accomplishments.)

Magic Johnson's performance as a professional athlete exemplifies what professional Go-To Leaders are: magical High Performers.

Understanding That Go-To Leaders Are Magical

Go-To Leaders stand out among the crowd, and people are drawn to them because they do amazing things and achieve great results, all the while working with a team. They do things that Genetic and Generic Leaders just aren't at a level to achieve in terms of talent and skill. Go-To Leaders are acknowledged for this ability, just as Magic Johnson was. Go-To Leaders in Corporate America are game changers. When an organization or team is down or under the gun, they are the ones you go to.

Go-To Leaders are acknowledged as magical and High Performers on their teams because they play several roles. Go-To Leaders function as multi-professionals or, as I refer to them, 3D Leaders. They play the roles of leaders of teams, individual contributors, and specialty talent. Just like Magic, their ability to play multiple positions increases their value to others and builds a reputation and a brand as the Go-To Leader who gets things done, especially those that are urgent, complex, and customer-centric.

In 2001, while working for Motorola in Schaumburg, Ill., I had the privilege to be a part of a team of Go-To Leaders. We were a part of the business transformation leadership team, a High Potential team recruited and retained, dedicated to developing solutions to integrate and rationalize cellular platforms, products, and infrastructure to improve customer satisfaction while becoming more effective, efficient, and profitable.

To achieve this task, the organization committed to recruiting hundreds of Go-To Leaders with leadership, individual contributor, and specialty talents in order to achieve their aggressive goals and desired business objectives. I was fortunate to be among the Go-To's.

Each day, this High Performing team would meet at what we called the "tower dome" and strategize on how we could achieve the targeted outcomes of the organization. The initiative was challenging in the sense that this group of leaders reported to the corporate organization. We were charged with creating transformation in the independently run business sector, all led by presidents and CEOs, each with independent control.

Given the vision and scope of the initiative, leaders at all levels and from all facets of the organization participated in "business transformation" meetings. There were engineers, financial analysts, information technology gurus, lawyers, project managers, accountants, operational experts, product designers, developers, software programmers, vendors, suppliers, salespeople, marketing staff, product developers...the list goes on.

There was one person, the vice president of market and product planning, who stood out among all of the Go-To Leaders. He was institutionally well connected and versed in all aspects of products, infrastructure, and organizational capabilities.

From a structural standpoint, within the business transformation team there were separate work teams collaborating but focused separately on products, infrastructure, finance, and market planning work streams. Each of the teams presented ideas, solutions, and business cases for solving complicated problems at the business transformation meetings. As you would expect, the process during each meeting was that each work group selected a presenter to present their progress report to the C-level committee. The presenters selected on behalf of the work teams had significant experience and were viewed as authorities and acknowledged as a leader by others.

I happened to be on the products work team and was heavily engaged with the Go-To Leader, Lester, the vice president of market and product planning. At a planning meeting, we received a request that the product team present their solution, approach, and plan for solving a problem associated with market confusion at the next C-level business transformation meeting. Many assumed that Lester would be the Go-To presenter because of his vast knowledge.

My role was to lead the team in developing the solutions, preparing slides, and making other preparations for the meetings. We walked through the slides as a team about two days before the meeting, making minor changes. As we reviewed the last page of the slide deck that included next steps, there was a pause. Lester asked the team, "So who's presenting?"

There was complete silence.

I thought two things were possible. Either nobody wanted to publicly say they could do what Lester did, or nobody wanted to step up and be the Go-To person for this particular meeting.

As I sat there thinking, "Should I volunteer?" a negative voice in my head said, "That is a career-limiting move. You are being set up to take the fall if the presentation sucks. After all, you just got here. Nobody is going to listen to you anyway. Let someone else volunteer!"

The positive voice in my head said, "You have to decide if you are going to sit on the sidelines or get in the game."

Fortunately, I listened to the positive voice that day. As nervous as I was about what the CEOs, vice presidents, and directors might think of our presentation and how it might impact my career, I raised my hand and made the decision that I would take the center position and get in the game.

During the next few days, I asked advice on presenting issues from other leaders on the team. I discussed how to verbally craft specific solutions to the C-level executives, all in an effort to thoroughly prepare for the meeting.

I asked one of the executive vice presidents who would be attending the meeting about how they viewed certain topics. His agitated reply was, "You will do just fine." To my dismay, he got up and left the room and never answered my question. In fact, he did not speak to me when I saw him during the next two days as I got ready for the meeting. I guess to him I appeared nervous and was over-preparing.

The day of the meeting, I arrived about 20 minutes early to have enough time to review my notes and prepare for the presentation. I thought I would be alone, but when I arrived, the boardroom was full of executives reviewing the materials that were released in advance of the meeting. They took their responsibilities seriously. I sat toward the front of the room and reviewed my material quietly.

Twenty minutes later, Lester took center stage. He made opening comments and introduced me as the leader of the team that would be presenting for the products team. I took the floor, and the rest is history. I presented the business case, the committee accepted it, and I received acknowledgement from my team and a few of the C-level executives on a job well.

Lester and the executive vice president, who had not answered my questions earlier in preparation for the meeting, walked up to me. The executive vice president said to Lester, "I told you he was our Go-To." He shook my hand and said, "Great work!"

I learned later that the executive vice president was aware of my specialty skills of communicating, presenting, and engaging others as a part of the business transformation team. He was also aware that I was a leader of a core function and a significant contributor. When planning the meetings with the C-level executives, both he and Lester discussed me as the presenter. Just as Magic Johnson volunteered to be on center court in that game against the Sixers, I, too, would volunteer, unaware that the acknowledgement of leadership potential was already established and I just needed to step into it.

Several things happened that day. Not only was the presentation accepted, but the company moved forward through a business transformation that would ultimately turn it around. But something else happened that day: I acknowledged my potential by getting into the game; others acknowledged my contributions as a leader; and I discovered I was a Go-To Leader, as well as the concept of the Go-To Leader. Like Magic Johnson, a Go-To Leader is acknowledged by peers for his actions and results.

Just as in basketball, when there is complexity, challenge, and chaos, people want Go-To Leaders whom they can rely on to achieve desired results. Leaders become Go-To Leaders when they make a choice to be the "go-to," when others acknowledge their potential, and when their performance achieves extraordinary results. They are High Performers who take dire situations and somehow produce the magic that achieves the desired outcomes.

Those who aspire to be leaders on the 3G Network, or wish to sustain operability on the network, must be able to lead others while producing results and must be acknowledged as a leader. And they must have magic. My experience with Motorola cemented me in the Go-To status as a leader, and the same potential and opportunities exist within you.

To explore and tap into your potential to be a Go-To Leader, take some time to think about your current leadership situation and career path, and answer the following questions:

- What opportunities, projects, and initiatives exist for you in your role as a Go-To Leader?
- What skills do you need to improve in order to increase your confidence in being a Go-To Leader?
- What special talents and gifts do you possess to make you feel magical?
- How do others acknowledge your leadership abilities? Do they see you as a technical, functional, or multifaceted leader?
- How can you become the "Magic" in and on your team?
- What Go-To Leadership opportunities are there when you can demonstrate your ability to lead others, deliver results, and perform as a specialty talent?
- What new leadership skills or behaviors can you further refine to be viewed as a specialty talent, multi-dimensional leader, and High Performer?

3G–Go-To Leader Profile and Traits

The 3G–Go-To Leader is the third network in the 6G Leadership System. To expand from the 2G to 3G Leadership Network requires several things: First, you must be acknowledged by others with regards to your leadership ability; second, you must acknowledge others' leadership potential; third, you must be sought after to lead critical business goals and objectives; and finally, you must be able to create magic and deliver extraordinary outcomes.

Go-To Leaders are not appointed. They volunteer and choose to be Go-To Leaders. The key difference between the 2G–Generic Leader and the 3G–Go-To Leader is that the Go-To Leader has been acknowledged as a leader by other leaders from networks 2G through 6G. In contrast, the 2G–Generic Leader has been accepted by peers and others as a one-dimensional leader with limited brand recognition who operates in a general and generic capacity.

If scores from your leadership aptitude identify your dominant network as a 3G–Go-To Leader, then congratulations are in order, because that means that leaders acknowledge your leadership actions, you've created magic like Magic Johnson, and you have taken risks that others run from, such as leading complicated assignments, functions, and tasks using teams and your specialized skills and talents.

To help you better understand the profile, Diagram 1 summarizes the profile of the 3G–Go-To Leader and the Acknowledgement App "mindware" that every 3G Leader needs to run on their leadership operating system.

• •

Diagram 1

High Performing, with the ability to lead others and produce desired results. Leaders allow you to influence them because they acknowledge your results.

Acknowledgement App—*Acknowledgement* is others recognizing your accomplishments as you acknowledge your strengths and weaknesses.

Overview of the Go-To Leader

- Go-To Leaders recognize the organizational need to get things done and their ability to do it, but they may forget to seek buy-in to limit impact on others.

- Go-To Leaders are driven by deadlines and a sense of urgency, but because of the need for results, they take on risks when not in the best interest of their career.

- Go-To Leaders love challenges, but in the absence of assigned challenges, they may become creatively anxious and initiate change projects without strategic rationale.

Maximum Potential—realized in situations that require transformation, planning, structure, and creativity.

Least Potential—created in a scenario that is routine, mundane, and unchallenging.

Core Leadership Value to Teams and Professionals

Professionals value you because they recognize your results. Professionals value you because others acknowledge your success.

- Embraces new assignments and direction.
- Brainstorms solutions and takes risks.
- Driven by challenges, deadlines, and urgency.
- High Performer with specialty and unique skills and talents.
- Change agent and game changer.

• •

Go-To Leaders have unique traits and behaviors that are easily identifiable in comparison to those in other leaders. They have the ability to connect with people in ways that challenge, motivate, and inspire them to perform to their potential. Go-To Leaders continue to advance in achieving extraordinary results.

Go-To Leaders are High Performers because they take the risk of challenging opportunities and doing the things that others are not willing to do. The 6G Leader Contained in Diagram 2 is a limited set of traits to help you understand the Go-To Leader in more detail and to give you guidance in forming Go-To Leader habits.

• •

Diagram 2

Go-To Leaders:

– Perform in multi-dimensional roles as leaders, individual contributors, and specialty performers.

– Are proven in leading teams and highly sought-after for the completion of complicated projects, assignments and tasks.

– Are often High Performers.

– Typically have a self-developed brand unique from other leaders.

– Rely on teams, relationships, and individual talent to accomplish goals and objectives.

– Constantly over-deliver.

– Have been given authority to lead others and empowered to make critical decisions, but choose to be the "Go To" when times get tough.

– Fully acknowledge and demonstrate their potential and work to improve strengths and weaknesses.

– Transform culture and leadership styles.

– Take action and seek feedback after results are achieved.

• •

Features of the Go-To Leader

Not every leader is the same, and there is no set profile for the millions of leaders in the world. However, the Go-To Leader listing of features gives a general sense of and helps identify and maximize the potential of Go-To Leaders. On the 6G Leadership System, you will find diversity and inclusion for leaders who have both similar and different traits. However, the key to connecting to the 3G Network is that Go-To Leaders respect and acknowledge others' leadership contributions, and in doing so, will earn them the opportunity to become Go-To Leaders.

Next are several key features that each user of the leadership system have access to—both those whose dominating network may reside here, and those who may expand onto other bands but visit this network often. It is important that every leader fully comprehend, optimize, and develop skills to navigate the network because those same skills allow leaders to operate on the expanded network. Remember the saying "A chain is only as strong as the weakest link"? The same is true for the 6G Network: "A leader is only as strong as its weakest network."

If this is not your dominant leadership network, it is critical that you grasp knowledge of how the network operates so that when you interact with others, you will be able to better connect with leaders and to operate on this network.

Should you be an aspiring leader, or if your aptitude results indicate you are operating on the 3G Network, I will share with you the key features, limitations, and applications of the 3G–Go-To Leader to help you maximize your potential.

As you review this network, celebrate other leaders you have collaborated with, identify what you can do to maximize your leadership potential, and get excited about expanding to the next network.

Go-To Leaders Lead From the Middle

There are an awful lot of concepts and varying opinions that exist on the best leadership style: leading from the top, leading from the sidelines, bottom-up leadership, and leading from behind. But none of these are effective for the Go-To Leader.

Go-To Leaders lead from the middle. Not from a hierarchy standpoint, but from a relational standpoint—relating to professionals and other leaders. Go-To Leaders have relationships with stakeholders, peers, teammates, and colleagues who give them a keen sense of ability to get right in the middle of things and lead others to achieving extraordinary results.

Go-To Leaders understand that professionals from all walks of life add immeasurable value because of their unique views, perspectives, ideas, and thoughts about life, business, and society. Go-To Leaders recognize that it is those varying opinions that make up the intellectual knowledge base in an organization, and they also acknowledge that the only way to extract the value from this reservoir of knowledge is to get in the middle of the flow.

Go-To Leaders have the special talent to lead, regardless of organizational structure—formal, informal, hierarchical, flat, or matrix. Others acknowledge them as the Go-To Leader for major projects, initiatives, and activities based on past accomplishments and results. They have the ability to work within all levels of an organizational structure and are often viewed as a leader. But, more importantly, they are viewed as a member of the team.

Go-To Leaders penetrate the minds, hearts, and souls of professionals by being a member of the team first and a leader second. They create a presence of collaboration, flexibility, mutual respect, and contribution while downplaying position, authority, and status.

The middle is where the action is. The middle is where you will find issues, solutions, challenges, and opportunities. Go-To Leaders are successful because they have the features and abilities to get in the middle of things. They have the presence to not be in the right place at the right time to take advantage of opportunities, but simply to be in the middle. When the ball of opportunity drops, they are in position to catch it.

Be a Go-To Leader, take center stage, and get in the middle. Once there, you can lead!

Go-To Leaders Cut Through Politics

Often, opportunities are created for Go-To Leaders because of the dynamics of organizational culture and politics. There are silos, pockets, and cultural walls existing in organizations that require a leader to cut through obstacles, build a team, and create engagement in order to achieve desired outcomes. Those things described as obstacles can also be described as organizational politics. "Trust," "transparency," and "agenda" are code words used to describe this dilemma. One of the Go-To Leader features is their ability to cut through politics, which we will discuss in a later chapter.

Go-To Leaders are often non-affiliated politically. They make decisions based on experience, observations, and facts, and predetermine their decision-making based on votes needed and favors returned. It is this independence that creates their brand collaboration, engagement, and openness with all parties and leaders.

People who are interested in improving both themselves and the business connect easily to Go-To Leaders because they know they do not have a hidden agenda or ulterior motive. Go-To Leaders are about achieving a desired outcome through leading a team, contributing along the way, and acknowledging the contributions and successes of others.

Go-To Leaders clash with leaders who are disguised as Go-To Leaders interested only in self-gratification, recognition, and reward through using others. After repeated self-promotion, other professionals and leaders soon recognize this behavior and their leadership goes nowhere—they become "No-Go" Leaders.

Recently, a Fortune 1000 client experienced tremendous growth and improvement in providing services to its customers. As a result, the organization wanted to recognize those who contributed to their success at an upcoming annual meeting. At the meeting, the master of ceremonies, who was also the executive division's officer, called up to the stage a leader identified as the person who "led" the successful growth effort. That person walked up on stage as others in the audience looked on in surprise. He accepted the individual recognition, said a few words about the difficulty of the project and how he achieved the results, then thanked the master of ceremonies for the award.

After the event was over, several other divisional leaders approached the master of ceremonies. They told him that they, too, and their entire divisions also worked tirelessly on the project and inquired as to why their teams were not recognized. It turns out the leader was acknowledged because he was a good friend and worked for him. In short, the division's executive officer wanted his organization to receive the credit for the company's success at the annual meeting.

This was not the Go-To Leader but rather a Go-To Leader in disguise who ultimately became a No-Go Leader. All of the leaders in the organization who attended the meeting categorized the leader as a No-Go for several reasons: he did not acknowledge anyone for their assistance, he did not contribute to the project but took credit, and he engaged in political theatre.

Go-To Leaders leave politics aside and go after business goals and objectives without affiliations, relationships, or aiming for personal gratification. They forget about themselves and take care of the customer first. Everything else is secondary—that's what Go-To Leaders do.

Go-To Leaders Are Franchise Players
Who Have Developed a Brand

Go-To Leaders are acknowledged by others because they have developed a uniquely defined positive image, perception, and brand of their ability to achieve extraordinary results. They are the Go-To Leaders for complicated, time-consuming, and high-pressure deliverables. Professionals and leaders acknowledge them as those who are willing to take the last shot with one second left on the clock. They are recognized for their ability to succeed in the most challenging scenarios: presenting in front of a high-prospect client, successfully implementing a system that every customer will experience, or creating a new product or service dubbed the "turn-around project" that everyone is relying on to put the company back in the black. They are risk-takers who worry about their careers last and place the company first, time and time again. Go-To Leaders are unique in that they are multi-dimensional, can lead others, deliver as an individual contributor, and possess a unique skill or talent in the areas of communication, innovation, strategic thinking, execution, problem-solving, and relationship management. They are franchise players. With them, the team grows, which makes them High Performing Leaders.

Go-To Leaders have the magic to make everything they touch succeed. They hit the free throws under pressure. They have a brand associated with taking risks, growing others as they grow themselves, and are best known for leading by getting in the middle of things and achieving by doing!

Go-To Leader Limitations

If you are a Go-To Leader, know professionals who fit this profile, or perhaps people in this category report to you, be aware that every system and network has its limitations. Operating on the 3G–Go-To Leadership Network is no different. Leadership is not absolute and it is not an exact science.

With limitations also come opportunities to improve on the 3G–Go-To Leader Network. Some limitations may be a result of personality, experience, chemistry with others, and organizational culture. You will find that as you explore and evaluate your leadership behaviors and skills, you will uncover weaknesses, organizational challenges, and blind spots that limit your ability to maximize your potential. As you uncover them, view them as an opportunity to improve your leadership aptitude and to expand to a broader leadership network. Remember, all of these skills, capabilities, mindsets, and principles also apply to other leadership networks, so there is always an opportunity to improve.

Good news comes in pieces. One piece of good news about the 3G–Go-To Leader is that others acknowledge them as the ones who resolve complicated matters and business issues. As mentioned earlier, there are several limitations existing on the network. The good news is that they can be transformed into benefits through coaching, professional development, and changing the operating environment of the Go-To Leader.

The next several pages identify areas you can focus on to expand your skills and abilities, avoid leadership limitation traps, and begin developing a plan with a dedicated coach who can help you explore and improve growth opportunities.

Go-To Leaders Are Heroic But Not Invincible

Go-To Leaders are professionals and can hold any leadership position, from team leader, manager, director, officer, and C-level executive in an organization. Most people see Go-To Leaders as heroic figures who fight the business "crimes" of uncertainty, doubt, challenges, and difficult issues in an organization. Some are seen by their peers as superheroes like Superman or Wonder Woman, who deal with business catastrophes.

My favorite superhero was Steve Austin, the Six Million Dollar Man, played by Lee Majors. He was a man with a bionic left eye, right arm, and both legs. He could run 60 miles an hour and had the ability to jump more than 60 feet in the air. Whenever there was a complex government matter to solve, Steve Austin was the go-to man, the "Six Million Dollar Man," called on to solve the problem.

The Six Million Dollar Man was not invincible. As with any superhero, there are weaknesses. Superman's was kryptonite; the Six Million Dollar Man's was atmospheric interference (such as weather) that impacted the functioning of his bionics. So is the case with leaders; with their extraordinary capabilities comes vulnerability.

The Go-To Leader is vulnerable to negative corporate environments. In Corporate America, the corporate weather is often referred to as corporate culture. A culture can be warm and sunny, gloomy, rainy, or stormy, and some can be described as blizzards and tornados. A warm culture provides the right environment for a Go-To Leader to perform, but a cold culture limits the leader's natural talent and ability to maximize his true potential.

In a negative, cold culture, the Go-To Leader is left incapable of achieving extraordinary results and objectives. Because of interference projected through negative behaviors and actions of others, they cannot produce at an optimum level. A culture of distrust, mischief, misalignment, and mediocrity are cold environments and make Go-To Leaders highly ineffective at achieving difficult objectives and challenging goals. However, an environment of centered change, cultural adaption, and success epitomize a positive culture that will assist the Go-To Leader in achieving their goals as expected.

The best Go-To Leaders are positioned for success by being placed in the right environment that will maximize their leadership potential. Being in the wrong environment makes a Go-To Leader vulnerable and highly susceptible to failure. What is the weather like in your corporate environment? If you are an aspiring Go-To Leader and are being limited by a negative boss, controlling leaders, impossible assignments, and a lack of trust, consider fighting business "crime" elsewhere—preferably an environment where the culture is warm and you can flourish and grow. If you are a leader and have Go-To Leaders on your team, and the culture is not conducive to their performance needs, either help change the culture or set them free so they can maximize their potential and help others who are ready to accept their heroic gifts.

Go-To Leaders Do What They Love, Not Love What They Do

If you think about it, do people love what they do or do what they love? If you were to ask my friend Brian Jordan (a two-sport pro athlete who played for both the Atlanta Falcons and Atlanta Braves) this question, he would answer that pro athletes do what they love, which results in loving what they do. I have found this to be true for leaders on the 3G–Go-To Leader Network. They do what they love first, which makes them love what they do.

It is the old "chicken or the egg" debate all over again. What comes first? Loving what you do or doing what you love?

Here is what I know. Go-To Leaders are consistently at their best when they choose to do what they love. When you do what you love, dedication, motivation, interest, energy, and joy are omnipresent.

A Go-To Leader's ability to deliver time and time again can sometimes be considered a dumping ground or solution center for all organizational issues. That can result in projects with low interest, stimuli, or meaning to the Go-To Leader. This can cause disinterest, demotivation, and disengagement. During my leadership experience, I have often witnessed leaders identified as Go-To Leaders and High Performers being bombarded with projects and challenges often outside their "interest zone." As a result, they don't perform well, or because of their generosity and courage, they are successful but drained after giving their all. They become empty.

This dilemma occurs because organizations often make the mistake of assuming that Go-To Leaders "love what they do," so much that they will do anything. This is far from the truth. Go-To Leaders do what they love. I always say that if you want to know what interests, excites, or piques leaders' interests, watch them. Through time, you will discover you are actually watching them do what they love, and that is where their talents and gifts lie.

I have discovered that Go-To Leaders resemble athletes. For example, Brian Jordan played strong safety for the Atlanta Falcons, his specific position on the team. He did what he loved and was the Go-To Leader because of his skill, knowledge, and talent. Now, if you were to place him in the role of a defensive lineman, it is highly unlikely he would have extraordinary results playing that new position, even though he is a professional. In one position (the role of safety), he is "doing what he loves," but in the position of defensive lineman (although he "loves what he does"), he would be out of position and unsuccessful. Leaders are always better off and more successful doing what they love rather than loving what they do.

The same is true for Go-To Leaders. Often, organizations will place the Go-To Leader in a position to resolve challenges, issues or complexities that they may not have the knowledge, skills, or abilities to do. This places the leader in a position of disadvantage and weakness rather than a position of advantage and strength.

To optimize your leadership potential on the 3G–Go-To Leader Network, make sure you are in a role that will allow you to do what you love, and as a result, love what you do.

Go-To Leaders Are Change Agents, But Also Agents of Risks

No leader ignites and initiates change like a Go-To Leader. But at the same time, they are agents of risk. Risk is a part of business. When I share this with professionals and leaders whom I coach, I refer to it as the "risk engine." The stock market, our economy, investments, entrepreneurial ventures, and even careers are facets of capitalism based on risk vs. reward outcomes. The same can be said of leadership, particularly for Go-To Leaders.

It is my view that change is the only constant in life. Change is the only thing you can count on happening every day. And with change comes risk.

In leadership, change is what separates the bad leaders from the good leaders, and the good leaders from the best. Change creates opportunities for Go-To Leaders to be identified and to demonstrate their leadership abilities. Because with change comes risk, Go-To Leader are change agents and agents of risk. Go-To Leaders take risks every day that are not taken by 1G or 2G Leaders.

To achieve desired business outcomes, whether implementing a new system, redesigning a process, delivering a new service or product, or going through a business paradigm shift, Go-To Leaders orchestrate change and underwrite risks. Go-To Leaders take more risks than any other leader on the 6G Leadership Network. Frequently, business change is placed on the shoulders of Go-To Leaders because they are fearless and accept risks in order to achieve extraordinary results. It is their ability to succeed in adverse situations that makes other leaders acknowledge their skills, talents, and successes.

The challenge with organizations and Go-To Leaders is that Go-To Leaders' fearlessness, risk-taking, and change-driven mindsets can often place them in situations where they are stretched too thin. They are stressed and sacrificed by organizations that have a limited number of Go-To Leaders with the skills to achieve the extraordinary results they are trying to achieve.

It is very difficult for a few Go-To Leaders in an organization to sustain and carry out an organization's initiatives without rotation with and relief from other Go-To Leaders. As with a basketball, football, or baseball team, an organization would not want to place all of the change and risk on one franchise player. The change and risk must be spread out among the team to ensure success. It is critical that organizations invest in developing other

Go-To Leaders on the team. An unrealistic level of change and risk can cause burnout and career injury to its leadership team.

The best organizations develop and grow Go-To Leaders to share in leading the challenging workload, assignments, and strategic initiatives. These initiatives require skilled leaders who can lead others, contribute individually, and provide specialty skills that help the business achieve extraordinary outcomes. A leadership development program supported by a dedicated organizational coach is a great way to begin developing a pool of Go-To Leaders.

The best Go-To Leaders understand that it takes a team to achieve extraordinary results. To sustain their connection on the 3G–Go-To Leader Network, leaders must recognize and acknowledge the potential of other leaders, then develop them by giving them the opportunity to become Go-To Leaders simply by sharing change and risk.

Summary

Go-To Leaders are High Performance leaders with the ability to create magic. Similar to Magic Johnson, others acknowledge their "magic" because of the results they produce and their commitment level to the team.

Other professionals are influenced by Go-To Leaders because they lead from the middle; they are non-political and are franchise players. Leaders admire Go-To Leaders because they take risks and drive results, acknowledge the contributions of others, and develop others while developing themselves.

Go-To Leaders are best when they are in an environment that recognizes that they are heroic, but not invincible. They operate optimally in politic-free, supportive, and flexible environments where there is balanced responsibility for change, risk, and reward. They are least optimized when they are not allowed to do what they love.

If you need to get something done, you will never err in going to a Go-To Leader!

The Acknowledgement App

The Acknowledgement App is the third "mindware" application that optimizes your ability to perform on the 3G–Go-To Leader Network while also preparing you for expansion to the 4G–Growth Leader Network.

When leaders become Go-To Leaders, they come into complete acknowledgement of their potential relating to their strengths and weaknesses. Because Go-To Leadership is a choice, leaders must be able to fine-tune areas of development. It is that acknowledgement that allows them to take calculated risks to pursue the opportunities that others avoid.

The majority of leaders are on this network because of one thing: They chose to be there. Nobody appointed them; they were presented with an opportunity and took it. Those who don't seize Go-To Leadership opportunities will never expand beyond a 1G or 2G Leader. It is the Acknowledgement App that provides the mindware to believe you can achieve those things that are extraordinary.

Famous scholar Napoleon Hill once said, "There are no limitations to the mind except those we acknowledge." Go-To Leaders understand that strengths are advantages and weaknesses are opportunities; this acknowledgement of opportunities triggers the action to become great leaders.

To maximize your potential as a 3G–Go-To Leader, you must have an application that routinely provides the following upgrades to your mindware:

- Acknowledges your strength zone as a leader.
- Acknowledges your weak zone as a leader.
- Acknowledges your opportunity zone as a leader.

Now that you get the gist of the Acknowledgement App, answer several questions about where you are in your professional and personal life journey with regards to acknowledging your leadership potential.

- What skills do your colleagues describe as your strengths?
- What flaws do leaders, peers, and teammates see in you?
- How would you define your leadership weaknesses?
- Identify three areas of opportunity that can improve your biggest leadership weakness.
- What would you define as your kryptonite when it comes to leadership?

Acknowledging Your Strength Zone

Acknowledgement is defined as the recognition of the existence of truth. Every leader has to acknowledge and recognize that within them exist both strengths and weaknesses. It is much easier to deal with strengths than it is to deal with weaknesses. Let's deal with strengths first.

Strengths can be ambiguous because they are viewed differently by each individual. Have you ever wondered why, when an employee works for a manager, that manager may view certain behaviors as strengths, and when the employee transitions to a new manager, the new manager may view those same behaviors as weaknesses? This is simply because each manager has a different opinion, perception, definition, and aptitude about what strengths are.

If you really think about it, strengths are—for the most part—situational. In any given situation, an action can be viewed as a strength or a weakness, which makes it very important for leaders to have their own independent understanding of their strength zones.

Several years ago, I was working for a Fortune 1000 company in the role of an executive leader. The leader I was working for had a top-down, command-and-control organizational leadership style. Because of a problematic business issue, the leader asked me to lead the challenge of developing an innovative solution before the problem began to impact customer service. It required me to work with a significant amount of leaders in management.

Because I was defined as the Go-To Leader for the enterprise initiative, I was assertive and proactive. I scheduled and conducted meetings, conversations, and conference calls with members of senior leadership to get their perspective on the issues and their thoughts on potential solutions. They thought I had superior leadership skills and publicly acknowledged my value.

But, when the leader who assigned me to the initiative caught wind that I was interacting and talking with senior leadership, my assertiveness and proactivity suddenly turned into opportunism, kingdom building, and grandstanding. Why? Because the leader was passive-aggressive, followed a top-down, command-and-control leadership formula, and had significant issues with self-confidence.

As with most organizations, people often believe what others say about you before they take the time to validate it themselves. I am grateful that—regardless of one person's views—others viewed me as being innovative, collaborative, and insightful.

The best Go-To Leaders have a pulse on how other leaders view their leadership strength zones and understand their true potential. To assess your strength zone, develop an Acknowledgement App that inventories your potential and removes the virus of perception.

Acknowledge Your Weak Zone

It was William James, an American philosopher and psychologist, who said, "A rule of thinking which would absolutely prevent me from acknowledging certain kinds of truth if those...truths were really there, would be an irrational rule."

The Acknowledgement App is a mindware that also helps Go-To Leaders acknowledge their weaknesses as they relate to potential. This is one of the most important features of the Acknowledgement App because without it, leaders cannot expand or develop to the next leadership network.

There is an undercurrent being pushed along by some experts in the field of professional growth that suggests that once you uncover a weakness, you should bury it and swear never to dig it up and bring it back to life. I could not disagree more with this mindset. This Acknowledgement App is specifically designed to kill that thought from the minds of leaders, because it is one of the biggest mistruths limiting the growth of leaders.

In earlier chapters, I established that everyone is a leader. Leadership is innate in each living person. Within each person is potential. The experts who push the philosophy of ignoring your weaknesses fail to realize that ignoring your weaknesses in turn ignores your potential.

Michael Jordan did not make his high school varsity basketball team. In fact, he was cut. If he had not converted his weaknesses to strengths, he would not have become one of the greatest basketball players of all time. If Michael Jordan had not worked on improving his weak teamwork skills and engaged other players in playoff and championship games, the Chicago Bulls would not have won six championship titles. Just as in basketball, leadership is not about ignoring weaknesses; it's about working to improve and fine-tune potential.

The basic skills of leadership—innovation, collaboration, engagement, inspiration, motivation, direction, compromise, relationship building, and value adding—are all things that each leader has the ability to improve.

Leadership is one-third talent, one-third gift, and one-third skill, and we all have the potential to develop each portion to be Leaders of Significance.

The Acknowledgment App has the ability to assess one's potential and to identify weak zones, based on perception and observation. With the understanding that our potential is unlimited, uncapped, and untested, Go-To Leaders acknowledge through the Acknowledgement App the areas they need to further refine and fine-tune. Go-To Leaders take a constant inventory of skills that are required for development, and assess the gifts and talents that require practice and refinement.

To assess your weak zone, develop an Acknowledgement App that inventories your potential daily and identifies the leadership areas you can further develop.

Acknowledge Your Opportunity Zone

Within each organization there are zones of opportunity. Once a Go-To Leader understands his strength zone and assesses his weak zone, the combination of both assessments creates what I refer to as "opportunity zones."

There are two types of opportunity zones. The first is an opportunity zone that allows a leader to maximize potential. The other is an opportunity zone that allows a leader to pursue an organizational opportunity as a result of acknowledging his potential. The Acknowledgement App is designed to pull all forces together to assist the leader in reaching his maximum potential.

Go-To Leaders understand that strength zones and weak zones create potential, and potential leads to organizational opportunities. The Acknowledgement App is always running in the subconscious mind and on the lookout for the right opportunity for the Go-To Leader to monitor and evaluate organizational opportunities. In order to sustain the connection on the 3G–Go-To Leader Network, you must stay connected to your strengths, weaknesses, and opportunities.

To maximize your potential, upgrade your mind with the Acknowledgement App that inventories your potential daily, identifies the leadership areas you can further develop, and alerts you to opportunities that can put you in the Go-To Leader opportunity zone.

Summary

Go-To Leadership comes with a choice, and that choice is acknowledging others so they will acknowledge your leadership contributions as a "go to" leader. The 3G–Go-To Leader Network requires "mindware" to keep you connected to the network and to create the potential to connect to the 4G–Growth Leader Network, if optimized effectively. If you acknowledge your leadership strength zone, weakness zone, and opportunity zones, others will acknowledge and respect your leadership.

6G Leadership Coaching is the art and science of retraining your brain through meditation, thought, action, and repetition. In this chapter, you will complete the exercise and put into action the concepts we have discussed.

Next are 10 ways to use the Acknowledgement App, including daily affirmations, action steps, and applications on your journey to becoming a Leader of Significance. Remember: the stronger your Acknowledgement App, the greater the potential!

* *

3G–Leadership Coaching Exercise:
Acknowledgment Affirmations, Action Steps, and Applications

1. Each morning when you rise, repeat three times, "I will enter my strength zone." Write down three strengths you will maximize each day. *This will open your mind to begin operating from a position of strength.*

2. Identify three areas in leadership that fall into your weak zone, which you will work on improving each day. *This will help you exercise your mind to acknowledge developmental opportunities.*

3. When leaders and professionals create negative perceptions of you, repeat three times in your mind: "I may not be able to change perceptions, but I can change outcomes!" *This will build your confidence. Write down three outcomes you can change that can rebrand your leadership.*

4. As a Go-To Leader, others may bombard you with over-challenging obstacles that may produce stressful situations. With confidence, state affirmatively: "I have the ability to

remove stress and to create the magic to produce results." Identify three leaders who can assist you in being a Go-To Leader and in achieving your desired results. *Doing this reverses stress into positive energy.*

5. During lunch and after the day is over, think about how you may be able to transform weak zone leadership behaviors into strong zone behaviors. Write down three things you can start doing today. *Following this action will transform conscious acts into unconscious behavior.*

6. Repeat daily: "Acknowledge others' leadership and they will acknowledge mine!" This serves as a reminder that if you want to be acknowledged by others, you must first acknowledge them. Write down three things you admire about others' leadership, and make it a point to tell them. *This will introduce an element of gratitude and expand your strength zone.*

7. During your commute home, introspectively reflect on your day. What things could you have done differently? *This will introduce your psyche to the concept of building the habit of excellence into action.* Write down the one thing you will do differently tomorrow than you did today.

8. Repeat daily: "I may have a seat at the table, but it does not give me the right to lead. I must earn it through my actions!" *This daily regimen will force you to take your leadership role seriously.*

9. You are magical because of your special talent. Assess daily your reaction to negative influences to ensure they are not impacting your potential and thoughts. Identify three things that make you magical. *This will increase your confidence in your potential to achieve extraordinary things and verify that your assessment is accurate with others' views of you.*

-   10. Before you leave the office each day, write down one thing you did that day that you loved; commit to doing it again tomorrow. *This will help to acknowledge and remind you to do the things you love!*

Now that you have completed this exercise, review each week and assess your progress. In the next chapter, we will explore the 4G–Growth Leadership Network and its profile, features, limitations, and Achievement App. Let's upgrade to the next network.

4G–Growth Leader and the Achievement App

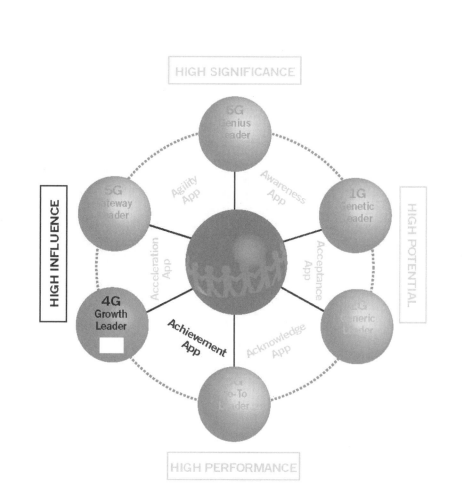

The team with the best players wins.
—Jack Welch, former CEO at General Electric

The Faces Behind the Growth

In 1984, a dentist and psychiatrist gave birth to a child who would grow up to be the leader of the world's third-largest nation, behind only China and India, if only what he led was a nation!

A kid born in White Plains, N.Y., began writing software in middle school. He was a techie at heart. He enjoyed developing computer programs and games while other kids played with or used them. In high school, he built a music player called the Synapse Media Player that Microsoft and AOL tried to purchase.

During college at the age of 19, he came up with a concept that now has approximately 845 million subscribers, turning a dream conceived in a dorm room into today's reality, estimated to be worth $75 billion to $100 billion. This miraculous accomplishment did not take 30 years to create and develop, but only seven, because of a strong leadership team.

Many analysts, critics, and futurists give limited credit to Mark Zuckerberg, Facebook founder, for the success of the organization. Yes, Mark Zuckerberg should be credited for Facebook's success; however, the credit does not end with Mark. It must be expanded to include his team, who was able to grow both the business and leaders simultaneously.

Limiting credit to a founder and CEO of a company completely over-looks the power and value of a leadership team. As I've said before, a leader is only as strong as his/her weakest leader. For Facebook to be as successful as it is, credit must go beyond the founder and CEO. It was not just the idea that made Facebook successful; it was the Growth Leaders (the leadership team) who had a vision, created a plan by developing leaders, and executed a strategy by empowering those leaders to act. The entire leadership team includes everyone—because everyone one is a leader—and should be credited for Facebook's huge success! It is very important to place your leaders' face on the book of success!

If you look closely at Facebook's leadership team, I am sure you will find that many of their leaders can be categorized as Growth Leaders who reside on the 4G Leadership Network within the 6G Leadership System.

Growth Leaders Grow Through Growing Others

It was Mark Zuckerberg, founder and CEO of Facebook, who was quoted in a recent article as saying, "When you give everyone a voice and give people power, the system usually ends up in a really good place. So, what we view our role as, is giving people that power." ("Facebook CEO Defends Company in ABC Interview, Advocates Democracy" 7/22/10, mrc.org) I could not agree more with Mark. I like to put it this way: in order for leadership to be effective, a leader must grow other leaders by giving them a voice, power, and an operating system so they can grow a business. The power is in building leaders, and that is exactly what Facebook did. They grew leaders.

Growth Leaders are highly influential leaders because they can grow the business by growing leaders. Professionals allow them to influence their actions because of their consistent business and professional development achievements.

The 4G–Growth Leader Network is the leadership effectiveness zone that separates High Performing Leaders from High Influence Leaders. High Performing Leaders, who reside on the 3G Go-To Leader Network, are acknowledged for their leadership as a result of achieving business goals through their individual contributions and their ability to lead teams. High Influence Leaders, 4G–Growth Leaders, are recognized for their achievements in influencing overall business results by growing leaders.

Leadership Growth Is Not Transactional; It's Transformational

Many organizations make a fatal mistake by following a real estate investment formula when investing in talent rather than a talent investment formula. Most organizations invest significantly in only the top 10 percent of the organization's professionals, typically defined as High Performers. These are the chosen few who are enrolled in leadership development and training programs, and are approved to attend the most desired seminars and workshops offered by top-tier providers.

The challenge is that most traditional leaders and organizations have adopted what I call the "80-10-10" transactional investment rule for reinvesting in employee and leadership development. This is very similar to a term in real estate called the 80-10-10 Mortgage Loan Program. The 80-10-10 loan program is based on an investment split three ways: 80 percent principle, 10 percent down payment, and remaining 10 percent second mortgage—all to avoid Private Mortgage Insurance (PMI), which is a slick way to avoid investment expenses.

Similarly, organizations have set up an "80-10-10" program for employees, not because they want to fully invest in them, but to avoid investment expenses with low returns. Here is why. A recent study indicated that most organizations' existing performance-based talent supply consists of 80 percent mediocre or competent employees, 10 percent low-performing employees, and 10 percent high-performing employees.

To provide an inside view, here is how the 80-10-10 Talent Investment Rule plays out in many organizations. Because of budget constraints and limited believed value in their talent supply, organizations rarely invest in 80 percent of its employees. They view that as a transaction and see a limited return on investment in mediocre resources. Second, organizations, more often than not, do not invest in the next 10 percent because those employees are viewed as being underachievers. And finally, the remaining 10 percent may or may not be invested in because attrition is highest among High Performing employees. They are so good that they may be recruited by competitors, and many organizations do not want to lose those investment dollars. This is a transactional view of investing in talent.

This approach is problematic and impedes the leadership development process for a couple of reasons. If an organization only targets investment in High Performers, that means the rest of the organization—roughly 90 percent—is not being developed or invested in. This transactional investment in only High Performers cannibalizes future leadership development and kills any organic growth that has been seeded.

Growth Leaders understand that leadership development is not transactional. It is transformational. They understand that development does not consist only of investment dollars, but also in time committed to training, independent coaching, development of career opportunities, and on-the-job experiences. Not investing in 90 percent of a talent supply is a sure way to stifle leadership growth and create a scenario of low leadership bench strength.

Recently, I was discussing with a senior leader at a Fortune 500 company their perspective on leadership development. I was surprised to hear him say that in today's market, they expect their leaders to come into their roles ready to lead. When I asked how they define leadership, his response helped me understand why so many companies have talent supply gaps in the foundation of their leadership.

This senior leader shared with me that their organization views employees as leaders only at the officer level, starting at the vice president level. It was no longer a mystery as to why customer service was at an all-time low, market share had dropped by double digits, and the organization had not been profitable in the last three years.

It is my belief that officer-level leadership is not enough leadership to build, sustain, or turn around a company. Top- and-mid-level management is not enough. What is needed is a system that invests in everyone's leadership potential, so that leadership is distributed throughout the fabric of the organization to every employee. If you look closely at Facebook, that is exactly what Mark Zuckerberg has done. He has established Growth Leaders throughout the organization.

Growth Leaders are High Influence Leaders because they recognize that in order to grow the business and achieve extraordinary results, organizations must grow leaders. That requires transformational, not transactional, investments. Successful organizations, such as Facebook, establish shared equity in leadership development for professionals, whether they are developers or officers.

To truly achieve extraordinary results, organizations must have a Growth Leader approach to identify, develop, and create leaders. Simply put, using this 80-10-10 Transformation Leadership Investment concept will help build a leadership talent supply by allocating investment dollars as follows: 80 percent (competent), 10 percent (High Performers), and 10 percent (low performers). In this model, everyone, not only High Performers, would be totally invested in as leaders, and leadership growth would occur top down, bottom up, and middle out.

If you aspire to be a 4G–Growth Leader or want to fine-tune your network leadership skills, take a few minutes and answer the following questions.

- How are you helping others to grow on your leadership team?
- What 80-10-10 growth and development plans do you have in place for leaders?

- How much time do you spend coaching and developing teams?

- What do you see other leaders doing that you admire when it comes to motivating, coaching, and inspiring leaders?

- How does your leadership development plan address becoming a better Growth Leader?

- What areas can you improve to becoming a better Growth Leader?

- How much do you rely on yourself vs. others in achieving significant results?

4G-Growth Leader Profile and Traits

The 4G–Growth Leader is the fourth network in the 6G Leadership System. To expand from the 3G to 4G Leadership Network requires leaders to consistently maintain all of the features of the 3G–Go-To Leader and, in addition, achieve extraordinary business results through leading others and developing leaders.

Leaders and professionals value Growth Leaders because of their achievements in business and performance. The key difference between the 3G–Go-To Leader and the 4G–Growth Leader is that the Growth Leader achieves a significant portion of his results not by individual contributions but by influencing the leadership and direction of others, which is one of the most challenging leadership skills. It is one thing to accomplish goals as an individual contributor; it's another to obtain goals while leading others. And it is on an entirely different network operating level that leaders lead a function or project—lead teams of leaders and develop leaders—that results in the achievement of extraordinary business results. That's the 4G–Growth Leader Network performing at its best.

The truth of the matter is that most leaders do not make it to the 4G Network because they have not mastered the skills of developing leaders, building trust and relationships, and creating the appropriate skills needed to achieve business goals.

This chapter will help you understand how to operate on the 4G Growth Leader Network. If scores from your leadership aptitude identify your dominant network as 4G–Growth Leader, then you are well on your way to becoming a Leader of High Significance.

To help you better understand the profile, Diagram 1 summarizes the profile of the 4G–Growth Leader and the Achievement App that every 4G Leader needs in order to run on this network.

• •

Diagram 1

High Influence Leader, with the ability to grow the business and grow people. Leaders allow you to influence them as a result of achievements in business performance and growth!

Achievement App—*Achievement* is reaching business success through leading and developing others.

Overview of the Go-To Leader

- Growth Leaders are competitive and goal-centered. Often their aggressive goal-setting can become overbearing to others.
- Growth Leaders work hard to achieve extraordinary results, but their passion for results may cause them to gloss over systematic details.
- Growth Leaders reward progress, which is a good thing; however, in their recognition and development of others, they may tolerate short-term failures and mishaps for long-term wins.

Maximum Potential—realized in scenarios requiring innovation, motivation, and transformation.

Least Potential—created in an environment that requires consistency and mediocre business goals.

Core Leadership Value to Teams and Professionals

Professionals value you because of the achievements in business, performance, and growth of others. Teams value you because your achievements and actions are associated with business results.

- Goal-centered.
- Takes risks on others.
- Influences decisions and directions.
- Promotes change.

- Delivers extraordinary business results.
- Motivates and rewards success.
- Develops others.

• •

Growth Leaders have distinct traits and behaviors that separate them from all other leaders on the 6G Leadership System. Simply put, Growth Leaders are the engineers of business growth and development of leaders. They cast vision, take risks, influence decisions, motivate and inspire, promote change, and deliver. Growth Leaders have a way of promoting growth in the organization and in its people.

For that reason, Growth Leaders are High Influence Leaders. They risk their career by taking risks on others, and as a result, achieve extraordinary results.

Contained in Diagram 2 is a limited set of traits to help you understand the Growth Leader in more detail and to give you insight into the habits of the 4G–Growth Leader.

Review each of these traits and indicate the ones that resonate with your actions, behaviors, and habits by providing a score in the box between 5 (often), 3 (sometimes), and 1 (rarely) for each leadership action description. After you have completed the exercise, for the traits rated as "sometimes" or "rarely," think about how you can transform those traits into daily habits.

• •

Diagram 2

Growth Leaders:
- Develop other leaders.
- Drive change.
- Are often High Influence Leaders.
- Have a brand of growing business results and growing professionals.
- Rely heavily on developing leaders to accomplish business goals and objectives.

- Have achievements that are constantly associated with business results.
- Choose to be internal mentors, coaches, and role models to other leaders.
- Inspire others to maximize their potential.
- Are transformational, not transactional, leaders.
- Provide real-time forward coaching.
- Promote risk-taking.
- Expand responsibilities and scope.
- Create stretch goals.
- Are planners and executors.
- Require speedy action.
- Influence decision-making.
- Reward others, both publicly and privately.
- Lead independently of culture and politics.
- Make it do what it does; they make things happen.
- Invest in the growth and development of themselves and others.

• •

Features of The Growth Leader

Growth Leaders on the 6G Leadership System have features that make them stand out from other leaders. Obviously, each leader is different, but they all work together and collaborate on the network while achieving extraordinary results. To provide a broader context around the positive aspects of Growth Leaders, this section summarizes several features that each Growth Leader demonstrates, which adds significant value to organizations, teams, and its leaders.

Next are several of the key features that each user of the leadership system have access to on the 6G Network, both those whose dominating network may reside here and those who may expand onto other bands but visit this network often. It is important that every leader fully comprehend, optimize, and develop skills for navigating the network, because those same skills allow leaders to operate on the expanded network. Growth Leaders rely on all leadership networks to achieve extraordinary business results, and they also develop leaders on all network bands from 1G–4G.

The features listed are most prominent with the 4G–Growth Leader. If this is not your dominant leadership network, it is critical that you grasp knowledge of how the network operates so that when you interact with others, you will be able to better connect with leaders. If you are an aspiring leader or if your aptitude results indicate you are operating as a 4G–Growth Leader, get ready to master the key features and benefits that others are expecting you to deliver.

Here are several primal key features of the 4G–Growth Leader.

Growth Leaders Operate Using the Leadership Law of Attraction

The Law of Attraction is a metaphysical belief that states "like attracts like." The usage of the phrase and terminology dates back to the beginning of the New Thought Movement and is noted in the early writings of Thomas Troward, William James, Napoleon Hill, and other great philosophers from 1904 to 1940.

In the 21st century, this metaphysical belief remains constant in leadership—"like attracts like." Make no mistake about it; leaders gravitate to other leaders. Simply put, good leadership attracts good leaders; bad leadership attracts bad leaders.

Growth Leaders attract other leaders who want to grow. For example, if you show me a leader who does not want to grow and develop, I guarantee that if you follow them to their home network of leaders, you will find others who do not want to grow and develop. And, chances are, that includes their leader. On the contrary, if you show me a leader who wants to grow their leadership ability, I guarantee you if you follow them to their home network of leaders, you will find others who want to grow and develop. That group will likely include their leader. That is the Leadership Law of Attraction—"like leaders attract like leaders."

Don't get me wrong. There are situations I have coached where the opposite occurred. A new leader whom I was coaching shared with me that he reported to another leader in the organization who did not want to grow and develop. That leader had become comfortable in his role and decided it was time to coast into retirement, given the number of years he had dedicated to the company.

The issue was that the leader I was coaching had aspirations to grow and develop into the next leadership opportunity. In this particular situation, the Leadership Law of Attraction was applied. Because the primary leader did not want to grow, the leader I coached decided that the organization was not the right fit and transitioned to another organization headed by a Growth Leader with a leadership team that wanted to advance and grow professionally. Why? Because like attracts like.

Growth Leaders operate under the Leadership Law of Attraction. With Growth Leaders, your organization will be full of organic growth potential. The other good news about this feature it that Growth Leaders have the tendency to expedite the transition of professionals who do not want to grow, creating new leadership opportunities for those with high leadership aspirations.

Growth Leaders Go Beyond Business Relationships; They Truly Know Their Leaders

It is one thing to have a business relationship with someone and a totally different thing to truly know someone. Growth Leaders know their leaders and teams, and their leaders and team know their Growth Leaders.

How often do you have conversations with your leaders or teams that have nothing to do with work? How personal do you get in sharing your aspirations, goals, challenges, or issues in your organization? How transparent is your professional life in your leadership role?

Several years ago, I was in a leadership role and one of the leaders I had just hired was having a significant challenge in her personal life. We had to deliver a proposal to a customer that day that, if accepted, would allow us to meet our business plan. The morning of the presentation, I received a call from human resources alerting me that my leader had left her office and was extremely emotional about a personal matter. I was advised that the employee was upset and might have difficulty getting through the day. Human resources also told me that if the employee brought the matter up, I should not engage in a conversation about it, and to direct the employee to the human resources counseling number—you know, the 800 number you call when you don't want to get involved in personal, non-work-related matters.

I suggested to the human resources person that perhaps discussing the matter with the employee would help. He responded, "Employees have to learn to leave their personal issues outside of the workplace." He continued, "We did not discuss the matter with her in detail and neither should you. Please direct her to the 800 number—often used when an employee faces the loss of a loved one. Have a great day!" He then hung up the phone as if this was a routine conversation. Obviously, this human resources person was not aware that dramatic issues like bill collectors, family and friend disputes, and even tragedies don't care if you are at home or at work; they follow you wherever you are until they reach you.

Ignoring his suggestion, I got up out of my chair and went to my leader's office. Immediately, I could see she was having a challenging day, as tears rolled down her cheeks. With concern and against the suggestion I was given, I asked her if everything was okay. She began to tell me something that changed my outlook on life forever.

She told me that a family member who had been with her for many years had passed. I asked who died. She broke down in tears and said, "Great Aunty." She went on to say that the chemotherapy had not worked and ultimately the radiation treatment had killed her that morning. I immediately asked her if she wanted to take the day off. It was then that she explained how human resources told her that she could only have a day off for immediate family deaths and that this death did not qualify. Plus, she did not want to miss the presentation that was scheduled for that afternoon.

I told her that life was more precious than any presentation or client proposal, and that she could take as much time as she needed. She thanked me, began to exit, and stopped and asked if I wanted to see a picture of the loved one she lost. Of course, I said yes.

She reached in her purse, pulled out her iPhone, and showed me a picture of her being licked by Great Aunty. I could not believe my eyes. Great Aunty was a Great Dane. They nicknamed her Great Aunty because she was a female Great Dane who lived to be 15 years old (with a life expectancy of eight). Thus, the name Great Aunty.

I wanted to laugh and I did, right in her face. She knew I had a sense of humor and did not take my laughing personally. She asked me what I was laughing about. I told her that I thought that her great aunt had died. She turned and said, "Oh, no, she has been dead for 20 years now!" Both of us burst into laughter.

She then turned and asked, "Will you come to the funeral?"

That was a breakthrough point in knowing the leader on my team. I came to understand her love for animals, how much she loved her pets, and how she likened her love for animals to her love for human beings. This allowed me to see a whole new side of my leader that I did not know existed.

Growth Leaders know their leaders, and their leaders know them. In order to grow and develop leaders, it is critical that Growth Leaders go beyond the firewall of work-related relationships and actually get to know the person in the leader. Understanding what makes them tick, their likes and dislikes, their values and beliefs, are all critical in growing and developing leaders. Acknowledging their strengths, as well as their weaknesses, helps produce stretch goals and assignments. Going beyond a business relationship and getting to truly know a leader opens the way into their minds and hearts.

The experience I shared with you, although funny, transformed a working relationship into a relationship of knowing and understanding the person behind the leader. Knowing a person is what makes Growth Leaders go above and beyond the call of duty for their team. It attributes to the business results—growth and outcomes that high-performing organizations realize—and it starts with knowing the person behind the leader.

By the way, I did go to Great Aunty's funeral. The experience was an example of what can be achieved when you go from a professional relationship to personally knowing and understanding a leader. But what changed my outlook on life was that this was a reminder that we all should show our appreciation for family, friends, and colleagues, as well as our beloved pets. Growth Leaders recognize that professionals are leaders and deserve love and appreciation. They recognize leaders are, after all, human.

Take time and get to know your leaders on a personal level. I can't tell you the number of leaders I know who do not take the time and effort to get to know their employees, professionals, and leaders personally.

Leaders who invest in getting to know their leaders inquire as to how they are doing, invest time outside of group meetings to get to know their leaders, ask questions to better understand their leaders' values and beliefs, and create an open and safe environment where the leaders can display who they truly are. Leaders who do not practice this often remain on the 1G3G leadership network, never becoming Growth Leaders.

Here is why. It is very difficult to lead a team, develop leaders, and achieve extraordinary results without understanding leadership potential. That requires understanding the person behind the leader. In many instances, leadership relationships are limited to working for the same company, in the same department, and on the same team. The relationship often doesn't go any further than that. It is difficult for someone to give their all if they don't know who they are giving their all to. Get to know your leaders. Open yourself to them so they can know you.

Growth Leaders understand that relationships within a team are not enough to reach extraordinary achievements. They realize that you have to know your leaders and your leaders must know you in order to achieve extraordinary results!

Growth Leaders Replace Themselves Rather Than Secure a Position

Many leaders have a philosophy that I call a "job security plan." They plan to hire people who are less competent, less qualified, and less intelligent than they are in an effort to create the illusion of being smarter, more knowledgeable, and invaluable compared to others. In their twisted minds, this is called a job security plan. Leaders who operate under the mindset of maintaining job security because of their lack of trust, insecurities, and low self-confidence, strip their leaders of power, authority, and information, leaving them defenseless, ineffective, undervalued and unable to bring about significant change.

Growth Leaders are completely the opposite. They trust, hire, and develop leaders, giving them full power and authority, and the proper training and information, to achieve desired results. On the contrary, leaders who operate in a job-security mindset can be observed doing things such as securing a perimeter around information they don't want others to have, locking up all knowledge and operational trade secrets with a code that only they possess, sharing as little information as possible, and building silos to limit collaboration with others. They are ineffective, though they believe concealing information makes them appear more valuable to others.

Growth Leaders replace rather than secure themselves. Growth Leaders understand that in order to increase business results, lead teams and develop leaders, you need leaders who are smarter, brighter, faster, and broader than one individual could ever be. They hire to replace themselves rather than to secure their place in a position or role.

4G–Growth Leaders on the 6G Leadership Network are confident enough in their role and potential to understand that their value is not in the execution of the business results, but in the orchestration of leading teams and developing leaders who produce extraordinary results. Ineffective and insecure leaders trap themselves into being doers, controllers, and executors, depriving themselves of the ability to grow. They recognize that to be an influential Growth Leader, they must:

- Grow the overall organization's capabilities through recruitment and development of other leaders.
- Empower others to maximize their leadership potential without hidden restraints.
- Provide opportunities for others to contribute.
- Share information to increase organizational knowledge.
- Promote the advancement of others regardless of self-impact.

Growth Leader Limitations

If you are a Growth Leader, know professionals who fit this profile, or perhaps people in this category report to you, be aware that this network has its limitations.

Growth and development can sometimes be painful and may have its limitations. Like an athlete who seeks to develop and grow to run faster, leaders have to find their limitations and seek to improve them. The beauty of this network, as well as others, is that the limitations on the 4G Network can become benefits if efforts are made to transform the natural limitations into benefits. Once leaders are aware of the limitations, they can create opportunity zones so that Growth Leaders can focus on improvement.

Many of the 4G–Growth Leader Network limitations have to do with recognizing that no leader is perfect and that each network has improvement zones for better managing risktaking. If you understand individual leadership quirks and develop a leadership support system, you will find that as you become more in tune with leadership emotional intelligence, you will be able to transform limitations into limitless potential.

The next several sections provide key limitations that leaders on this network must experience, along with strategies and techniques to turn the limitations into benefits for every other leader operating on the 6G Leadership System.

As you review this section, identify areas you can focus on to expand your network capabilities by understanding its limitations. Also think through the accompanying suggestions that will improve your connections to other leaders operating within the leadership system.

Growth Leaders Like to Push the Envelope, but Must Operate in a Fail-Safe Mode

Because Growth Leaders are exploratory in nature, they often push the envelope from a business-results standpoint in pursuit of unchartered success. It is the discovery of the unknown that creates business growth opportunities and results.

Growth Leaders learn, develop, and grow the organization and others from the lessons learned by failure. I am reminded of Thomas Edison who, as he was trying to invent the light bulb, said, "I have not failed. I've just found 10,000 ways that won't work." That is a great way to look at it. Growth and results do not occur instantly. They have to be tested, and sometimes those tests result in failure. But it is the experience of failure that ultimately results in success. I like to put it this way when I coach and speak to leaders: "Let's not let the fear of failure get in the way of success!"

Growth Leaders have the courage to fail in pursuit of the need to boldly succeed. This does not make them change agents (people who implement a desired change), but rather change idealists (people who are the genesis of the idea of change). It is that action that creates the pushing of the envelope that tests organizational potential. They are integral in the sense of influencing success measures, and developing and executing plans of action to achieve the desired change, whether it is a new product, project, or process. For that reason, Growth Leaders are not risk adverse, but risk tolerant. It is the risk that excites and drives them to achieve extraordinary business results.

With the pushing of the envelope also come limitations. Growth Leaders' need to grow the business and feed their desire for change often potentially places the organization at risk of failure. Because of their personality and growth role in the organization, Growth Leaders need to operate in a "fail-soft mode." A fail-soft mode is often referred to in operations and technology as a characteristic of computing that creates the ability of a system to fail in such a way as to preserve as much capability and data as possible. The same strategy holds true and must be applied in leadership. I like to call it fail-soft leadership.

Fail-soft leadership is getting other leaders to agree on risk tolerance levels prior to exploring new efforts and strategic changes for achieving desired extraordinary business results. Often this is done via a controlled rollout, phased release, and in some instances, as a pilot. It provides advance notice, takes the shock and awe out of the equation, and allows the organization to develop contingency plans as appropriate. Ultimately, this also protects the leader from fatal career damage as a result of potential implications.

It is no doubt that success is often found in failures; however, Growth Leaders must adopt a fail-soft leadership approach to balance the growth of the organizations with its tolerance for failure in pursuit of success. For Growth Leaders to maximize their full potential, they need to operate in a supportive organization that recognizes that success is not automatic and understands that achievements are the result of attempts, misfires, and in many instances, outcomes from previous failures.

Thomas Edison operated every now and again on the 4G–Growth Leaders Network. He was on this network when he invented the light bulb. It was his 10,000th failure that led to his number one success. Like Mr. Edison did, Growth Leaders need to push the envelope and not be afraid of failure, while at the same time balancing the risks by operating in a leadership fail-soft mode.

Growth Leaders Have Pet Peeves and Quirks Too, Requiring Leadership Emotional Intelligence

Growth Leaders are unique in that they do three things very, very well: they lead teams, develop leaders, and achieve extraordinary business results. Most Growth Leaders have a systematic way in how they accomplish these extraordinary results, which makes them great role models for other leaders to follow.

Growth Leaders each have unique qualities, skills, and traits. Most organizations would love to be able to clone Growth Leaders. It seems so easy to identify a great Go-To Leader as a role model for everyone else to conform to, but it is not as simple as setting up a cookie-cutter for leadership. Because Growth Leaders are human, they are not perfect. They also have pet peeves and quirks, just like everyone else. Cloning other leaders is not the best way to build a Growth Leader talent supply chain, and here's why.

Have you ever wondered why people have pet peeves? Pet peeves are described as a minor action that an individual identifies as particularly annoying to him or her, to a greater degree than others may find it. Everybody has their own set of pet peeves, usually unknown to everyone else. Individual leader pet peeves are vast and could range from not starting meetings on time, ending meetings early, not ending meetings on time, not immediately responding to e-mails, interjecting before someone completes a sentence, completing sentences for people while they are still talking, pacing back and forth, or checking your phone during meetings. The list goes on and on.

If you really study it, the action performed by another that is annoying to the leader produces a response or action that takes the offender by surprise and may seem strange to them because they are not aware of that leader's pet peeve. Often, the response is so strange to the offender that the leader's behavior is referred to as a quirk. I define a leadership quirk as a peculiarity of action, behavior, personality, or mannerism displayed by a leader and not understood by others, in response to another leader's action toward them.

I remember some time ago in a C-level leadership meeting, two very senior-level vice presidents, both Growth Leaders, got into a heated exchange. At one point, the senior vice president of business administration, Kevin, lashed out at the senior vice president of operations, Jennifer.

What initiated the chain of events was that the business growth meeting was designed to isolate opportunities and associated problem areas that needed to be addressed. Because Growth Leaders are very competitive, this created additional pressure and stress on the meeting. The triggering of the exchange occurred because whenever Jennifer raised issues about the services Kevin had oversight of, she would look at him and smile while describing the issues. This occurred a couple of times, and the third time Jennifer raised an issue and smiled at Kevin, he got so irritated that he got up out of his seat, turned and screamed at the top of his voice, "Would you take that smirk off your face? I don't see anything funny!" Jennifer became so irritated that she turned purple, folded her arms, and did not say another thing the rest of the meeting.

After the meeting, I asked one of the other leaders why Kevin got so upset. Some leaders said it was just Kevin's personality. Another leader told me that it was Kevin's pet peeve when people smile while criticizing someone, because it is a sign of disrespect. Still another leader dismissed it as just a behavioral quirk. He went on to say that we all have quirks. It is just a matter of time until someone eventually triggers ours.

Later, I saw Jennifer and asked what happened. She went on to say that it's her inclination to smile while discussing issues so others know you are not attacking, disrespecting, or being critical of them.

Which person is right?

It really doesn't matter. What matters is that each person did something that resulted in behavioral "quirks," paralyzing both leaders from moving forward and stopping them from adding value to the meeting.

The reality is that Growth Leaders are not perfect. They are competitive and thrive to achieve significant business results; they are on the 4G Network for that reason. Yet, at the same time, they have their quirks, which is why leaders should not be cloned. We don't want to be in the business of cloning quirks and pet peeves. For that reason, each leader has to be individually developed and refined, including the 4G–Growth Leader.

The key for Growth Leaders is to recognize each person's uniqueness and effectively utilize emotional intelligence as much as possible to ward off competitiveness that negatively impacts emotions, actions, and behaviors, triggering pet peeves and quirks that impede progress and results.

The best Growth Leaders have emotional intelligence tools that help to manage and provide a better understanding of self-awareness, self-management, social awareness, and relationship management concepts, which enhance emotional intelligence levels critical for business leaders. Highly influential leaders and high-performing organizations understand that leaders are not clones, drones, or robots, and that they require a significant investment in coaching, training, emotional intelligence, and competency development in order to maximize their leadership potential.

Growth Leaders Bet on Others; Leaders Must Bet on Them

Growth Leaders are unique in that they bet on others. Here is what I mean. Growth Leaders believe so much in their leaders' potential that they are willing to put their professional career on the line. They believe that their organization, teams, and leaders can achieve extraordinary results. Because Growth Leaders move the business beyond expected results, when it comes time to commit to business goals and objectives and the development of an enterprise scorecard, Growth Leaders don't sandbag goals, they "up-bag" them. Growth Leaders raise the bar and up the ante to challenge the status quo. They strive for significant results and rely heavily on High Performing and High Influence Leaders at all levels to achieve them.

The best Growth Leaders have an extreme amount of confidence in their team to deliver during tough business cycles, downward trends, and difficult economic climates. They believe in their people. However, for various reasons, sometimes confidence in the Growth Leader may not be consistent among other leaders who operate on networks 1G–6G on the 6G Leadership System. Those reasons could stem from distrust, inexperience, a lack of confidence, and many other things causing Growth Leaders to feel unsupported. In order to achieve extraordinary results, all leaders must be willing to fully hedge their bets on one another. When this fails to happen, it creates a limitation on the Growth Leader's ability to perform, which impacts their confidence level.

One of the most inspirational things happening around the world in businesses every day is when a leader places confidence in another leader. The most disappointing thing is when leaders lose confidence in Growth Leaders and publicly do not bet on them. Sandbagging, lowering goals, and creating an environment of mediocrity are all signals of not betting on the leaders' ability to win. This can be devastating to all leaders, particularly the Growth Leader.

Can you image a championship football game between two rival teams when the coach says to his quarterback in front of the team, "We are going to get creamed, so we are going to ask the other team to spot us two touchdowns to make it fair." Unheard of in football, right? That is exactly what sandbagging is in business. By telling the organization your team of players and leaders are not that good, the goal can be lowered so it looks like a win in the end—sandbagging. This happens every day in leadership.

When this occurs, it impacts several facets of the organization: morale, engagement, teamwork, and commitment to excellence. In short, Growth Leaders and their team may begin operating in fear of failure and lose established momentum. One of the worst things a leader can do to a Growth Leader, regardless of the network or leadership position they operate in, is not to bet on them. The best Growth Leaders operate in environments that have signs of support, commitment, and engagement. They strive for stretch goals to be achieved, which in the long run positively impacts performance, productivity, profits, and the professional development of others.

To ensure leaders are strategically positioned for success, here are several things that should exist in order to create and maintain an environment that bets on Growth Leaders:

- All leaders are committed to achieving stretch deliverables and goals influenced by Growth Leaders.
- Growth Leaders are empowered to make decisions throughout the organization.
- Multiple leaders are not required to approve Growth Leaders' decisions.
- Growth Leaders' decisions are rarely overturned or changed once committed to.
- Senior leaders macro-manage rather than micro-manage.
- Growth Leaders have appropriate resources to pursue organizational goals and objectives.
- Authority and trust is given to Growth Leaders to achieve extraordinary results.

Growth Leaders are in the business of betting on leaders to reach extraordinary results. In turn, Growth Leaders need leaders who bet on them!

The Achievement App

The Achievement App is the "mindware" application on the 4G Leadership Network that motivates leaders to achieve extraordinary results from a business and personal perspective. Having a mindset to achieve your personal best is a significant distinction for leaders on this network. This App prepares leaders to expand to the 5G–Gateway Leader network.

Leaders on the 4G Network must have a constant drive to achieve results that have not been reached previously by other leaders. Their competitive spirit pushes the organization forward and creates an environment of extraordinary results. It was Eleanor Roosevelt who said, "You must do the thing you think you cannot do!" 4G–Growth Leaders push the organization, teams, and leaders to do the things they think cannot be done!

The term "achievement" is defined as something accomplished, especially by superior ability, special effort, or great courage. Accomplishing achievements requires motivation mindware that continuously runs on our operating system (the human brain) and challenges the status quo.

The Achievement App helps drive Growth Leaders to achieve extraordinary results by optimizing:

- Effective catalysts of change.
- Attitudinal intelligence fluency.
- Goals and success sharing.

Now that you get the gist of the Achievement App, answer several questions. Think about what things you can do as a 4G–Growth Leader to improve your optimization on the network.

- If you think of leadership as a game, are you winning or losing? How many points are you scoring each day?
- What is your personal best in achieving business results as a leader?
- If you were playing against the leadership challenges you encounter on a daily basis, what would you say the score is (leader vs. challenges)?
- What growth and development barriers do you see requiring elimination? How would others describe you as a catalyst?
- What goals do you not share currently with other leaders that should be extended to them?

Catalysts of Effective Change

There has been a lot of emphasis on change when it comes to achieving extraordinary results in business. Some experts on the topic suggest that professionals and leaders have to embrace change because, if change is not embraced, it will roll over you like an avalanche. To some extent, I would say in the past they were right. But in today's fast-paced, competitive business climate, simply embracing change isn't enough. By the time you have spread your arms to embrace it, change has hit you and flung you aside.

Leaders today have to be ahead of change in order to achieve it. Leaders have to be the catalysts of change. The best way to achieve change is to be on the front side of it, influencing it, directing it, and driving it. Growth Leaders operating on the 4G Network require an application that constantly identifies business opportunities to change processes and platforms through the creative use of people for improving performance, productivity, and profits.

It is never good to change just for the sake of change; there must be a desired achievement or outcome. It was Winston Churchill who said, "There is nothing wrong with change, if it is in the right direction." He was absolutely correct.

As an independent consultant for an organization, I coached a professional who made me aware of significant changes that the organization was considering implementing during the next few months. They had achieved great success and maintained consistent service and market share with customers. However, new leaders in the organization thought that by shaking things up, performance, productivity, and profits would improve. Of course, they were planning the only thing that could shake up an organization—that massive earthquake: reorganization. According to the professional I was coaching, the objective of the reorganization was to align resources to better meet the needs of the customers.

Several months after the reorganization, the company experienced record customer service complaints, lost a considerable amount of market share, and employee morale plummeted. Why? Apparently, the organization rotated all of the leaders and their support teams to new roles with no transition plan in place, causing confusion, misdirects, and misalignments in serving both internal and external customer needs that ultimately resulted in a reorganization implosion.

The change failed because there was no purpose or targeted measurable results of the organization's achievements. Growth Leaders must validate both the qualitative and quantitative value of change before implementing it. The assurance that change is not being initiated just for the sake of change, or to flex power and authority, propels the business to the next level of success.

Change measured in achievements is critical to a 4G–Growth Leader's success!

Attitudinal Intelligence

Maintaining a positive outlook on life is critical for a leader. In organizations, there are daily issues, personality challenges, and power and control battles. As a Growth Leader, you will be challenged by other leaders who do not take the professional road. They will challenge your decision-making authority, attempt to undermine you, question your knowledge, and even challenge your heart! That's right—they aim to determine if you are a mouse or a lion. I encourage you to use attitudinal intelligence and project the image of a lion!

Attitudinal intelligence is a term I coined several years ago while working for a healthcare organization with significant culture issues within the organization. Attitudinal intelligence is the art and science of managing your thoughts, feelings, and actions with the intent of projecting a positive mindset regardless of the situation. This is one of the most challenging things to do in life! It was particularly challenging in this organization because the organization's culture was silo-based, and rumors, perceptions, and mistrust ran through every crack in the organization.

Here is what having attitudinal intelligence can do. It gives you the power to change the culture, one person at a time. By maintaining a positive attitude, regardless of how toxic an environment may be, you can change the climate of those leaders and professionals who have positive attitudes, but are influenced by the negative behavior around them. I used to think that one person could not change a culture, but I have found that one person can change a culture for a period of time. Perhaps the culture will not stay positive after you leave the environment, but the culture does transform into what you inject into while you are in it.

I recall walking into a meeting where the tone was completely negative. As I projected positive energy through communication and gestures, I could see the culture of the meeting change. Suddenly it turned from being negative in the beginning to being positive throughout. Having attitudinal intelligence creates the ability to change the culture for a moment in time.

Growth Leaders must have an attitudinal intelligence mindware to influence positive behavior and cultures given the challenging human dynamics that many leaders have to manage daily. Without attitudinal intelligence, obtaining extraordinary results will be difficult.

Goals and Success "Shareware"

Do you ever wonder why there is employee burnout, frustration, and high attrition among highly influential performers? The primary cause is that many leaders do not share goals or successes; they exploit their control over resources to reach their personal goals that are hedged against the divisional and corporate scorecard.

Growth Leaders must maintain "shareware" that monitors all goals and ensures that leaders are recognized and rewarded for achievements. When leaders don't set clear goals and share a vision, professionals may think they are being exploited by leaders who are trying to reach their own personal goals. There is a saying that there are two types of leaders, those who are users and those who are sharers.

I remember when I first discovered a leader who was a user. This person I reported to would often come to my office and assign me specific projects for solving certain organizational problems. As I completed and resolved one problem, he quickly assigned another.

One day, about six months later, I asked that leader a simple question. "Since these assignments are taking a significant amount of time, do you think it is appropriate for me to add them to my personal performance plan as goals for the year?" The response from that leader was, "No, they are not significant enough to be added as goals. These are to be done in addition to your current assignments." About three months later, I was in a meeting with my boss and the CEO. The CEO complimented my boss on the success of several projects and mentioned that it allowed both of them to reach their corporate goals and that their bonus payouts would be at the highest tier.

After the meeting, I realized the projects they were referring to were the projects my boss had given me that he suggested were insignificant and not to be included as goals on my performance plan. In short, they both took credit for goals they did not personally achieve while I—and the other leaders on the team—was not recognized for the achievements by the senior leaders.

4G–Growth Leaders must have shareware that creates harmonious goals among leaders, and identifies, shares, and rewards team achievements. Leaders who exploit resources to reach their own goals will never reach the leadership network level of a Growth Leader, Gateway Leader, or Genius Leader on the 6G Network. They will forever be cast into the network of a 1G–Genetic Leader or 2G–Generic Leader because sooner or later, leaders will drop their calls and not allow them to connect again.

In order to achieve extraordinary results through development and rewarding of leaders, a shareware must be maintained at all times on the 4G–Growth Leadership.

Summary

Growth Leadership comes with a price. To become recognized for extraordinary achievements, the 4G–Growth Leader Network requires mindware that keeps 4G Leaders connected to the network and creates the potential to connect to the 5G–Gateway Leader Network, if optimized effectively.

If you, as a leader, can maintain attitudinal intelligence, establish goals, share success, and operate as a change catalyst, you will achieve extraordinary results through leading teams and developing leaders.

6G Leadership Coaching is the art and science of retraining your brain through meditation, thought, action, and repetition. In this chapter, you will complete the exercise so you can immediately grasp and put into action the concepts we have discussed.

Next are 10 ways to use the Achievement App daily, including affirmations, action steps, and applications on your journey to becoming a Leader of Significance. Remember, the stronger your Achievement App, the greater the potential!

• •

4G–Leadership Coaching Exercise:
Achievement Affirmations, Action Steps, and Applications

1. Each morning when you rise, repeat three times, "I will achieve my goals today." Write down three daily goals you have. *This will open your mind to setting daily goals.*

2. Identify two leaders on your team who need to improve in areas of leadership. *This will help exercise your mind to understand weaknesses in your leadership team.*

3. What transformation leadership investments can you make in your team of leaders?

4. As a Growth Leader, state three times a day, "I am a transformational leader." *Doing this speaks truth to reality.*

5. Think about how you can create an independent coaching program to help your leaders reach their maximum potential. Write down three things you can start doing today. *Following this action will show leaders you value them and are willing to invest in them for the short- and long-term.*

6. Repeat daily: "Leaders follow the Law of Attraction; I want positive leaders in my inner circle!" Write down the names of three positive leaders whom you want in your inner circle. *This will begin the process of building a positive infrastructure of leaders around you.*

7. During your commute home, introspectively reflect on your day. How could you better use emotional intelligence and attitudinal intelligence to deal with negative scenarios and situations that occur routinely? What things could you have done differently? *This will introduce your psyche to the concept of turning the habit of excellence into action. Write down the one thing you will do differently tomorrow than you did today.*

8. Repeat daily: "Relationships are good, but knowing my leaders is even better!" *This daily regimen will force you to take your leaders more seriously.*

9. What pet peeves and quirks do you have that other leaders suggest you control and manage better? *This will begin the process of replacing pet peeves and quirks that can impede your career with healthy leadership habits.*

10. Before you leave the office each day, write down your vision for the organization, along with three goals. *This will help you achieve those objectives and remind you to communicate to teams and execute on the things you love!*

Now that you have completed this exercise, review each week and assess your progress. In the next chapter, we will explore the 5G–Gateway Leadership Network, its profile, features, limitations, and Acceleration App. Let's upgrade to the next network.

5G–Gateway Leader and the Acceleration App

• • • • • • • • • • • • • • • • •

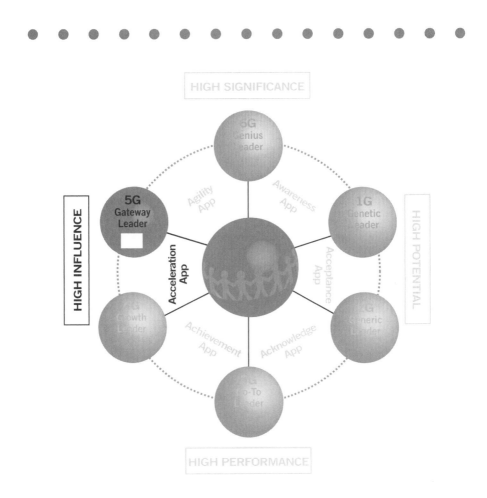

We know that leadership is very much related to change.
As the pace of change accelerates, there is naturally
a greater need for effective leadership.
—John Kotter, leadership expert

Defining the Gateway

In today's global economy with accelerated change, it is more important than ever to have transformative leaders. With the downturn of the economy and its much-anticipated recovery, change is needed now more than ever. On Capitol Hill, the debate is not that we need jobs to turn the economy around, but how they should be created. What does not get discussed during the debates is what actions actually create jobs. Jobs are a result of pursuing opportunities. Without this, there is no demand, no products, customers, sales, revenue, expenses, and, therefore, no jobs.

In the 6G Leadership System, there is the 5G–Gateway Network, which serves as an igniter of change, transformation, and opportunities benefitting both business and its people. Gateway Leaders create accelerated growth opportunities for the business and their leaders—they, in essence, create jobs.

The Free Dictionary defines *gateway* as: 1) A means of entry or access; 2) Computing hardware and software that connect incompatible computer networks, allowing information to be passed from one to another; 3) A software utility that enables text messages to be sent and received over digital cellular telephone networks.

I like to define Gateway Leaders as leaders who create an entryway and accelerate success through the pathway of change. They realize the opportunities for change and connect incompatible capabilities together, resulting in value to customers.

Gateway Leaders achieve this through innovation and creativity. According to the IBM 2010 Study, the most significant leadership qualities that an organization will need during the next five years (as rated by the world's top 1,500 CEOs) are creativity, integrity, and global thinking, in that order. To address speed of change and overwhelming business complexities, leaders will need to become less traditional and more original in meeting new expectations and demands. Gateway Leaders bring into existence something new, based on creativity and innovation.

Gateway Leaders break through traditionalism and challenge the status quo to pioneer new frontiers of success. It was John Kotter who said, "We know that leadership is very much related to change. As the pace of change accelerates, there is naturally a greater need for effective leadership." For this reason, 5G–Gateway Leaders are highly influential leaders, with the ability to accelerate positive business results by influencing decisions and actions. Leaders use their influence because they create opportunities to accelerate change while creating wins and improving business processes, teams, and leaders.

The Power of Creativity

Gateway Leaders break through barriers to create opportunities and, within their success, change the landscape. Gateway Leaders are visionaries and accelerate outcomes that benefit the industry, organization, and teams.

There was one person who set out on a journey, based on a dream, which created an entryway that transformed the consumer market for years. His mother was still in her teens when he was born in Albuquerque, N.M. From an early age, he would display a striking mechanical aptitude. As a toddler, he became known for rigging electric alarm clocks and made his younger siblings late for school. He converted his parents' garage into a laboratory for his science projects. In high school, he fell in love with computers and was an outstanding student, becoming valedictorian of his class. In his college years, he attended Princeton University, planned to study physics, but instead pursued his passion, obtaining a degree in computer science and electrical engineering.

After graduation, he found employment on Wall Street. While working for a company called Shaw, he met his wife, also a Princeton graduate. He rose quickly in leadership, becoming a senior vice president, with a career in finance.

While looking at the top 20 mail-order businesses, he asked a simple question: "What is more effective in the selling process, the Internet or traditional means?" and transformed sales around the world.

The next day he flew to Los Angeles to attend the American Booksellers' Convention to learn about the book business. He observed that major wholesalers compiled electronic lists of their inventory. He envisioned the electronic list on the Internet, where consumers could search the available stock and place orders without physically visiting a store.

The rest is history. In 1994, he wrote a business plan while he and his wife, MacKenzie, drove to Seattle. Later that year, he founded his company and set up shop in a two-bedroom house with electrical wires running to computers in the garage. He took action, formed a team, and started his business dream compiling electronic lists of wholesalers' inventory and placing the lists on the Internet.

Today, 18 years later, the company's market value is approximately $81.4 billion and earned revenues totaling $48 billion in 2011. Just about everything you can imagine is sold on this Internet site—from books to clothing to tools, to almost anything imaginable. The name of this Gateway Leader is Jeffrey P. Bezos, president, CEO, and chairman of the board. His company is Amazon.com.

Jeffrey is what I call a Gateway Leader and hired other Gateway Leaders to create opportunities based on a casted vision. He was able to use innovation, creativity, and potential to connect what seemed to be an incompatible wholesale business model to the Internet, and transformed the commerce and publishing industry at an accelerated pace.

Gateway Leaders are far more advanced than other leaders; other leaders are driving with a roadmap while Gateway Leaders soar to new heights with a flight plan for success. In today's competitive business, traditional roadmaps will not push organizations or leaders to define their breakthrough zones, success zones, or end zones. It is the pressure to soar that can be a defining moment for an organization. The formation of diamonds requires very high pressure. The same is true of leadership. When pressured to reach maximum potential, leaders create breakthrough zones, success zones, and end zones. To achieve these zones, leaders need to be creative in the development of a "flight plan" to accelerate the transformation of business processes, people, and platforms. Gateway Leaders are innovative and creative, and pursue avenues to success that others do not when building leaders and teams.

Organizations need a transformational shift that stretches to the limits the capabilities of the organization. That's what great Gateway Leaders do: they stretch an organization's limits by stretching the potential of its people.

Change for Gateway Leaders Can Be an Advantage or Disadvantage, Depending on Who Is on the Receiving End

There are many organizations whose leaders do not prefer the status quo and want to become Gateway Leaders but are not able to expand their actions to do so.

It is not the success of the company that defines a Gateway Leader but the successful behaviors of the leadership team. Amazon is an American success story. Created in 1994 in founder Jeff Bezos' garage, Amazon now employs 33,000 leaders within their employee base. The same ideas, innovation, and thoughts that Jeff Bezos had can exist in all employees (I call them "leaders") in every organization. The challenge for organizations is to create an environment that feeds creativity and starves normalcy. To create an environment where people are not "paid to do" but "paid to think" requires Gateway Leaders.

Here is what can happen when you have an organization built on "paid to do" leadership, and Gateway Leaders are nonexistent. The organization can be mired in traditional thinking, and traditional delivery of services and products, while an innovative-thinking competitor comes by and penetrates market share. The company has to try to get transformational leaders to turn the company around, but often it can be too late. The best companies maintain Gateway Leaders who embrace change in order to re-energize the company. Sometimes this is reactionary change that can overcome an organization and make recovery difficult to achieve.

Some years ago, I had the great leadership opportunity to be recruited by a Fortune 500 company to become a member of a turnaround transformation team. At the age of 30, I made the decision to uproot my family and move from Baltimore, where I grew up, to a city called Crystal Lake, Ill., to step into my leadership position as the senior manager of the strategic business transformation team.

My first day at the headquarters was amazing. The orientation was so powerful that it inspired all of us who were new employees to perform at our maximum potential. The training was delivered in three parts: first, completion of the necessary forms to make sure you received your paycheck and benefits; second, an overview of the company; third, the big finale, a walkthrough of the company museum. As we followed the trainer into a huge, two-story building and walked through the doors, I could not believe my eyes. Standing before me was a museum that contained all of the great inventions and products the company was responsible for, thus creating the world as we know it today.

We all stood looking around at the large, two-story museum in amazement of all of the company's accomplishments. In each section was a dedicated area of pictures, products, and illustrations of each innovation, invention, and transformational breakthrough the company was responsible for, releasing into the world and changing lives. In each section, there was a presentation describing how the company was among the first to invent and successfully market everything from the color television, car radio, pager, mobile cell phone, transmitter that communicated sound from the moon, hands-free mobile cell phone, broadband cable network standards, the original Six Sigma Quality Program, HDTV, GSM cellular system, 2-way pager, GPRS cellular system, and wireless cable modem. The museum of accomplishments goes on and on. If you are ever near Schaumburg, Ill., I would encourage you to visit the museum, which I call the "gateway of success," to witness what can happen when High Performing teams work together.

What company is it, you ask? Motorola! Their success was phenomenal. As a new leader in the company, I could not help but feel the innovation and creativity that ran through the fabric of the organization. Little did I know that the accelerated path the company was on was destined to change because innovation, change, and creativity, through time, escaped the grasp of leadership. During the next two years, the company went from being innovative to mediocre. The transformation from a three-generation, family-run business, to a company run by new leaders and officers, produced a bureaucracy that blurred vision and organizational goals, and for a number of years became a revolving door of officers and CEOs.

The once-treasured open leadership system shifted to a top-down leadership model that resulted in each business segment being converted into a Strategic Business Unit (SBU). Each ran independently, operating separately from the others. There was so much command and control that there were three appointed presidents and CEOs for each of the SBUs. To make matters even more complex, a president and CEO of Motorola, Inc., who had little to control or influence, was appointed, and each sector president and CEO reported to him. As I've said in earlier chapters, appointment, position, and title do not equal leadership. This is an example where awareness, acceptance, acknowledgement, achievement, and acceleration were missing from the leadership equation.

In all instances, the sector presidents had more power and control than the Motorola, Inc., corporate president and CEO. The business transformation leadership team that I was a part of began to add collaboration, creativity, and innovation into the fabric of the organization. However, the downward spiral was about to be accelerated by market and competitive complexities that would catch the company off-guard.

As the organization shifted from a concept of "everyone is a leader" to a "top-down" command-and-control model as a result of the new regime, one of the most recognized and innovative companies in the world was paralyzed, unable to respond to a competitor that came out of nowhere and drove Motorola's stock value down to record all-time lows.

Who was the company that unleashed that unwanted and unexpected change on Motorola? It was a company from Finland that, prior to entering the telecommunications market, had produced rubber products—galoshes, tires, rubber bands, and raincoats. They knocked Motorola completely out. The little-known company that no one took seriously was Nokia.

What was a rubber-band manufacturer's competitive advantage over Motorola? It was not capital assets, it was not trade secrets, and it was not breakthrough, industry-changing technology or innovation. Motorola had all of that. It was simply leadership!

Nokia had Gateway Leaders and Motorola had Standby Leaders, thereby losing its leadership edge. They had drifted to a "top-down" leadership style and a non-collaborative organizational personality creating silos. It was the business transformation team's role to tear down the silos. As mentioned earlier, however, there was limited influence and authority over the silo culture. Motorola was on the brunt of the receiving end of change from outside forces and external factors. By the time they recognized they were in a downward spiral, it was too late for the five sector presidents and CEOs of Motorola to recover from the blows delivered by Nokia, Samsung, and other competitors. It was a TKO—a technical knockout.

This is just one of many case studies that supports that leadership is everything. It can make or break a company. Gateway Leaders can "make" companies and they can "take out" companies. In this instance, Motorola was taken out by Gateway Leaders. If closely studied, the rise and fall of companies, ultimately their successes and failures, can be measured by their degree of innovation, creativity, and ability to embrace industry changes. I remember a senior executive making the comment in a leadership meeting that, "We don't have to worry about being first to market; we can always catch up." That is a sure way to become obsolete, implode, or fold.

Gateway Leaders push the company in a direction that other competitors doubt, question, or run from. It is the Gateway Leader who is the critical element in achieving extraordinary success in an organization.

Today, more than a decade later, Motorola has transformed. It has a new CEO and other leaders who have torn down silos and repackaged and rebranded the company into two separate, publicly traded companies, Motorola Mobility Inc. and Motorola Solutions, Inc., with market caps of $12 billion and $15.7 billion, respectively. Google purchased Motorola Mobility for $12.5 billion. Included in the acquisition are Motorola's 17,000+ patents, along with half of the museum I toured the day I joined the company in 2000. Gateway Leaders create opportunities, and I assure you there are many Gateway Leaders at Google.

Based on my experience, I have observed that transformational journeys such as Motorola's are created by leadership lapses that can be fatal to any organization. If you are on the reactionary side of change and not driving it, change can be so powerful that it overcomes you and slowly paralyzes your every move, before you get the chance to react to the competitive threat or internal chaos. The best approach is not just to embrace change, but to ignite it. Being on the receiving end of change is no fun. That is why it is always better to give change rather than receive change!

In the competitive economy, it is imperative that Gateway Leaders are developed and fully supported to innovate, change, and catapult organizations to the next level of success. Having a Gateway transformation team working in a culture of anti-change paralyzes leadership's ability to accelerate business results. That maintains the status quo, and by not pushing the organization and its leaders to be transformational, causes the organization to go backward.

As Johann Wolfgang von Goethe said, "He who moves not forward, goes backward." Perhaps for a split-second, Motorola did not move forward, and therefore, went backward. Here is what I know—Gateway Leaders can protect organizations from takeovers as well as create organizational takeovers if leaders and the organization are ready to accelerate change! Which position do you and your organization want to be in? Do you want to go backward or forward?

I encourage you and your organization to be Gateway Leaders and to initiate innovation and change by bringing things together that are viewed as incompatible, following the lessons from Amazon and Motorola.

If you are (or aspire to be) a 5G–Gateway Leader, I invite you to take a few minutes to answer the following questions and determine your gateway for connecting to this network and expanding your ability to transform your organization, team, and you.

- How are you helping to define innovative opportunities in your role as a leader?

- What areas can you improve on that would build your leadership creativity skills?

- How much time a day do you spend identifying breakthrough opportunities to improve processes, platforms, and people? What are your transformational goals for the organization and for yourself?

- How would you define your organization's tolerance for change (high, medium, low)? What is your tolerance for transformation (high, medium, low)?

- Do others view you as an accelerator of change, transformational, and results-driven?

- How do you transform leaders to help them maximize their potential? How many leaders have you transformed?

- What percentage of time do you spend leading, developing others, or doing work-related tasks?

5G-Gateway Leader Profile and Traits

The 5G–Gateway Leader is the fifth network in the 6G Leadership System. To expand from the 4G to 5G Leadership Network requires leaders to accelerate the achievement of business results through casting a vision, influencing decisions, igniting change, leading teams, and developing leaders. Leaders and professionals value Gateway Leaders because they create opportunities for the business, its leaders, the industry, and the economy. Gateway Leaders are the force behind innovation, breaking through barriers to achieve unprecedented services, products, milestones, and performance.

The key difference between the 4G–Growth Leader and the 5G–Gateway Leader is that the Gateway Leader's value is in his creativity in achieving accelerated results through change and by tapping into assets, relationships, and capabilities that are unproven, innovative, or thought to be incompatible. 5G–Gateway Leaders change the paradigm and challenge the status quo.

According to an IBM study completed in 2010 by 1,500 CEOs, organizations have a significant capability gap in the leadership supply system in the areas of: a) creativity (60 percent), b) integrity (52 percent), and c) global thinking (35 percent). The fact is, with the complexity in today's marketplace, the traditional approach—"build it and they will come"—is outdated. Successful organizations are co-creating with their customers, products, and services, and integrating their customers into their core processes. In order to compete successfully in this global market, Gateway Leaders are needed more than ever to transform organizations into flexible and diverse companies like Google, Amazon, and Apple.

This chapter is designed to help you understand how to connect and operate on the 5G Gateway Network. Becoming a 5G–Gateway Leader does not require a leader to be a CEO, officer, director, or manager, but does require high influence, creativity, and acknowledgement by others. One cannot join this network unnoticed. It is not that you need an invitation, but it is critical that you study, develop, and master through your actions the features and benefits of this network, and also understand its limitations so you can maximize your leadership potential and become the innovator and creator you were born to be!

If the scores from your leadership aptitude identify your dominant network as 5G–Gateway Leader, then I would encourage you to pay particular attention to weak connections and traits that you may need to shore up to maximize your connection to other leaders.

To help you better understand your profile, Diagram 1 summarizes the profile of the 5G–Gateway Leader and the accompanying Acceleration App, motivational "mindware" every leader needs in order to run on the 5G Network.

Diagram 1

High Influence Leader, with the ability to accelerate positive business results by influencing decisions and actions. Leaders allow you to influence them because you create opportunities and accelerate change!

Acceleration App—*Acceleration* is creating success wins while improving business processes and teams.

Overview of the Gateway Leader

- Gateway Leaders inspire leaders by their ability to accelerate positive business results. However, their passion to pioneer new frontiers may not align with organizational strategic direction.
- Gateway Leaders enjoy collaboration, which is usually of significant value. However, in situations where collaboration and comprise cannot be reached, they may appear confrontational in tearing down silos.
- Gateway Leaders are great at influencing others, but because of their persuasiveness, they can appear to be manipulative.

Maximum Potential—realized in initiatives requiring accelerated outcomes and matrix team collaboration.

Least Potential—resides in situations with rudimentary activities, anti-change culture, hierarchical structure, urgency, and limited complexity.

Core Leadership Value to Teams and Professionals

Professionals value you because you create opportunities and accelerate change for others. Teams value you because your actions accelerate business performance and results.

- Sets clear vision with clarity in action.
- Breaks through obstacles and barriers.
- Challenges and heals culture.
- Leads matrix and informal teams.
- Accelerates outcomes.
- Creates new opportunities.
- Promotes innovative thinking.

Gateway Leaders have distinct traits and behaviors that separate them from all other leaders on the 6G Leadership System. Simply put, Gateway Leaders cast vision, clarify vision through actions, break through obstacles while challenging and changing cultures, and accelerate outcomes. They are the group of leaders that challenges the status quo and creates new opportunities for success. 5G–Gateway Leaders grow leaders by providing growth opportunities through role expansion, coaching, and developmental training.

For these reasons, Gateway Leaders are high-influential leaders. They are experts in leveraging matrix resources to achieve mutual goals and are effective collaborators in executing activities that are outside of their span of control. They are company turnaround agents!

Contained in Diagram 2 is a limited set of traits to help you understand the Gateway Leader in more detail and to give you insight into the habits of 5G Leaders. Review each of these traits and indicate those that resonate with your actions, behaviors, and habits by providing a score in the box between 5 (often), 3 (sometimes), and 1 (rarely) for each leadership action description. After you have completed the exercise, for the traits self-rated as "sometime" or "rarely," think about how you can transform those traits into daily habits.

• •

Diagram 2

Gateway Leaders:

- _ Create opportunity for others.
- _ Operate with integrity and commitment.
- _ Are often creative, high-influential leaders.
- _ Challenge culture and change it.
- _ Develop and lead matrix teams.
- _ Accelerate business results and outcomes.
- _ Engage in debates and not politics.
- _ Push buttons to ignite change.
- _ Are always enthusiastic in helping others reach their potential.
- _ Are transformational, not transactional leaders.

- _ Influence leadership systems.
- _ Promote innovative thinking.
- _ Redefine and create unique leadership roles.
- _ Challenge the status quo and tear down silos.
- _ Redefine achievable goals.
- _ Cast vision and execute strategies.
- _ Break through barriers to success.
- _ Influence results.
- _ Recognize others' contributions.
- _ Lead from the middle.

Features of the Gateway Leader

As on the previous networks, the Gateway Leader on the 6G Leadership System has both features and limitations that make them stand out from other leader networks. Gateway Leaders are uniquely different from other network leaders because they operate on networks 1G to 5G, meaning they have a wide network advantage and are able to perform all actions on each of the networks. To provide a broader context around the positive features of Gateway Leaders, this section summarizes their top three most beneficial values to organizations, teams, leaders, and their customers.

If this is your dominant network or if you aspire to operate on this network, as you review the key features, make an effort to introspectively evaluate your performance. Are you truly maximizing your potential in your position, role, or assignment? Determine how well you are accelerating change and achieving extraordinary business results. Identify what may be holding you back. Is it you? Is it the culture? Both? What is blocking your gateway to extraordinary success?

If this is not your dominant network, review these features closely so you can grasp the knowledge of how the network operates. When you interact with other leaders that reside here, you will have a better appreciation and understanding of their leadership aptitude, style, and approach.

Let's review the key features and open the Gateway to becoming a stronger 5G Network Leader.

Gateway Leaders Have 5G Vision
(Hindsight, Nearsight, and Farsight!)

Gateway Leaders are unique in that they have 5G Vision. They have the ability to see and reference those things in the past, present, and future. When I speak to organizations and coach leaders, I refer to this as 5G Vision using the terms: 5G Hindsight, 5G Nearsight, and 5G Farsight. These terms provide insight as to how Gateway Leaders accelerate change by looking through multiple lenses of vision.

5G Hindsight

According to Webster's Dictionary, *hindsight* is the ability to understand, after something has happened, what should have been done or what caused the event. Gateway Leaders do not let the past paralyze or slow them down, like some leaders do. Because of bad experiences or failures, leaders can allow hindsight to cause them not to act. Not Gateway Leaders. Gateway Leaders use Hindsight to accelerate action.

Gateway Leaders have the unique feature to not only analyze what happened, but to see what should have happened; they have the unique vision to analyze past events and accelerate change based on their determination of future direction. Hindsight allows Gateway Leaders to predict the future, cast a vision, and accelerate change to achieve extraordinary business results.

5G Nearsight

Gateway Leaders also have the ability to understand the short-term to the degree that they can see and understand any myopic change. I refer to this as 5G Nearsight.

I like to refer to Gateway Leaders as also being nearsighted because, in addition to hindsight, their vision gives them the ability to understand exactly how market, industry, and regulatory changes can have subtle but fatal implications on business processes, procedures, and platforms today.

Gateway Leaders understand the details and changes within an organization and use their short-distance vision to identify business challenges and how they impact and create opportunities for change. Those changes are a result of current performance, productivity, and business, both internally and externally.

Gateway Leaders use their nearsighted vision to shift their attention from the past, away from what they anticipate in the future, and focus on the changes in the organization that are occurring in the present. They have the ability to put in place short-term, 30-, 90-, and 120-day plans to address issues, challenges, and obstacles requiring immediate resolution. Gateway Leaders are also operational leaders.

Gateway Leaders have the vision to understand and adjust to short-term changes and limit errors, failures, and poor decisions that impact the present!

5G Farsight

Gateway Leaders have the gift of intuitiveness and the ability to predict and see into the future based on industry trends and innovation. I like to refer to this as 5G Farsight. One of the definitions of farsighted is wisdom in seeing future developments. Gateway Leaders have exactly that. They not only have a rearview mirror view of the world and see the short-term change around them, but they also have the ability to cast a vision of the future in a way that professionals and leaders understand and believe to be achievable.

Traditional visionaries are people who work on the top floor of a building and only come off the floor to go to the restroom, get something to eat or drink, or to go home at the end of the day. They also move downstairs to present to operational people what they have been working on for months in isolation, the enterprise vision and strategic plan. These folks are called strategists. Their job is to present business strategies to the people who actually perform the work while they plan the direction of the future in closed-door sessions with the CEO.

This is not what Gateway Leaders do. They collaborate with operational and tactical professionals and leaders to develop long-term plans. Gateway Leaders are aware that, with accelerated change and the complexities of business, the best strategy is to develop long-term plans of no more than 24 months. Because it is no longer time or cost effective to plan further out because technology changes so quickly, some industries' long-term planning has gone from the traditional five years to one to two years.

Gateway Leaders have the ability to predict, envision, and create vision for the organization on an accelerated timetable, creating opportunities for the organization and its leaders to capitalize on by using 5G Vision to work in the present. The combination of 5G Hindsight, 5G Nearsight, and 5G Farsight allows them to accelerate change and business results that can be realized in the present.

As one of my mentors shared with me on a recent radio program, "If you do the things today that others won't do, you will have the things tomorrow that others won't have!" Gateway Leaders use the 5G Vision to accelerate change in the present moment to achieve what competitors want in the future!

Gateway Leaders Set C.H.A.N.G.E. Goals

Gateway Leaders transform vision into goals. One of the hardest things for a leader to do is to transform a vision into a series of goals, objectives, and steps, and to determine how to achieve that vision. What makes Gateway Leaders unique from other leaders on the 6G Leadership System is their ability to align their vision and goals with the minds, hearts, and hands of their teams.

Gateway Leaders make sure their goals are **S.M.A.R.T.** goals, not **D.U.M.B.** goals. **S.M.A.R.T.** goals refer to a process used by many organizations and professionals. It is an acronym for goal setting that is:

- Specific: The goal is a clearly defined project, activity, initiative, or effort for a desired outcome.
- Measurable: The goal has a standard to determine if the desired outcome was obtained.
- Achievable: The goal can be realized by an organization, team, or leader.
- Realistic: The goal is not far-fetched and unable to be accomplished.
- Time-Bound: The goal has a start and completion date.

Does this sound like a **S.M.A.R.T.** way to develop goals for all professionals, leaders, and teams?

I describe **D.U.M.B.** goals as:

- Duplicative: The goal is duplicative in the sense that other organizations, teams, and leaders are pursing the same objective with resources that could be assigned to other activities, projects, and initiatives.

- Untargeted Value: The goal does not have a targeted performance standard to measure improved customer service, customer satisfaction, performance, productivity, quality, or sales (or any other goals that have been set).

- Mediocre: The goal set does not challenge the organization or its people to define and develop new capabilities or maximize organizational potential.

- Blame Free: The goal, initiative, activity has no clear organizational or personal accountability; typically, these are cross-functional or enterprise goals that professionals, teams, and leaders cannot influence.

The **S.M.A.R.T.** goal process is antiquated, and its robotic nature does not ensure that goals are aligned with those of the customers, suppliers, organizations, teams, and leaders. By default, this produces **D.U.M.B.** goals. After presenting at a conference where I was the keynote speaker, I had a CEO come up to me after my speech and say that he agreed with my definition of D.U.M.B. goals. He went on to say he would change one thing in my speech, "I'd put 'ass' after 'dumb.' We have a lot of people in our organization who have **D.U.M.B.** A.S.S. goals," and he gave me the acronym for the last three letters. I can't share those with you in this book, but if you want to try and figure it out, email me at Robert@6GLeader.com, and I will let you know if you are right. But I digress.

To address this, I have developed a goal-setting system that will help ensure alignment across organizations and within teams, and will allow leadership to accelerate change and create results that Gateway Leaders can apply and leverage. I refer to this as **C.H.A.N.G.E.** Setting Goals, which stands for goals that are Congruent, Healthy, Action-Based, Necessary, GrowthOriented, and Excellence-Driven.

- Congruent: Goals must be developed and written in a form that aligns with the organization's overall strategic direction, operational plan, and departmental objectives, down to the professional development plan for leaders and professionals engaged in the effort. Many organizations make the fatal mistake of individualizing goals and disconnecting them from the "big picture," causing vision impairment and organizational misalignment. Gateway Leaders ensure there is goal congruence for the organization, suppliers, leaders, teams, and professionals.

- Healthy: Simply put, goals should be healthy. Gateway Leaders create goals that are of value to customers, suppliers, partners, leaders, teams, and organizations. Goals should be designed and written so that they produce healthy results that can be measured and compared with both past and future goals. Many organizations fail to measure past, present, and desired future performance when crafting and designing goals, making them ambiguous and difficult to compare. Gateway Leaders design and develop healthy goals that improve and accelerate organizational value to internal and external customers.

- Action-Based: If there is no action, there is no progress. Gateway Leaders define goals that are action-oriented and results driven. A goal that is not action-oriented indicates that leaders and professionals are riding on the coattails of the actions of others. Often, organizations create departmental, cross-functional, and enterprise-wide goals that require limited action from professionals and leaders and create a scenario with little to no action, engagement, or commitment. This can result in mediocrity. Gateway Leaders design goals and objectives for their teams and ways to measure results that are directly actionable for leaders to demonstrate and achieve desired outcomes. This increases engagement and commitment levels.

- Necessary: When determining and influencing corporate, divisional, departmental, and professional goals, Gateway Leaders ask a tough question: "What is necessary?" I've noticed that a significant amount of work is based on historical activities that departments routinely perform, work that is created by leaders who have limited external value, and work that is just "busy work" or unnecessary. Gateway Leaders set goals and objectives to find ways to eliminate activities, projects, and assignments that are not needed to deliver value, services, or products to external customers, regulators, or partners.

- Growth-oriented: Gateway Leaders help craft and design organizational and professional goals that foster creativity, innovation, and change, creating a gateway to achieving extraordinary results. Gateway goals are big, audacious, and challenging, and consist of projects that professionals and leaders commit to in order to accelerate the transformation of the organization toward their future vision. Gateway Leaders influence the level of commitment to their goals through collaboration, departmental partnering, and team-building and development. Gateway Leaders also help create leadership development and training programs in influencing, running, and directing programs, initiatives, and projects for current and aspiring Gateway Leaders to participate in. Gateway Leaders recognize that in goal-planning, a commitment to personal growth and professional development is critical for an organization's success. Gateway Leaders ensure that goal-setting also creates opportunities for leaders to develop to their maximum potential.

- Excellence-Driven: Goals are a measure of improvement. Gateway Leaders influence organizational and professional goals to ensure that objectives stretch the organization and its leaders toward pursuing excellence from several perspectives: market position, cost position, service position, and brand position. Reaching and maintaining a strong market position is the desire of every organization. The key to succeeding in that goal is to continuously drive toward excellence. Determining ways to do more with less and becoming more effective and efficient with resources is the way to drive down costs to create a position of strength over competitors.

Developing measures and goals to improve delivery, resolution, and communications to customers is a leap toward reaching a position of excellent service. And focusing on building, expanding, and optimizing brand recognition is the pathway to being recognized as the best in the industry. Gateway Leaders pursue excellence in all they do without regard for career risk. The proof can be found in their organizational, team, professional and leader goals!

Setting goals tied to key performance and driven by the pursuit of excellence is what separates long-term, successful companies from those with short-term success. Gateway Leaders continuously strive for excellence and have specific goals for market position, cost position, service position, and brand position.

Gateway Leaders Don't Typecast; They Recast

Job descriptions serve many purposes. Primarily, a job description describes the activities expected to be performed in the position and the skills required to fulfill those expectations. A job description defines "what," not the "who, when, where and how."

One of my favorite actors is Denzel Washington, a two-time Oscar Award winner for his roles in *Glory* and *Training Day*. His believable portrayals of broad characters place him as arguably one of the greatest actors of all time. His performances are the gateway to his notoriety and success in the industry. Why? Because he does not allow himself to become pigeonholed or typecast into recurring roles, as many other entertainers have done. Denzel does not change what he is as an actor; he changes who, when, where and how he selects the scripts, characters, and films he is featured in. Denzel does not let his job description as an actor limit him, which underlines the value he brings to the entertainment industry and to his fans.

Leadership is no different. Leaders are actors performing roles and they, too, have fans. People either like a leader in the role they are playing or they don't. Gateway Leaders recognize this and place themselves and their leaders in the right roles so they are successful and liked by other leaders and professionals for their value to the organization and for their results.

When it comes to job descriptions, leaders and professionals are more than they appear on paper. The job description is the "what," but the "who, when, where, and how" is up to the leader to define. Job descriptions do not create extraordinary results regardless of position, title, or grade. It is the person, not the job description, who does not limit the creativity of professionals, leaders, or teams.

Gateway Leaders do not typecast themselves or other leaders by limiting them to a job description; they allow role creation and flexibility in assignments, initiatives, and projects. Gateway Leaders allow the development of their leadership role, just as an actor develops his role. They allow leaders and professionals to tap into strengths and develop weaknesses. Gateway Leaders let their teams, professionals, and organizations explore outside an assigned role or job description to uncover opportunities, innovations, and potential change.

Because the range of leadership is so broad, leaders have to play different roles or take different approaches to solving business complexities and dealing with professionals. Gateway Leaders understand that leaders cannot be typecast and provide the opportunity for each leader to create what they want their role to be, rather than defining it based on past perceptions, prejudices, and pressures.

Much too often, organizations, professionals, and leaders limit themselves to operating in predefined roles based on job descriptions. Many organizations hire people to perform in a role that limits their ability to grow, explore, and become the born leader they were meant to be.

I recall a friend of mine telling me a story about being typecast in a role that took him several years to escape. Larry was promoted to a new executive-level position by a Fortune 500 company. From a structural standpoint, he was hired by and reported to the person who previously held the position. That leader had been in the role for more than a decade.

As they began the transition process, Larry could not help but notice that his leader would constantly describe how he had performed in the position. In a meeting they both attended, someone raised a concern on a matter in an area over which Larry had oversight. His boss jumped in, answered the question, and gave direction before Larry could respond. The next day, Larry mentioned to his leader that he had discussed a different solution to the problem with the person who had raised it. His leader became irritated and inflexible to the change in the approach discussed at the meeting. He then demanded that Larry follow the process they had outlined because it was how it had always been done.

As time progressed, his boss checked with others on the team who had previously reported to him. The majority said that Larry was making good changes and had great ideas on how to make things better and accelerate results. Larry began receiving phone calls and meeting requests to explain why processes were being eliminated, questioned, or changed. Each time, Larry would explain the value and acceleration of the results that would be realized with the change, but his rationale was never quite good enough to gain his boss' support.

Here is what we discovered. We learned that each person in the organization, including Larry, had been assigned a predetermined typecast role based on previous job descriptions and the past of professionals in that position. The organization did not allow leaders to explore and define their roles. They wanted to control direction, energy, and focus by typecasting their leaders. The organization wanted to dictate to the leaders the "what, who, when, and how" of a role.

As a result, the organization ended up with a bunch of bad actors. The professionals were trying to play roles they were not familiar with; they had no knowledge or understanding of them. The leader wanted Larry to play the role he had played for a decade, line by line, word for word, as written by his previous actions. Can you image playing the same character, starring in the same movie every day for over a decade? Unfortunately, in business there are a lot of leaders who are acting in typecast roles.

It was clear that this leader was not a Gateway Leader. He did not want creativity, innovation, or the exploration of opportunities. He was only interested in maintaining the status quo. Because of this typecast leadership style, the organization's service scores, employee morale, and customer satisfaction plummeted to an all-time low. No competitor had launched a surprise attack on the company. It was the result of typecasting leaders who stymied the overall potential of the organization. It was not until a new leader was recruited—who recast and redefined leadership roles allowing leaders to stretch and grow—that the organization began to achieve extraordinary results.

Gateway Leaders recognize that organizations and leaders cannot be typecast; they must be recast. Recasting their roles against the backdrop of business complexity, customer demands, and industry challenges can constantly create value.

Recasting means providing the flexibility, range, and authenticity to redefine the "who, what, when, where and why" in the quest for change, new opportunities, and accelerated results so that leaders can maximize their true leadership potential in the organization. The best Gateway Leaders don't prescribe to "typecasting"; they "recast" by allowing themselves and leaders to:

- Redefine how to accelerate change and measure results.
- Define leadership roles by allowing the leaders to answer the "who, what, when, where, and why" questions of success.
- Implement resolutions to institutional challenges, obstacles, and breaking points without negative implications from veteran leaders.

- Create roles, opportunities, and pilot programs to foster leadership development and growth.

- Build trust, relationships, and partnerships with key stakeholders.

- Restructure command-and-control leadership organizations into nonhierarchical distributed leadership systems.

- Develop a coaching program to develop, grow, and build leaders today who can connect the network tomorrow.

As in acting, the key to success is not in typecasting but in recasting. Take a page out of Denzel Washington's playbook and define your leadership authenticity. Don't get typecast.

Gateway Leader Limitations

If you are a Gateway Leader, know professionals who fit this profile, or perhaps people in this category report to you, be aware that, as with the other networks, this network has its limitations.

Gateway Leaders have an awesome responsibility; they catapult organizations, teams and leaders to new, unchartered territory. Gateway Leaders create organizational breakthroughs by maximizing the potential of all resources. Limitations are similar to weakness: they can be improved through time, but it takes focus and commitment. Given no leader is perfect and that we all make mistakes in life, these limitations can actually result in leadership strengths if investments are made in professional and personal development through training and coaching programs. Many of the 5G–Gateway Leader Network limitations have to do with dealing with the high-profile position of Gateway Leaders. Knowing how to manage the associated stress and still accelerating as a team is critical to the success of the Gateway Leader.

The next several sections provide some of the key limitations that leaders on this network experience, along with strategies and techniques to turn the limitations into benefits that will be applicable to every other leader operating on the 6G Leadership System.

Gateway Leaders Act Quickly, but Must Remember to Accelerate Together

Gateway Leaders have the ability to anticipate windows of opportunity. They are brilliant in that they can address an opportunity, envision a solution, and predict when the solution must be deployed in order to realize those calculated benefits often referred to as the "window of opportunity." Because Gateway Leaders operate under this premise of short amounts of ideal time, they act quickly. At the same time, because of their accelerated pace, their actions, decisions, and influence can be out of step with the rest of the organization, leaders, and teams. Their unique, rapid-fire strategic and operational thinking often is more advanced than others, and their ability to understand nuances, complexities, and draw conclusions can become confusing to their teams.

Gateway Leaders accelerated actions and ideas can become an organizational challenge. Using their 5G Vision, they are able to process historical events, current trends, and future projects and, as a result, suggest a chartered course, while others may be still trying to understand historical events. The 5G Leader, because of his ability to operate at a much faster rate than most people, can cause directional misalignment given that others can't keep up. This may cause his team to become uncommitted and disengaged.

It is critically important that Gateway Leaders understand that they operate at an accelerated pace and often make quick decisions that impact the daily routines of leaders, professionals, and teams in the organization. It is critical that they understand that quick directional decisions be strategically communicated in the form of collaboration and not misconstrued as dictation.

In order to be effective, Gateway Leaders must take into account that other leaders may have varying opinions, ideas, and suggestions that should be considered before final decisions are made. Without proper vetting, engagement, and feedback, it is unlikely the defined charted course would be accepted and supported comfortably by others on the leadership team.

So what is the answer? Do Gateway Leaders slow down or do others speed up? The answer is both must be done!

First, to maximize efficiencies with regard to focus, time, and performance, there may be situations where Gateway Leaders may need to slow down so others can catch up. There is no value in communicating a new plan to the entire company if the leaders on your team still don't understand the direction. Slowing down would help in that regard. The best Gateway Leaders can sense when there may be a disconnect and can slightly reduce their accelerator, allowing others to catch up so they are in sync.

Second, there also may be situations when other leaders, teams, and professionals—recognizing the urgency and limited window of opportunity—need to accelerate their mindware to catch up to the Gateway Leader's approach and rationale. Sometimes leaders must be able to accelerate change, action, or results when clarity and understanding are a work in progress. Getting behind the Gateway Leader is not as important as accelerating alongside him. Commitment and support is critical if there is a disconnect. All leaders need to speed up or slow down so that the team can accelerate change and reach end results together.

The worst feeling in the world is to have a great plan, but because everyone is moving in different directions and speeds, the plan has the potential to fail. The Gateway Leaders allow everyone to accelerate together!

Gateway Leaders Are the Stars of the Team, but Must Be Careful Not to Become Prima Donnas!

I owe a great deal to one of my mentors. If you are wondering, he isn't a famous author, thought leader, motivational speaker, or celebrity. He is someone I am sure you've never heard of. His name is Coach John Buchheister. He coached three great players in high school. Two went on to be NFL players: Brian Jordan, who played for the Atlanta Falcons, and Reggie White, who played for the San Diego Chargers.

Who was the other great player? It was me! I can't tell you I was a better player than my friends Brian and Reggie. But I will tell you that in high school, I tackled both of them at the same time. That's right. Both of them!

Reggie was a lineman, 6-foot-6-inch, 300 pounds; Brian was a running back with each leg the size of a maple tree. I was playing defensive back in a practice scrimmage, and Brian and Reggie were on offense. Coach Buchheister called a play up the four hole where Reggie blocked and Brian got the ball. When the ball was snapped, I was there and took all three of them out! Who was the third person, you ask? The coach—I took him out, too. As Coach Buchheister got up, he yelled at both of them, "How the hell can McMillan tackle both of you at the same time? Run it again." That's when I got up, picked up my shoulder pads that flew off from the blow during the collision, and left the field!

That is my story and I'm sticking to it. Now if you ask Brian and Reggie what happened, they would tell you that I was already lying in the hole when they got there. According to them, I was knocked out from the prior play and they tripped over me. And that's when Buchheister screamed, "Run it again!"

Buchheister taught us a valuable lesson about excellence through his "run it again" philosophy. His lesson was that there was no room for "prima donnas" on the team. Coach pushed the starters on the team just as hard as he pushed the second-, third-, and fourth-string players. That is why he always made us run plays again when we did not hit the excellence mark. He wanted to make sure his stars did not become prima donnas, and that we maintained team chemistry where everyone was seen as a leader and equally valuable!

The same is true in leadership. Gateway Leaders are the stars of the team, just like Brian and Reggie were star athletes. Gateway Leaders are accepted, acknowledged, and recognized for their talents, gifts, skills, and accelerated results, but their success cannot become fuel for them to be prima donnas. Prima donnas, often temperamental and believe they are better than others, cause distractions, misalignment, confusion, and chaos, whether in sports or in the office. Gateway Leaders must make sure their star status and achievements do not signal a behavior of elitism, privilege, and petulance toward other leaders and teams. The best Gateway Leaders treat everyone equally and participate in projects, activities, and initiatives—not as a star, but as an equal contributor to the team.

Prima donnas in leadership do not last long. Demanding too much attention, the spotlight and special recognition can be the cause of infighting, distrust, and low morale. The key to organizational success is managing stars in a way that does not create a leadership team of prima donnas but a team of Gateway Leaders.

Gateway Leaders Are Under High Pressure and Must Have Low Stress Levels!

Have you ever heard these statements from leaders? "There is not enough time in the day." Or how about, "It is what it is," or "I need it yesterday"? These are all what I call "stress signals." These are signals from the organization and its people that indicate the pressure to succeed is creating an environment of stress that can impact performance, productivity, and profits.

Gateway Leaders are under a significant amount of pressure to accelerate change and achieve extraordinary business results. They are tasked with the critical assignment of doing more with less, creating efficiencies, and building gateways into the future of the organization, all while leading teams and developing leaders. In an organization that has C.H.A.N.G.E. goals as I described earlier, this can create a stressful atmosphere. Unmanaged stress can be a limitation of a Gateway Leader.

The Gateway Leader's role comes, of course, with celebrity, but with celebrity also comes the pressure of delivery. If Gateway Leaders are not careful managing pressure, the pressure can ultimately turn into a limitation: leadership stress.

I define "leadership stress" as the result of mental, emotional, or physical strain or tension placed on a leader to achieve a desired goal or objective. Because Gateway Leaders have close interaction with other leaders, professionals, and teams, the level of stress placed on them can result in frustration, impatience, and imbalance, impacting the overall morale of the organization. Gateway Leaders must manage the pressures of accelerated change and business results, not allowing them to result in organizational stress that can be crippling to an organization and team.

Organizational stress does three things very well: it creates mistakes, promotes indecisiveness, and stalls progress. Here are several strategies that Gateway Leaders can do to limit organizational pressure from turning into organizational stress:

- Create office fun and a mood of positive energy by focusing not specifically on the goals or objectives, but by celebrating positive outcomes as a result of efforts.

- Establish C.H.A.N.G.E goals throughout the organization to make sure that goals are Congruent, Healthy, Action-Based, Necessary, Growth-Oriented, and Excellence-Driven.

- Limit negativity from entering your leadership circle by dismissing it upon arrival. Intentional or unintentional negative comments must be stopped immediately, because they are contagious and an incubator for stress.

- Every morning, start your day with a positive attitude. Having a favorable outlook on life results in an impactful day!

The Acceleration App

The Acceleration App is a mindware application similar to other applications defined in the previous networks. The 5G Acceleration App is the mindware that motivates teams, leaders, and organizations to accelerate change and business results by maximizing the potential of the organization through creativity and innovation. Leaders on the 5G Network must have a motivational "g factor" to accelerate business results and change. It is this motivation that fuels the positive energy of the Gateway Leader.

Accelerate can be an ambiguous term. In the context of the 5G Leader, "accelerate" has several meanings: 1) To cause faster or greater activity, development, progress, advancement; 2) To hasten the occurrence of an event; 3) To change the velocity or the rate of motion; 4) To reduce the time required by intensifying the work or eliminating detail. Gateway Leaders do all this. Simply, they accelerate positive results! Unfortunately, this does not happen on its own; it takes motivation and the right mindset. The fact of the matter is, most people, professionals and leaders stop before they discover their organizational and personal limits. It was William James, American philosopher and psychologist, who said, "Most people never run far enough on their first wind to find out they've got a second." This is so true in leadership.

Gateway Leaders push leaders, teams, and organizations beyond their first wind to the discovery of their second wind. This is sometimes referred to as the breakthrough point. Every organization has one, but it requires motivation to get there. To maintain their motivation, Gateway Leaders require mindware that runs on their operating system and that helps them achieve extraordinary results by programming their mind with:

- An attitude to overcome insurmountable odds.
- An unconscious ability to think of the team first.
- The courage to turn personal failures into lessons for others.

An Attitude to Overcome Insurmountable Odds

Each morning we all wake up to an environment with one constant: change. Within change whirl challenges, obstacles, and barriers outside our control. Mergers, government regulations, economic challenges, and customer expectations all create an environmental shift impacting the daily lives of leaders. Many of these are viewed as insurmountable odds.

Sometimes leaders are not in a perfect position to stop, slow, or initiate change. For the most part, leaders do not have knowledge of external changes, and therefore, obviously cannot control them. External change is a shift outside a leader's control that forces the leader to take action once they have knowledge of the event. An external change can be market, industry, supplier, customer, competitor, government, or regulatory based. An internal change is the action taken by a leader as a result of their response to external changes such as a project initiation, reorganization, downsizing, rightsizing, upsizing, or in some cases, an uprising. It is those changes that ultimately initiate the internal organizational changes we have all come to love.

Sometimes external and internal changes are so significant that they are viewed as insurmountable odds and appear to overcome some leaders. With the degree of complexity and accelerated change in the global economy, Gateway Leaders must have an "overcome" attitude that provides a positive outlook when faced with significant challenges.

Presenting something as insurmountable impacts an entire organization's morale, confidence, and energy level. Can you imagine a leader shaking his head and looking toward the ground, communicating to an organization the following motivational words: "A competitor has penetrated and taken a significant amount of our market share that we worked for 20 years to build. We are under insurmountable odds." It would take the air out of the room and fill it with fear.

Gateway Leaders must present issues as both challenges and opportunities in order to inspire, influence, and inject proactive action throughout the organization to surmount challenges viewed as insurmountable. People are competitive by nature, and when someone takes a customer from them, they want that customer back! People love issues presented as challenges and opportunities. That creates energy and excitement. Now imagine that same leader saying, "A competitor has come into our back yard and taken 20 percent of our market share. What do you say we go over there and take it back and then some!" Wow! I want to work for that leader.

Gateway Leaders turn insurmountable odds into surmountable opportunities using a mindware that produces and maintains positive thoughts. This results in creating the required motivation to accelerate change and drive business results. Once teams, leaders, and professionals within the organization experience triumph over a significant obstacle and break through challenging barriers, they accelerate toward more extraordinary success.

Unconsciously Think "Team"

Leaders typically have access to tangible and intangible resources: budgets, people, capital, knowledge, power, information, and so on. The access area that is often missed is teambuilding. Teambuilding is one of the most critical requirements from leaders that can accelerate change and business results that are effective, efficient, and extraordinary. To become a high-performing team, the leader must have mindware that generates unconscious team thoughts, because if you have to think about it, chances are the opportunity has been missed.

Too often, leaders expect teamwork to exist without investing in teams. In order to build a team, one must first think "team." In the global economy, the individual contributor, star performer, and high-performing leadership concept is not enough to accelerate change and produce significant business results. Pursuing opportunities that require innovation, creativity, cross-functional disciplines, collaboration, enterprise skills, and leveraging internal and external business partners requires teamwork.

Unfortunately, I have observed organizations and leaders who spend an inordinate amount of time focused on individual accountability rather than group and team accountability. They often think of teams as an afterthought. Critical decisions, direction, projects and activities are already set and planned by a few leaders. As an afterthought, someone suggests—because people and teams are impacted—that someone should communicate and let them in on the decisions made. So, a meeting is held with the decision-maker present, facing a crowd of uninformed leaders staring like deers in headlights.

In these environments, feedback and ideas from the group are sometimes nonexistent. The issue lies with the traditional leadership approach of focusing on the individual. This approach dissects the concept of teamwork to the extent that organizations become reliant only on individual contributors and a few high-performing leaders to do the heavy lifting, while the organization as a whole becomes weaker in leadership. How often have you heard a leader say when there is a significant project or an assignment, "I'll get it done myself!" Or how about, "I'll work on that project!" In this scenario, it is common that only a few leaders in the organization have access to and understand the information, make decisions, and control all factors of a project that impacts an entire organization. This is an example of an organization that is not team centered and does not unconsciously think team. But when Gateway Leaders automatically considers the efforts of and benefits for their teams, the organization is imbued with camaraderie, trust, commitment, and engagement.

Gateway Leaders on the 5G Network must have a "mindware" to accelerate results and produce team leadership thoughts of:

- Defining and maintaining the joint purpose of team existence.
- Developing, creating, and improving team chemistry and composition.
- Building trust and commitment.
- Fostering and nurturing the development of personal team relationships.
- Developing team connectivity through ensuring challenging assignments to accelerate business change and results.

Gateway Leaders understand that teams do not become teams because of quarterly team meetings, dinner outings, or after-work events. Gateway Leaders understand teams are not developed offsite; they are created onsite and require work-related interactions. Unconsciously, the best Gateway Leaders have a mindset that instinctively initiates teambuilding: group collaboration, assignments, activities, and workshops. They ensure that teams have portfolios of enterprise, department and personal goals that are congruent, shared, challenging, fun, and professional-development focused.

Courage to Turn Personal Failures Into Lessons for Others

My grandparents and older family members would often say, "What doesn't kill you only makes you stronger!" to a family member or friend who was going through tough times—stress, marriage difficulties, financial hardship, work issues, unemployment, and just dealing with failures in general. As the conversation neared its end, they would always reiterate, "What doesn't kill you only makes you stronger!" The person would feel inspired and their energy level perked up because there was hope in the air. As a child, I would ask my grandparents, "What happened? What was about to kill them?" Of course they would say, "Stay out of grown folks' business. This is not for a child to know!" At 10 years old, I could not appreciate or understand what they were discussing or what the saying meant.

As I got older and began working in business, I realized that one of the keys to life and leadership success is sharing the gift of personal failures as lessons to others. Those people who visited my grandparents were sharing a gift. How could a failure be a gift? Well, because the failure did not kill them! They lived through the failure and were able to share with others so they would not fall prey to the same mistakes!

Leadership works in the same manner. In order to accelerate business growth and change, leaders must share personal lessons and failures with their teams so they can avoid missteps and mistakes. Leaders have to have a mindware that gives them the courage and self-esteem to be transparent so others can learn from them.

I can't begin to tell you of all the failures I experienced during my career as a leader. What's the point, you ask? The point is, we all make mistakes. We all miss the mark. We all come up short. When we miss, we fail. The question is, must leaders cover up misses and failures? Externally it appears that leaders are perfect and failure-free, but the fact of the matter is, they usually have more misses and failures than they have hits and successes.

Gateway Leaders must have the courage to share their failures with others and continue to keep going! One of the most powerful transformative things a leader can do is not just share their successes. Oh, no. They should share their failures as well. This creates trust, confidence, transparency, and commitment for team success!

Summary

Gateway Leadership is the springboard for an organization and team's extraordinary success. It is the launch pad for innovation, creativity, and team performance, which results in accelerated change and business results. The 5G–Gateway Leader Network is a High Influence Leader, with the ability to accelerate positive business results by influencing decisions and actions. Leaders allow their influence because they create opportunities and accelerate change simultaneously!

The best Gateway Leaders maintain an Acceleration App that allows them to create success and wins, while improving business processes and teams. If you as a leader can maintain an attitude to overcome insurmountable odds, create high-performing teams, and share failures as gifts to others, you are well on your way to becoming a 6G–Genius Leader!

6G Leadership Coaching is the art and science of retraining your brain through meditation, thought, action, and repetition. In this chapter, as well as others, you will complete the exercise to immediately grasp and put into action the concepts we have discussed.

Next are 10 ways to use the Acceleration App, including affirmations, action steps, and applications on your journey to becoming a Leader of Significance. Remember, the stronger your Acceleration App, the greater the potential!

● ●

5G—Leadership Coaching Exercise:
Acceleration Affirmations, Action Steps, and Applications

1. Each morning when you rise, repeat three times, "I will accelerate today." Write down three acceleration goals you have. *This will open your mind to setting daily goals.*

2. Identify two leaders on your team who need to improve in areas of accelerating processes, programs, or services. *This will help identify those leaders on your team to share acceleration goals with.*

3. What failures can you share with your team that will make them stronger as leaders?

4. As a Gateway Leader, state three times a day, "I am a star, not a prima donna!" *Doing this speaks truth to reality.*

5. Think about how you can create a C.H.A.N.G.E. goal-setting program to help your leaders reach their maximum potential. Write down three things you can start doing today. *Following this action will show a commitment to investing together in the success of the organization.*

6. Repeat daily: "Leaders don't typecast; they recast!" Write down the names of three leaders you have typecast and develop a plan that allows them to recast their role. *This will begin the process of building a positive infrastructure of leaders around you.*

7. During your commute home, introspectively reflect on your day. How could you better use 5G Hindsight, Farsight, and Nearsight to accelerate change and growth in the organization? *This will introduce to your psyche the concept of building the*

habit of excellence into action. Write down three things you will do tomorrow differently than you did today.

8. Repeat daily: "Stress free!" *This daily regimen will force you to manage pressure and eliminate stress from your mind.*

9. What D.U.M.B. goals can you and your leaders eliminate to free up time and resources to pursue more valuable opportunities? *This will start the process of challenging the status quo.*

10. Before you leave the office at the end of each week, write down two leadership traits you will work on the next week to improve.

• •

Now that you have completed this exercise, review each week and assess your progress. In the next chapter, we will explore the final network, 6G–Genius Leadership Network, and its profile, features, limitations, and Agility App. Let's maximize our potential by becoming a Genius Leader!

6G–Genius Leader and the Agility App

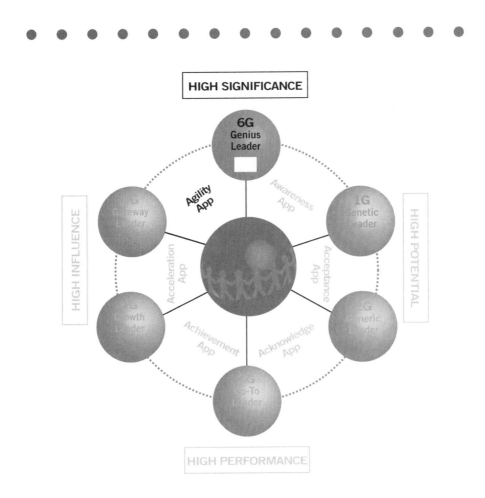

There's a genius in all of us.

—Abraham Maslow, psychologist and scholar

Genius People Do Complicated Things Really, Really Well with Agility!

I discovered leadership genius when I hit the most important man in the world with a golf ball—the President of the United States! I failed in golf that day but made a life-changing discovery. I discovered that Genius Leaders see the genius in everyone!

Sports figures are leaders in their own right, and many of them have reached the genius level because they have taken something complicated and made it look effortless with their remarkable agility. As a collegiate athlete and an admirer of those pro sports athletes, like my friend Brian Jordan and his teammates, Deion Sanders and Bo Jackson, I know there is no doubt that genius runs through their blood, just as it does in yours. To become a pro athlete requires elements of genius, particularly if an athlete plays both football and baseball during the same season, as Brian, Deion, and Bo did. Like them, you have to have an element of genius in what you do as a professional leader. The question becomes, "Are you demonstrating it?"

Of all sports, I would contend that golf is the most complicated and the most like leadership. One can definitely see the athletic genius it takes to accurately hit a little white ball with a stick. That is why I admire Jack Nicklaus, Arnold Palmer, Tiger Woods, and all the other golf greats.

In my opinion, golf is more complicated and requires more agility than football. In football, bodies crash into one another and a man in a black-and-white shirt measures if there is a loss or gain in yardage, all in an effort to score points so the players, coaches, and fans can decide whether to celebrate. In football, there is a clock, yard markers, allotted downs, and an end zone—simplistic and fairly easy to follow. Golf is not that simple. Golf does not have any of those things. You have to guess how far you are from the green. And to have a chance at a birdie or eagle, somehow you figure out how to hit that little white ball at the right angle with the right club to sink it into a hole you cannot see. Now that is complicated. And there is no scoreboard or referee. You become the referee and you keep your own score. If you play with my friends, that creates a whole other set of challenges.

Golf demands unique coordination and skills that other sports—such as baseball, soccer, or basketball—do not require. I believe that professional golfers are athletes and geniuses primarily because of their ability to master a complicated sport and make it look so simple.

The Same Genius in Golf Is Found in Leadership

Leadership can be just as difficult as golf and is very similar in terms of complexity. Navigating on the 6G Leadership System and connecting to every leader, regardless of pay, position, or power, is challenging. It requires a constant twisting and turning motion. The key to golf is your swing: being able to twist your body in a particular motion while staying on plane, and hitting the golf ball with force and acceleration at an exact angle. This requires significant athletic agility. Size, age, or strength doesn't matter in golf—just acceleration, precision, and consistency. Size, age, and strength doesn't matter in leadership, either; but acceleration, precision, and consistency is critical in leading others. I call that having "leadership agility." As with golf, when a leader's agility is missing in action, their performance and ability to influence others becomes significantly lowered.

In golf, poor agility results in hooks, slices, duds, scorches, and putting errors. In leadership, poor agility results in misfires, misjudgments, bad decisions, and rework. In leadership, a dud is when a leader attempts to move a matter forward by assigning it to someone or resolving it himself. Unfortunately, the issue does not change. It just stays there in the same spot where you found it. A leadership slice, hook, or scorch is the opposite of a dud. The leader attempts to take action and move a matter forward, only to send it off in an unintended direction, creating negative results and more problems. Golf and leadership are complicated but similar; the lack of agility (acceleration, precision, and consistency) can create overwhelming challenges.

It was because of the lack of agility that I almost hit one of the most powerful men in the world with a golf ball. That experience exemplified the characteristics of a Genius Leader.

You Can Fail and Still Be a Genius

In April 2009, I had an opportunity to play golf with a business partner at Andrews Air Force Base in Suitland, Maryland. The sun was blazing; the temperature was in the 90s. I was struggling to duplicate the success I had warming up on the driving range, hitting the golf balls far and straight. For some reason, I couldn't hit them as straight that evening on the course. I guess you can say I was not a golf player that day; I was a golf hacker.

After playing terribly the first several holes, hitting a lot of hooks into the woods, I decided to alter my shot by overcompensating for the hook. I would intentionally hit the ball to the left, hoping it would hook back into the middle of the fairway. I did this on the 10th hole, a Par 5, and it worked perfectly. I drove that ball 250 yards dead center. I can't tell you how surprised I was that I hit it that far. As we drove up to the ball in the cart, my business partner James questioned if it was my ball and I confirmed it was because it was a Titleist with black dots I had marked on it. I only played with one brand of balls, Titleist, because that's what the pros do!

As I approached the ball for my second shoot, I couldn't help but hear a foursome of golfers about 200 feet to the left of me on the 8th hole. They were laughing and giggling, and I really couldn't concentrate. "Hey, I'm trying to hit here!" I yelled. Against golf etiquette, they continued their loud and annoying conversation.

Trying to block out the distraction, I took my new two wood and lined up with my ball. Because of my success with my last swing, I decided to do the same thing. I hit the ball to the left near where the foursome was playing, waited for it to start to turn and hook back into the middle of the fairway. This time the ball refused to go where I wanted it to go; it just kept going toward the loud foursome. As it got closer and closer to them, I almost instinctively screamed "Fore," but my alter ego said to my subconscious with a smile, "Let's see what happens." One of the players picked it up and looked around to see where it had come from. Like little kids, James and I jumped in the cart and sped off to the next hole before they realized it was us.

As we were driving to the next hole, we saw a bunch of military officers and soldiers in golf carts, driving from hole to hole. The hole we were going to play was blocked and we had to wait 20 minutes to play the hole, backing up the entire course. Boy, was I frustrated. James asked one of the soldiers why they had blocked off the hole, and they told us that there were some very important golfers on the course. We asked who was so important that the hole was blocked, and they declined to tell us. I said to them, "If they were that important, they should play on a private course. This is public and a taxpayers' course!" I exclaimed

After approximately 20 minutes, we were finally allowed to approach the hole. As we got out of our carts to approach the tee box, an old man who worked the grounds drove by in a work truck. He stopped to collect the trash from the can and whispered quietly, "Do y'all know who you're playing with? The President." Still frustrated, I said, "President who?" He said, "Obama!"

Excited, I asked what hole they were on. I thought I could get close enough to get my ball autographed. He said, "I don't know which hole, but they are right over there!" He pointed to a foursome group that was about 150 yards away. Jokingly, James said, "Man, I sure hope you didn't hit the President with a golf ball. Secret Service will have your ass!"

For the next two hours, it felt as though the military and Secret Service were following us, creating a boundary between that foursome and us. We finally finished the 18th hole, about 25 feet from the front of the club-house. We returned the cart and walked into the clubhouse, noticing the Secret Service doing a security sweep on everyone. They announced that the President was on the grounds playing a round of golf, headed for the clubhouse after he finished the 18th hole. They had to secure the place. So they screened us, and invited everyone to watch the President complete the 18th hole from our great clubhouse view.

As the President completed the hole, he got in his cart, drove about 20 yards, stopped and waved at everyone watching in the clubhouse. Somebody shouted, "Mr. President, how did you play today?"

The President responded, "My putting could be better but what's important is I had fun!" Then he said, "I'm much better than the guy who hit me with a Titleist golf ball!"

That's when James did the dumbest thing. "Mr. President, it was him. He hit you with the ball," he yelled, pointing at me!

The President laughed, reached in his pocket, pulled out a Titleist golf ball. He looked at it and said, "What ball do you play?"

I answered, "The ones that go straight."

"Man, you know you only play Titleist," James said.

"With black dots?" asked the President.

"Yes," James answered.

The President took a pen, scribbled on the ball, and tossed the ball toward us while driving off in the golf cart.

At that point, I realized I was a genius, because I had gotten the President to sign my golf ball without even planning it. I don't have the ball to prove the story, because as the ball was in the air, I was trampled by 50 other golfers trying to catch the ball, all claiming they played Titleist with black dots, and they had hit the President with their ball.

Discovering the Genius in Leadership

What I discovered about golf that day did not have much to do with the embarrassment of being one of many golfers hitting the President with a golf ball; it had more to do with continuing to play through. I had countless failures on the course, but ultimately hit a good shot on the 10th hole, driving the ball 250 yards, my personal best.

What I've discovered about leadership is similar. What makes Genius Leaders are not their successes, but their courage to continue swinging after failure and their ability to see and maximize that genius in others! I learned that the genius is not in the results; the genius is in the attempt, the swing. Most leaders look for genius in the result, but it is the actions, behaviors, and traits of a genius that produce redefined success. Just as in golf, leaders must swing every day. Sometimes they miss, err, or fail, but the key is to keep swinging, and sooner or later they will hit the shot that redefines success and their personal best!

Regardless of obstacles, challenges, complexities, or failure, Genius Leaders continue to swing into action with a focus toward a specific vision, objective, or goal; that is what makes them different from other leaders. Even though there are obstacles and challenges outside of their control, Genius Leaders continue to redefine success, improve business results, and learn from failures.

The definition of genius is broad-based. According to Dictionary.com, *genius* is defined as 1) An exceptional natural capacity of intellect, 2) A person having that capacity, 3) A person having an extraordinarily high intelligence rating, 4) A natural ability or capacity, and 5) Distinctive character or spirit.

Genius Leaders are Leaders of Significance because they have defined their genius by redefining success, transforming industries, maximizing potential, growing leaders, and taking organizations to new levels of growth. Leaders value them because of their ability to inspire, impact, and institute change.

On the 6G Leadership System, there are very few leaders who have mastered this network. However, I want you to know that it is possible. As difficult as it is in golf to master every club, stroke, and possible scenario, and shoot an excellent score at or below par, that same level of difficultly exists in mastering the game of leadership—but it can be done.

Becoming a Genius Leader requires knowing every leadership network (1G–6G), and demonstrating the right behaviors and actions in every possible scenario with acceleration, precision, and consistency. The key to mastering the Genetic, Generic, Go-To, Growth, Gateway, and Genius Leadership traits and characteristics is having the courage to fail and taking those failures and transforming them into lessons for success. That is what makes a Genius Leader.

The fact that there is a Tiger Woods and a Jack Welch, a Steve Jobs and a Phil Mickelson, an Arnold Palmer and a Barack Obama, lets us know that there are not only genius professionals in their fields but genius professional leaders! The reality is that we all have a Genius Leader within us; it is just a matter of discovering, fine-tuning, and unleashing it to the world.

This chapter sets out to describe the features, traits, habits, and limitations of Genius Leaders, and to provide strategies, secrets, and techniques for dealing with some of the human, cultural, and leadership limitations found in most organizations. In short, you will discover that Genius Leaders are valued by others because of their demonstrated ability to:

- See and develop the genius in everyone.
- Balance long-term, short-term, and mid-term visions.
- Bounce back from challenges and defeat.
- Catapult over failure to success.
- Redefine new measures of success.
- Collaborate on multiple networks and levels.
- Navigate around organizational politics and theatre.
- Build leaders while building themselves.

Genius Leaders are viewed as Leaders of Significance by others because they are leaders with:

- Beliefs in maximizing full human potential in themselves and others.
- A natural capacity of intellect in a specific field.
- The ability to process, learn, and execute things others cannot.
- High intelligence in an industry, market, and organization.
- Unconscious abilities, habits, and traits with the capacity to achieve extraordinary success.
- Unique character and spirit that attracts and grows others.
- Agility that propels failures into launching pads toward significant business results.

I invite you to challenge yourself to begin operating on the Genius Leader Network, and in doing so, regardless of what your current aptitude may be, soar to new leadership heights by stretching yourself to be more, do more, and achieve more. Before others see genius in you, you first must see the genius in yourself!

I encourage you to take time answering the following questions and begin your journey to becoming a leader of genius you were born to be.

- What would you define as the genius in you?
- What unique talent and gift do you possess that could help you become a genius in your role within the organization or team?
- What opportunities exist in the organization that could allow you to demonstrate your genius and agility to redefine personal and business success?
- How do you help others discover their genius?
- Do you view yourself as a multi-dimensional leader who can play two or more professional roles? What are the roles?
- How are you maximizing your potential and others in your current role?

6G-Genius Leader Profile and Traits

The 6G–Genius Leader is the sixth and final network in the 6G Leadership System. To expand from the 5G to 6G Leadership Network requires leaders to demonstrate agility in connecting to every leader in the organization, creating a vision, redefining success, and pursuing opportunities to achieve extraordinary results and provide inspiration for success by having the courage to fail. Genius Leaders are masterful servers, leaders, and doers. They have so much agility in their leadership style that they are not known for leading from the top or middle; they are appreciated and valued by others because of their unique ability to lead from the back.

Leaders and professionals value Genius Leaders because they are visionaries, creators, developers, executors, and acknowledgers. Genius Leaders are the catalyst forces that transform organizations to redefined success. The key distinction between the 5G Gateway Leader and the 6G Genius Leader is that the Genius Leader has the profile, traits, benefits, and features of the Gateway Leader, as well as the ability to foster innovation, redefine levels of success, and influence the actions of others to achieve extraordinary results. 6G–Genius Leaders singlehandedly, by inspiring others, create a new beginning for organizations, leaders, and teams.

Given the current complicated business structures, market changes, and global competition, leaders need to have agility to initiate action in response to business challenges and customer needs. Flexibility in products, services, supply chains, delivery, and services is critical to the overall business success and directly reflects on how effective the organization's leadership system is. According to the IBM study that interviewed more 1,500 of the world's most-admired companies, many CEOs indicated that they could not afford the luxury of detailed studies before making decisions; 54 percent of CEO responses indicated that they are more likely to rely on quick decision-making than on longer, more thorough studies.

CEOs are expecting leaders to make faster decisions with the courage to fail and learn from results, rather than spending an inordinate amount of resources, time, and energy conducting analysis and studies. This requires creative and innovative leaders. In an organization where there is group think, collaboration, trust and the recognition that everyone is a leader, the future looks bright with leaders ready to step up to the challenge. In organizations where this is not the case, the future looks grim, filled with leaders who step down from the challenge.

Becoming a 6G–Genius Leader takes six generations, and the sooner you begin to understand, accept, and adopt the behaviors into your routine habits, the more benefits you will realize from the system. Becoming a Genius Leader within the 6G Leadership System does not require you to climb a hierarchical ladder over other leaders to get there; on the contrary, the 6G Leadership System is simply built on behaviors, actions, and characteristics that create the Genius Leader. Remember: Bill Gates, Michael Dell, Jeffrey Bezos, Steve Jobs, and countless others were not always in the spotlight. They became CEOs or entrepreneurs worth billions of dollars because their Genius came first and success followed. You, too, can become a Genius Leader. Remember, in every instance, the Genius comes first and the success follows.

I invite you to become agile, resilient, and relentless in your pursuit to be a Genius Leader, and I look forward to seeing you on the leadership network.

If the scores from your leadership aptitude identify your dominant network as 6G Genetic Leader, then I would encourage you to re-evaluate how you perform on each Leadership Network and re-assess how you can maximize your potential.

To help you better understand the Genius Leader profile, Diagram 1 summarizes the profile of the 6G–Genius Leader and the accompanying Agility App, a motivational "mindware" every leader needs in order to run on the 6G Network.

• •

Diagram 1

High Significance, with the ability to redefine success through vision, inspiration, and learning from past failures. Leaders allow you to influence them because they respect your leadership agility and connect with you.

Agility App—*Agility* is achieving business, organizational, and professional outcomes.

Overview of the Genius Leader

- Genius Leaders are Leaders of Significance. In their passion to redefine success, they have a tendency to create stretch goals that may cause leaders to become frustrated or burn out.

- Genius Leaders challenge culture and status quo, but sometimes they may forget to listen to reasoning for the current state.
- Genius Leaders have unique agility to navigate through complicated matters and view issues from multiple angles. Their ability to cast a vision may impair their ability to ignore details.

Maximum Potential—realized in scenarios requiring visionary thinking, extraordinary results, and engagement.

Least Potential—created in situations that limit creativity, risk-taking, and agility.

Core Leadership Value to Teams and Professionals

Professionals value you because they respect your leadership agility and ability to connect. Teams value you because your actions create agility to grow the business, the organization, and its people.

- Visionary leader with focused execution.
- Possibility explorer and resource irrigator.
- Agile and extremely flexible to significant change.
- Redefines boundaries of success.
- Transformational catalyst.
- Embraces learning through failure.
- Challenges the norm and cultivates culture.
- Grows leaders through personal coaching and development.

• •

Genius Leaders have distinct traits and behaviors that separate them from all other leaders on the 6G Leadership System. Simply put, Genius Leaders are extremely agile and are able to move between being visionaries, creators, executors, cultivators, and leaders. They are the catalyst to redefining and maximizing an organization's potential.

Genius Leaders are hands-on leaders, in tune with leaders and professionals to the extent that they inspire them to maximize both professional and business performance. They also challenge those things that are routine in nature, questioning their value in order to focus more effort on increasing value-added activities that impact the customer.

For these reasons, Genius Leaders are High Significance Leaders whose success results in a legacy of service to the organization, its customers and leaders that continuously provide extraordinary results and personal accomplishments that stand the test of time.

Contained in Diagram 2 is a limited set of traits to help you understand the Genius Leader in further detail and to give the mind a place to begin forming the habits of the 6G Genius Leader. Review each of these traits and indicate those that resonate with your actions, behaviors and habits by providing a score in the box between 5 (often), 3 (sometimes), and 1 (rarely) for each leadership action description. After you have completed the exercise, for the traits self-rated as "sometime" or "rarely," think about how you can transform those traits into daily habits.

• •

Diagram 2

Genius Leaders:

- _ Redefine the measures of success.
- _ Have clear vision with clarity in action.
- _ Are engaging Leaders of Significance.
- _ Personally coach and develop leaders.
- _ Operate and connect on networks 1G to 6G.
- _ Are multi-transformative; they turn companies and leaders around.
- _ Accelerate critical facets of the organizations.
- _ Motivate and inspire other leaders to achieve extraordinary results.
- _ Maximize their leadership potential.
- _ Build diverse leadership teams driven by purpose and passion.
- _ Align success with legacy.
- _ Promote failing as a way to learn.
- _ Create challenges to build core competencies.
- _ Lead from the front, middle, and back.
- _ Are visionaries, innovators, and executors.

_   Accelerate business results.

_   Influence the achievement of extraordinary results.

_   Lead from behind and unravel politics.

_   Eliminate silos and build cathedrals.

_   Break normalcy.

_   Invest in others as they would invest in themselves.

• •

The great news is that anyone can be a Genius Leader. One does not have to be a C-level executive or an officer. The 6G Genius Network is accessible and available to you!

Features of the Genius Leader

As on previous networks, the Genius Leader has features and a few minor limitations. 6G–Genius Leaders are the most agile and impactful leaders in the 6G network, uniquely different than other network leaders because they have mastered the operation of the entire 6G Leadership System. They are Genetic, Generic, Go-To, Growth, and Gateway Leaders. They have the ability to connect on each network and maximize the usage of the system's benefits and features. Genius Leaders are Leaders of Significance, and their limitations are few and far between.

As with any leader, there is always room for development and growth. Many leaders have not reached perfection within the Genius Leader Network. Some have developed certain skills to connect to a network, but do not remain consistently connected for very long. On the other hand, there are those who operate very well on the Genius Leader Network— leaders I have described throughout this book, Genius Leaders you know of in your organization, or even you.

This section is designed to help aspiring leaders reach and stay connected as Genius Leaders, using simple measures developed to provide practical, action-oriented steps and strategies that leaders can master to become a Genius Leader. To provide a broader context of the positive features of Genius Leaders, this section summarizes several of the most beneficial values they provide to organizations, teams, leaders, and their customers.

Because this is the most valued network, it is critical for you to understand, challenge yourself, and put into practice the concepts and behaviors you need to maximize the untapped leadership potential within you. Each feature will help you grow as a leader and advance your ability to influence and improve yourself, your organization, and your team.

As you review these key features, make an effort to introspectively evaluate the value you provide to others and how your performance reflects the benefits, traits, and behaviors of the 6G network. Evaluate if you are truly maximizing your potential in your position, role, or assignment. Think about it, then determine what steps you can take to become more agile in redefining business and professional success for you, your team, and organization. I encourage you to take that journey and identify what may be holding you back from being the Genius Leader you were born to be.

Remember, you have the potential to be a Genius Leader. Tap into your infinite well of potential; prime it and discover what awaits you. I invite you to explore and discover the Genius Leader in you.

Genius Leaders Lead From the Back (Ubuntu)

There are many great political figures in the world, from Presidents Reagan, Obama, Clinton, Lincoln, and Nelson Mandela to CEOs Steve Jobs of Apple, Ron Williams of Aetna, and Bill Gates of Microsoft. In that esteemed group is a spectrum of iconic human rights leaders as well—Mahatma Gandhi, Nelson Mandela, Martin Luther King, and Mother Teresa.

There is one thing all of these leaders have/had in common: the ability to lead from the top, center, and bottom. But what makes them unique and highly successful is their genius ability to lead from the back. The best example of this is demonstrated by Nelson Mandela, because of both his human rights and appointed leadership successes. He once said, "It is better to lead from behind and to put others in front, especially when you celebrate victory when nice things occur. You take the front line when there is danger. Then people will appreciate your leadership."

Leading from the back can be traced to an African philosophy called *Ubuntu*. Ubuntu literally translated means: *I am because we are*. In summary, it represents the following system of beliefs:

- Human expression should be genuine in relationships with other humans.

- Consultation is a form of valued orientation and expression.
- Interdependence is a superior value to independence.
- Humanity and group solidarity is valued.
- Decision-making and leadership are participatory.
- Opportunities, responsibilities, and challenges are shared and collectively owned.

From a leadership perspective, I view Ubuntu as a philosophy and idea that people can be empowered by others and become better as a result of unselfish interactions with others based on the willingness to let them take action and lead.

Leading from the back requires our trust and confidence in others, as well as a respect and appreciation for them. Genius Leaders follow the Ubuntu ideals. They are not interested in rewards, recognition, or profit; they are merely interested in and admire the success of others. To admire and recognize the success of others requires a leader who gives up control, attention, recognition, and accolades to provide others an opportunity to lead, contribute, and shine. In order to create this environment, leaders have to be agile enough to lead from the back, and when necessary, move to the front alongside other leaders to face challenges together.

When Mandela was a young boy, well before he became the famous leader we have come to know, he spent long hours every afternoon leading (herding) cattle. He explains that if you want to move cattle in a certain direction, you stand in the back and send several of your smartest cattle to the front. You then move the back in the direction you want the cattle to go. The leading cattle will adjust and the others will follow them. This is so much like leadership. When an organization has to move at lightning speed to respond to market pressures and customer demands, leaders don't have the luxury of leading from the front. Why? Because Gateway Leaders understand that they themselves can sometimes get in the way of acceleration.

If you are leading from the front, that means many people are watching your every move. Genius Leaders understand that this can limit progress and, in some instances, become a distraction. Do you know any leaders who have to be involved in everything, in front of every issue or action, in hopes of gaining attention or credit?

Genius Leaders recognize that there is a time to be in the front, casting vision, but often leaders stay in the front position too long. The secret to and the most difficult part of leadership is not leading from the front but having enough trust in your team to move from the front to the back so other leaders can take their natural leadership positions and become empowered to lead and accelerate business results and change. Sometimes direction, commitment, motivation, and engagement are better received when leaders lead from the back. From the back, a leader can see another leader out of step or out of position much more easily.

The true value of leadership from the back is exhibited when leaders influence other leaders, changing the direction of their thinking, and providing support with subtle influences and guidance. Here are several strategies that leaders can use to begin leading from the back to becoming Genius Leaders:

- Develop a broad range of leaders in the leadership group so there is an array of leaders, where everyone will have a rotational opportunity to lead and develop.
- Empower others to voluntarily make decisions that accelerate change and results.
- Transmit a synergistic leadership spirit with emphasis on ethics, integrity, and excellence.
- Focus on building a system of shared beliefs, values, and standards.
- Show genuine concern for others, and recognize and reward achievements.
- Ensure alignment with personal and business goals.
- Emphasize the necessity of strengths and weaknesses, and commit to coaching, mentoring, and goal-stretching.

Genius Leaders Have 11 Genius Rules and a Personal Mission Statement

Several years ago, my then-10-year-old son shared with me several statements that equate to defining your mission in life as a Genius Leader. That's correct. My 10-year-old son taught me about leadership! Genius Leaders have a professional mission statement that allows them to focus on those things that align with their reason for living, their purpose in life. When speaking and training leaders, I define a personal mission statement as *the moral purpose, work, agenda, and focus of a person's life that guides action.*

Children are precious gifts, and my son and daughter have led both my wife and I since their birth. If you pay very close attention to children, you will discover that they are, in fact, leaders, and they are leading you whether you realize it or not. Children are Genius Leaders. My favorite script of life says: *"And a little child will lead them."* (Isaiah 11:6) It is true; they are leaders!

Several years ago my son decided that he wanted to wrestle. Being as I was the 1991 NCAA wrestling champion, watching my 10-year-old son wrestling just like his daddy was one of the proudest moments of my life. As I watched my son practice with his teammates, I saw some of the same quickness, balance, and agility that was in me when I wrestled more than 20 years earlier. One difference between me and my son was that I did not start wrestling until I was a junior in high school. I had never wrestled before and did not know I had the potential to be great. For some reason, after a great football season in 1987, I decided to give wrestling a try. In my first year, without any formal training, I was undefeated, placed third in the state championship, and was crowned the "Takedown Champion of All Time." In my mind, I was the Muhammad Ali of wrestling. You see, I had the innate ability to take people down and let them up. I was not a technical wrestler with a bunch of moves; I was just fast, strong, and agile. I had the gift of balance and instinct that, as Coach Palmer told local reporters after my championship matches, cannot be taught.

As I watched, my son displayed the same characteristics—speed, agility, balance, and strength. He took people down and let them up. I never coached him to do that; he just did it unconsciously. I felt everything he felt, as my wife, daughter, and I cheered him on when he wrestled opponents during matches. I couldn't help but reflect on my own wrestling career.

Between my son's matches at the tournament, I recalled my senior year in high school. I practiced hard, learned wrestling techniques, and went on to place second in the state championships that year, beating others who had wrestled since they were 8 years old. The same thing happened in college. I was recruited to wrestle and play football at Virginia State University, and when the coach pulled my wrestling scholarship, I retired from wrestling and focused on football during my freshman and sophomore years. My junior year, the football coach reneged on a long-awaited full scholarship. Just like professional athletes do today, I held out for a scholarship that never came.

The coaching staff was upset with me because I decided to "retire" from football. They could not understand how a 20-year-old could retire. Retiring for me meant moving on in pursuit of life's mission.

A new wrestling coach who heard about me asked if I wanted to be on the wrestling team and offered me a scholarship. I told him I would come out of "retirement" and wrestle only to become the champion in my weight class. The rest is history. I went on to beat countless opponents with my signature "Shuffle Shot," which was the Ali Shuffle.

When I would get ready to take an opponent down, I would shuffle my feet as a distraction and shoot. When reporters would ask me about the move, I called it the "Rob Mac Shuffle"! In 1991, after being out of wrestling for three years and never wrestling at the college level, my arms were raised as the 187-pound NCAA Wrestling Champion. It was the "Shuffle Shot" that won the championship for me. When presented with the trophy in front of 1,000 fans, I screamed just as Ali did when he beat Sonny Liston, "I'm a bad man, and I must be the Greatest!" The crowd roared! That day, I announced my retirement. I decided to move on in pursuit of life's mission!

As I saw my son on the mat, like any parent, I saw myself. Because he was starting out as a 10-year-old, he had a 7-year head start on me and could exceed my success in wrestling, which is what every parent wants for their children.

As I drove my son to wrestling practice after his most recent tournament victory, I noticed he was very quiet. We reached the high school where he practiced, and I parked the car. I looked at his expressionless face. His excitement and energy were gone. When I asked him what was wrong, he asked me a question. "Dad, would you still love me if I didn't wrestle anymore?"

"Why, yes, son, I love you no matter what you choose to do in life. As long as it is moral and legal," I joked.

With tears in his eyes, he looked at me and said, "What if I decide not to wrestle anymore?"

Now I was getting teary-eyed. I have this thing I can't control. When people I love cry, I start to cry. I put my hand on his shoulder and said, "I just want you to be happy and enjoy what you are doing. If you don't enjoy something, then don't do it."

"Well, I don't want to wrestle. The only reason I did it was because I wanted to be like you. You always talk about how good you were and I wanted you to be proud of me."

His courage moved me so much that the tears I was holding back rolled down my face like a river. He asked me why I was crying. I used the classic line that there was something in my eye. And something was in my eye—the sight of a child leading and trying to control his own mission in life, with his vision blurred and influenced by others. In leadership, Genius Leaders have a clear mission and vision for their life and challenge those things that obstruct it.

I said these words to my son: "You don't have to be like someone in order for them to be proud of you."

We wiped our tears, promised we wouldn't tell anyone (especially my wife and daughter) that we both had a "moment," and drove off. We never went back to wrestling again. We were at the mall a few weeks later and when a former teammate he saw asked him why he wasn't wrestling, he looked at them without hesitating and said, "I retired from wrestling!"

What was the leadership lesson? Genius Leaders have a clear mission, and when activities don't support their mission, they retire from them.

My son went home and wrote *"Eleven Genius Rules"* that will help bring clarity to your vision, provide focus on your life mission, and retire those things that decelerate growth:

1. You can't go through life doing something you do not love!

2. A person must experience something before they decide that they don't like it!

3. Never do something you do not like to please others!

4. If you retire from something, it does not mean you are a quitter. It just makes you a "Go-Getter"!

5. We don't quit anything; we redirect our energy to our life mission!

6. If we start something, we finish it!

7. You don't do something for someone else; you do it for you!

8. Courage is knowing when to walk away!

9. Love is the greatest gift of all!

10. Love what you do!

11. Be who you want to be, not someone you don't!

Genius Leaders have clarity and help others bring it to their mission in life. They understand that everyone is a leader and each person is on the planet to maximize their potential. Genius Leaders see other leaders as whole individuals and not just as employees. Genius Leaders have a moral purpose and commitment to helping others during their leadership journey.

Genius Leaders do not let others define them; they take the time to discover who they are. They do not engage in activities that don't align with their personal mission in life; they retire from those activities and invest time and effort in new activities that support their mission, goals, and objectives. It is those traits that other leaders, professionals, and teams respect, admire, and appreciate that make them want to be part of a genius team.

Many leaders are not successful because they are leading someone else's legacy, agenda, or mission. They don't truly have a mission of their own in their professional life. They are, in many instances, lost in their professional life. They attempt to replicate the behavior, actions, or accomplishments of another leader, relative, or friend. As my son demonstrates through his "genius statements," people can easily fall prey to other people's dreams and be successful but miserable because they've discovered emptiness in their achievements.

Genius Leaders recognize this quagmire and help other leaders discover their mission in life without retaliation, prejudice, or envy. Genius Leaders help other leaders discover their maximum potential, which results in the discovery of their mission in life. Because of this ability to connect and relate to the whole humanistic side of professionals, Genius Leaders have the ability to nurture and develop leaders, multiplying potential, performance, and possibilities within the organization.

Leaders value Genius Leaders because they help bring clarity to their mission in life and accelerate personal development, change and transformation. Having a Professional Mission Statement is critical to the success of a Genius Leader. Here is an example of a mission statement crafted for a recent client.

Personal Mission Statement

To become the best leader I can be, maximizing the potential of myself, others, and the organization by redefining success, learning from failures, and being a catalyst of change. I will lead projects, initiatives, functions, and activities in pursuit of accelerated change and business results with agility. My team and other leaders recognize me for adding value to them and the organization. My family, work, and personal life are in balance. I recognize and capitalize on opportunities to improve myself, the organization, and team, which define my legacy.

What is your personal mission statement? I invite you to take the time to craft and develop a professional mission statement for you and your team, and initiate the action to becoming a Genius Leader!

Genius Leaders Are Continuously Coaching and Learning Leaders

In a complex environment, it is critical to be effective in utilizing resources and maximizing the areas that impact the customer most. Measuring standards such as customer satisfaction levels, percentage of defects, call abandonment rates, customer service, market share, and customer value are all important key performance indicators that are reached by Genius Leaders to continuously coach and learn from others. Genius Leaders must keep a pulse on the industry, markets, innovations, solutions, and strategic and operational challenges and opportunities by continually giving and receiving as a coach and teacher.

In the never-stagnate competitive and global economy, Genius Leaders never stop learning. In organizations that are command-and-control driven, leaders typically hoard information in an attempt to use and leverage the information as power and control over others. They request their leaders to leave their thinking at the door. These organizations typically end up with leaders whom I refer to as Dumb Down Leaders, opposed to a Continuously Coaching and Learning Leader.

A Dumb Down Leader is a leader who lacks self-confidence and motivation, and maintains a full supply of arrogance. He knows all of the answers before questions are asked, and he retain all of the critical information so others cannot be a part of the decision-making process. He believes he is the authority as it relates to all operational activities, never empowering others to take action or lead without his approval of every step. Typically, these organizations deplete growth, knowledge, intellectual capital, and morale. Knowledge transfer is maintained at the top of the organization and rarely filters downward.

Genius Leaders are Continuously Coaching and Learning Leaders. They create a culture of knowledge-mining, transferring, and sharing information throughout the organization for all leaders to learn and develop. Genius Leaders view every employee as a valuable asset and in a leadership position. These leaders do more than orchestrate breakfast meetings with the CEO and a half-dozen employees who have been screened, prepped, and warned not to communicate any issues or concerns to the CEO.

Genius Leaders create an environment where the CEO, officers, director, and managers interact with all leaders who are employees or associates at the organization. Companies such as Dell, HP, PepsiCo, GE, and others are known for creating workshops where leaders of the organization identify issues and solve problems together. Genius Leaders understand how to use their personable and intellectual agility to bring people together and allow them to raise the bar, redefining success, inspiring action, and becoming Leaders of Significance.

Genius Leaders explore opportunities to improve significant business results and increase value to the customer by implementing initiatives such as Six Sigma, Total Quality Management, and Zero Deficiency Management programs. They also ask the right questions of other experts in order to evaluate the return on investment on such programs. This ensures that there is optimal customer value and that organizations don't become chasers of non-valued KPIs (Key Performance Indicators), but pacers of invaluable KPIs.

Organizations must appropriately manage the amount of time and resources they invest in these areas to ensure they ultimately add value to the customer and that significant investments have not been made in areas that have diminishing returns.

Several years ago, I performed in the role of a consultant to a company that was having a diminishing return problem. In short, diminishing return is when the cost of achieving a business result exceeds financial and customer value. Simply put, the organization had a problem with overachieving.

This organization, a Fortune 500 company, had a group of officers who ran a top-down, control-oriented leadership system and dictated implementation of a key performance indicator (KPI) goal of 120 percent for customer satisfaction. The organization was able to achieve that service level profile for more than three years with a lot of effort and investment. To accomplish the goal, the organization spent millions of dollars chasing the KPI.

Because the company was losing money, a suggestion was made to conduct an analysis of the cause of the losses. It was determined that to keep a customer, the customer satisfaction level needs to be only 85 percent. In essence, the company was pouring millions of dollars down the drain so that a senior executive could tout that they were able to drive customer satisfaction up to 120 percent. It turns out that the additional 35 percent (120 percent minus 85 percent) over and above the amount needed to maintain their customer base cost the organization more than $100 million during a three-year period—diminishing returns. Because of that ongoing issue, unfortunately the executive vice president was viewed as a diminishing return and was ousted from the company.

Genius Leaders pull the right people and information together to understand and make the right call on setting business capacity, defining customer expectations, and establishing categories and metrics around diminishing returns. In my more than 20 years of leadership experience, I have seen an awful lot of leaders and organizations chasing performance metrics, service-level agreements, and performance-based incentives without clear knowledge of the maximum penetration of excellence relating to reaching diminishing returns on those investments in quality and accuracy.

Genius Leaders leverage continuous coaching and learning to ensure the organization is investing in the right initiatives. Genius Leaders understand when "good is enough"! They understand when to raise the bar, when to keep it flat and when to lower it.

Here is a list comparing a Continuously Coaching Learning Environment to a Dumbing Down Environment. To become leaders and organizations of significance, build an environment using the cultures and behaviors in ***bold italics*** while eliminating the unwanted antigrowth descriptors in **bold.**

Dumbing Down Environment	Continuous Coaching And Learning Environment
Top-only knowledge base and sharing.	*Leaders coach other leaders.*
Command, direct, and control.	*Leaders engage in learning workshops.*
Undistributed learning.	*Leaders learn from other leaders.*
Depletion of intellectual capital.	*Leaders mine, transfer, and share knowledge.*
Limited group satisfaction and value.	*Leaders recognize others' expertise, talents, and skills.*
Demotivation, individualistic, low morale.	*Leaders inspire, motivate, and foster collaboration.*
Low organizational confidence and leader self-esteem.	*Leaders have self-confidence and self-esteem.*
Silos, decentralization, duplication.	*Leaders build and develop teams.*
Disrespect, fear, and mistrust.	*Leaders respect, trust, and acknowledge the rights of others.*
Prejudicial thoughts based on top-down leadership.	*Leaders value diversity, groupware & heterogeneous thoughts.*

Genius Leaders recognize that to gain a competitive advantage requires an innovative and open coaching and learning environment where everyone can grow and develop together, even Genius Leaders. Genius Leaders have a zeal for learning and coaching others. It is that continuum that makes organizations such as Apple, Dell, HP, GE, Amazon, Facebook, and several others great. This has catapulted them into leadership positions in their industry.

Study these areas and begin to transition your teams, organizations, and yourself into the 6G–Genius Leader you were born to be! Invest in a coaching system to create agility in your leadership skills and build yourself an organization to operate on the Genius Leader Network.

Genius Leader Limitations

The Genius Leader does have a few limitations. It is unlikely that you know professionals who fit this profile exactly, and it is highly probable that no leaders in this category report to you. That is the bad news. The good news is that you will likely be the only person in your organization who will be able to operate on this network and truly understand how to navigate the limitations that exist on it, differentiating you from other leaders in your organization and team.

Genius Leaders redefine success and inspire others. They are leaders of High Significance. They are accountable for achieving extraordinary organizational results, which is an awesome responsibility! As with any human, they have their limitations. Because of the interactions and reliance on others, Genius Leaders are only as good as the leadership system and information they use to significantly influence their direction and decisions. Many of the limitations have to do with the soft side of leadership. The soft side of leadership means engagement, commitment, interaction, conflict, politics, and confidence, all of the things that affect the mind, heart, and hands, and result in the actions of Genius Leaders.

Because the Genius Leader is operating on several networks at one time, 1G to 6G, there are several interdependent limitations I would like to share with you that can also be used as benefits to other leaders on the network. As mentioned previously, limitations are similar to weaknesses; the good news is that they can be improved through time, though it does take focus and commitment. Each limitation creates opportunity zones for the entire leadership system, and each limitation is not limited to an individual leader. It expands and is dependent on other leaders and the culture the leadership system operates in. Simply put, even Genius Leaders need to be in the right environment to release their brilliance.

As you review this section, identify areas you can focus on to expand your network capabilities by understanding its limitations. Then implement the accompanying suggestions to improve your agility to connect to others on the network, thus redefining success for you, your team, and organization.

Genius Leaders Can Become Info-Intoxicated

Genius Leaders are sought after by an awful lot of people, leaders, professionals, and teams to give information, feedback, and ideas, and to present solutions to challenges and obstacles, all simultaneously. They have capacity constraints to transmit, receive, and process information, just like every other human, but their success is limited to their ability to zero in on key data points and make the right call to action. This differentiates them from other leaders. However, because they are limited to information provided to them, they must control the flow of information they receive so they do not become info-intoxicated. Genius Leaders must make sure that they are not drawn into the weeds (which I refer to as tall fescue), blinding them from a vision linked to redefining success, challenging the status quo, and inspiring others to achieve extraordinary results.

One of the keys to maintaining leadership significance as a Genius Leader is to mitigate the risk of becoming paralyzed by invaluable data and information produced by organizations, teams, and leaders. Genius Leaders must manage the level of detail and flow of information they allow to enter their passageway. Have you ever heard the saying, "On a need-to-know basis"? This is a leader's attempt to manage detail. The problem is that others define what you need to know; they determine the detail and often have a tendency to leave out important information that can easily change or alter a significant decision. Many leaders make the mistake of trying to counter this by requiring or placing an edict that they know every gory detail. They decide what information they will use in making decisions, setting strategy, or planning. This approach handcuffs and paralyzes leaders to the extent that they become rigid in their thinking.

Genius Leaders strategically make decisions based on knowledge and information provided by others. Because of the cycle of business change, Genius Leaders rely heavily on information from their teams. To limit decision-making errors and information overload, it is critical that leaders receive information that is accurate and at the right level of detail. Otherwise, they lose focus on the big picture and begin to focus on the small frame. Information must be gathered and presented accurately on a need-to-know basis. The old saying is true: "Garbage in, garbage out." If information provided to a leader is garbage, then it is highly likely that the output of a decision will be garbage as well. The same is true with detail—if information provided to a leader is too detailed, the output from the leader is likely to be a request for more information and/or unusable detail—"Detail in, detail out!"

Detail is a limitation for all leaders. Enough details allow leaders to make good decisions, but more often than not, they get too much detail, which causes leaders to become information overloaded. An overflow of information and detail is just as bad as consuming too much water. When someone consumes too much water, it triggers a chemical imbalance referred to as water intoxication. Water intoxication is a potentially fatal disturbance in brain function that results when the normal balance of electrolytes in the body is raised to unsafe levels as a result of over-consuming water. This can cause a system to crash and sometimes results in death.

Information overload can have similar impacts on leaders. When speaking at conferences or when coaching leaders, I refer to this as "info-intoxication." Info-intoxication occurs when leaders go into information overload. It would be like drinking from a fire hose. There is so much information coming at a leader from different angles, perspectives, and hidden agendas that the leader goes into information shock, unable to make any rational decisions.

I remember a leader who reported to me some time ago, and he practiced info-intoxication faithfully. Not only did he have this problem, he passed it along to others, including me. One day, several hours before a meeting, he was so concerned about providing real-time information that he reached under the bathroom stall to hand me several reports he thought were essential for preparation of the meeting. Not to be embarrassed further, I only took the report from his hands to stop him from talking to me from behind the door as other people entered the restroom.

Info-intoxication runs rampant in many organizations, and teams and Genius Leaders must manage the flow of information that they consume. It is logical to think that the last thing that would harm a human being would be information (and water), but anything over-consumed eliminates benefits and causes harm. The same is true in leadership—too much information can cripple an organization, team and its leaders.

Next are several steps that Genius Leaders can take to limit info-intoxication:

- Pre-define the level, type, and frequency of information you want your leaders to provide to you. Provide them with an understanding on the level of reporting you want, and make sure the reports provide a strategic decision-making purpose and are not reports with non-value-added data.

- Schedule meetings with your leadership team for them to present to you issues, challenges, and opportunities by directing them to present information at a high level, only "hitting the top of the wave." As you need more information, request it from them, but remember not to get trapped in the tall fescue weeds.

- Coach your teams and leaders to extract specific details that accelerate the decision-making process, and do not handicap it with information overload.

Following these steps will help Genius Leaders maintain their focus and ability to redefine success, inspire others to act, and to identify opportunities for exceptional success.

Genius Leaders Have a Finite Amount of Time and Must Guard It Wisely

Genius Leaders are sought after by countless people, leaders, professionals, and teams. They have a finite amount of time, and how effectively they use their time can make or break them. This finite amount of time can make Genius Leaders appear to be unpredictable, time sensitive, and aggressive. The fact is that those are all true attributes of Genius Leaders. Because they recognize the value of time, they think outside the box, appearing to be unpredictable. They want quick and fast answers, and they deal with challenges by aggressively confronting them, all because they recognize the value of time.

Because Genius Leaders are on a personal mission in life, they have a desire to leave a legacy based on their accomplishments, and what they accomplish is predicated on how effectively they utilize their time to redefine success, inspire others, and leverage failures to assist them on their journey to discovering success. Time is the key to success, and Genius Leaders must maximize its use.

Genius Leaders have to guard their time and be sensitive to it. At the same time, they cannot appear to be insensitive to others' needs, uninterested in what others have to say, or unyielding in receiving feedback and suggestions. They must find a way to connect to others while managing their own internal clock. The key to a leader's success is effectively leveraging the use of everyone's time to the best benefit of the customer, team, organization, and themselves.

Many leaders spend an enormous amount of time connecting to others to transmit and receive information. They run from meeting to meeting, conference call to conference call, responding to voicemails, e-mails, and handwritten notes, as they deal with drive-bys (those unplanned and unscheduled meetings when people corner a leader in the bathroom, office, lunchroom, at the water cooler, parking garage, and in the lobby to get or give information).

Genius Leaders, like anyone else, have the limitation of time as a factor. If their time is not strategically allocated, then there is no recovery of that lost time. Leaders are bombarded from every direction, almost like celebrities are hounded by paparazzi trying to get the perfect photo. Getting hit with question after question can eventually wear on a leader. This can become to much to bear for Genius Leaders. To balance this, Genius Leaders need time to think and digest overwhelming and complicated information, and draw their own conclusions to complex matters. What I have found as the best way to do this in a leadership role is to disconnect from the network to establish down time.

Genius Leaders need to allocate time to be disconnected as well as connected: connected to their teams, leaders, and network to accelerate change and deliver extraordinary business results, and disconnected from the network to free up time to process, question, and ponder strategic and unorthodox solutions to complicated and overwhelming business challenges without distraction. This is often where genius takes place. Genius Leaders can be so connected that sometimes the connection can be ineffective and create a limitation requiring the Genetic Leader to disconnect from others to reconnect to himself. I know that sounds weird—to disconnect from others in order to reconnect to yourself—but it is so true.

Each of us is accountable for our time, and how we spend it determines our success. The genius Albert Einstein once said, "The only reason for time is so that everything doesn't happen at once." He was spot on. Every question cannot be answered at the same time and every thought cannot run together. Disconnecting allows the leader to resynchronize his own thoughts, ideas, and strategies, and begin the process of bringing those strategies, ideas. and solutions together.

Nobody manages your time but you. To help remind me to strategically leverage my time, I start out every morning with a poem I wrote called "Time."

Time

Time, stand in the glass in yours and mine.

It is up to us to use or lose if we so choose,
but suffer an infinity if we abuse.

So have the courage to change every day,
stand in the glass from dirt to miry clay.

For it is mediocrity that leads to life's calamity,

But if I pursue possibilities,
with purpose and passion alongside of tenacity,

That same sand in the glass is but yours and
mine can make dreams a reality!

E-mail, Blackberry, Skype, and all of the other connection tools and devices we use must be managed so that they do not become a distraction and impede creativity. Remember every now and then to disconnect from your network to recharge and resynchronize. Effectively leveraging your time to accelerate change and business results is key to becoming the Genius Leader you were born to be.

Genius Leaders Have Leadership Critics

Genius Leaders attract critics. Because of their vision, approach, and ability to connect things that perhaps others cannot understand, Genius Leaders are often criticized and questioned by colleagues, leaders, and teams. It was Aristotle who said, "Criticism is something we can avoid easily by saying nothing, doing nothing, and being nothing." I like to put it like this: you can always tell a person who takes progressive action and does something others wouldn't dare to do, because all you have to do is find a critic, and in front of that critic you will find a genius.

Critics in leadership are people who criticize others for taking action. Unfortunately, this is a major challenge in leadership and one of the reasons why many leaders do not take bold, decisive action. They fear the critic. Critics can be CEOs, CIOs, officers, directors, managers, a boss, a subordinate, or any professional. And as I've said before, leadership is not based on position, power, or title. Anyone can be a Genius Leader, which most critics don't understand!

Here is what I have discovered about critics in leadership. Critics criticize things that they have a fear of doing, have not done before, or do not know how to do. Critics come in all shapes, sizes, levels, and positions. Some critics are disguised and others are transparent in stating their opinions, but the fact remains they are critics, nonetheless. With the goal of redefining success and turning poor performance into great results, Genius Leaders are often on the attack and must not allow critics to impact their self-confidence and belief in their potential and their desire to achieve extraordinary success.

Some years ago, I had the opportunity to experience working with an organization that had an issue with critics. Several leaders in the organizations were given the nickname "leadership critic" by their peers and, in some instances, subordinates. These leaders were responsible for building their reputation of being critics, primarily because they were controlling, lacked self-confidence, devalued others' contributions, and capped the growth of Genius Leaders in the organization. They viewed themselves as the evaluators of solutions and ideas, and made it difficult to redefine success and inspire others. It was those behaviors that fueled the beginnings of a culture that was highly critical of change.

The behaviors were so strong that when other leaders presented solutions and ideas to increase customer service, order fulfillment, and financial results, the critics would openly criticize them—so much so that many of the leaders attending the meeting began to disengage from the conversations because of fear of being criticized.

After the meetings ended, the critics would make negative comments to other leaders that the ideas and suggestions presented were unlikely to succeed. One of the interesting things I observed was that these leadership critics never volunteered to lead any initiatives or provide ideas or suggestions; they simply criticized leaders who were trying to take action.

These critics existed because the organization had a culture that criticized change and challenged new ideas. Some people went to meetings just to play the role of "devil's advocate." I was amazed at how many people in meetings would line up and wait for a turn to play that role. Some of them should have been nominated for an Emmy or an Oscar for their performances!

Have you ever been in a meeting and watched someone wait for a moment of silence, then take the floor and say, "Let me play the devil's advocate," and people responded, "Please do"? This seemed to be a role everybody wanted to play. If you really think about it, the role of a devil's advocate is that of a critic in disguise. They come up with irrelevant scenarios, hypotheticals, and negative points only to tear down, destroy, and poke holes in a solution or concept they do not understand, did not come up with, and don't support. Because of this limitation, aspiring and Genius Leaders will have to combat critics and devil's advocates so that the negative criticism doesn't impact their growth, potential, or aspirations for success.

Several weeks later, the leaders got back together to review the results of the activities they initiated at the previous meeting. In attendance were the same leaders from the last meeting, including the leadership critics. As one of the solution leaders presented the results of the action plan, they communicated performance scores that indicated customer service, orders, and financial results were improving at an accelerated rate; they were on their way to redefining success! The leaders in the meeting began to give high-fives and congratulate each other on their success. As I observed the critics' corner, I noticed it was as quiet as a tomb. The critics were not celebrating; they were astonished at the results achieved. Rather than allowing them to continue to be disengaged, one of the leaders made a genius gesture. She looked at them and thanked them for their feedback and participation. She indicated that if they had been accurate in their critiques, then the team would not have made the adjustments and been successful. She went on to say that they were valued team members. All of a sudden those critics came from their corner and joined the team in celebrating results, giving high-fives to everyone. They, too, were members of the team!

Genius Leaders must mitigate critics from adding additional stress or pressure, or allowing their actions to cause indecisiveness and hesitation in accelerating change and business results. Gateway Leaders must find ways to use critics to fuel the teams' success; create roles for critics on the team; and use critics' systematic questioning as test scripts for a valid solution.

I learned three things from that experience: First, critics are our best friends. They truly make us perform better because we want so badly to prove them wrong. Second, a sure way to silence a critic is to perform and show results. Finally, critics want to be a part of a winning team!

Genius Leaders deal with critics by showing resolve, resiliency, and results because one thing is for sure: critics are not going anywhere. Leaders must manage the limitations that they bring to the organization and continue to create other Genius Leaders!

The Agility App

The Agility App is a mindware application similar to other applications defined in the previous networks. It is a motivational application that helps the Genius Leader maximize his potential and the potential of others by connecting to all leaders, regardless of position, pay, power, or their current aptitude on the 6G Leadership System. Genius Leaders must have the agility to connect on all leadership facets with organizations, teams, and leaders.

Within the 6G Leadership System, agility is defined as the ability for the organization and its leaders to think and draw conclusions quickly; demonstrate intellectual acuity by accelerating business results; be nimble, cutting through organizational bureaucracy, politics, and challenges; and pursue significant change through the achievement of extraordinary business results.

To be a Genius Leader requires an Agility App, mindware that unconsciously helps Genius Leaders navigate through all the different nuisances of leadership, creating relationships and engaging with people of different backgrounds, ideas, philosophies, and cultures, in pursuit of redefining business and personal success.

There Is a Genius in Everyone

The foundational belief of 6G–Genius Leaders is that everyone is a leader and that there is a genius in every person. Genius Leaders require repeatable applications that are used to bring out the genius in others, helping them connect to the hearts, minds, and hands of leaders and teams. It was Harvard University's William James, America's first psychologist, who said, "The essence of genius is to know what to overlook." Genius Leaders do not determine the success of others by measuring their failures; they redefine success based on unlimited potential. According to James, humans only use about 10 percent of their overall potential. Genius Leaders understand that there is a genius and untapped potential in every human being, and they are committed to helping other leaders discover their genius and release it, resulting in extraordinary team and organizational results.

The key to a Genius Leader's success is building strong leadership connections throughout the organization that require agility. High Significance Leaders must develop leaders who can redefine success, create High Potential, High Performance, High Influence, and High Significance, which requires agility and connecting to others. When coaching and speaking, I refer to this as leadership connection agility.

Genius Leaders must maintain a mindset that is programmed to define and demonstrate leadership connection agility, improve leadership connection agility in other leaders and teams, and establish a culture of leadership connection agility in the environment. The Agility App sets out to help aspiring and current Genius Leaders do just that.

Leadership Connection Agility Defined

Have you ever experienced a conversation on a cell phone when the other party had a weak connection?

In that situation, there is no engagement or commitment reached because neither party is connected. The same is true in leadership. When there are no mutual connections or goals, objectives and expectations are rarely reached. For Genius Leaders to redefine success and become leaders of High Significance, it is critical to have strong leadership connection agility with leaders and teams.

Many of the issues that exist within leadership can be easily traced to leadership connection agility. Like on an iPhone or any cell phone device, when there is a connection to a network with a strong connection, both parties have clarity. The connection is crisp and runs without interference. However, if one party has a weak connection, then there is no clarity, resulting in a poor connection. This ultimately results in a dropped call. Leadership works the same way. Leaders have both strong and weak leadership connection agilities that determine a level of engagement and commitment for achieving extraordinary goals. Strong leadership connection agility provides clarity, quality, and reliability. Weak leadership connection agility produces confusion, frustration, and wasted resources.

During my 20-year career in Corporate America, I have discovered that few leaders have strong leadership connection agility and, as a result, are not able to get full commitment, engagement, and support from leaders. Often they allow the pressures of the business and their personal agendas to cause stress and disconnect with other leaders and teams. On the other hand, strong leadership connection agility enables Genius Leaders to balance pressures against commitments, engaging in relationships resulting in high performance, growth, success, and mutual respect among their peers. Weak leadership connection agility results in the opposite: low performance, stalled growth, failures, organizational chaos, and confusion.

Improving Leadership Connection Agility

Can one transform weak leadership connections into strong leadership connections? The answer is yes! Once Genius Leaders begin to demonstrate what strong leadership connection agility is, they can begin to improve their abilities in this area, as well as have other leaders begin to improve their connection agility.

The fact of the matter is that connection agility is an area that is often avoided and rarely discussed within departments, organizations, and teams. This issue is rarely referenced or examined in business settings or addressed in best-selling books on leadership authored by those referred to as experts in the field. Building stronger leadership connection agility in leaders and organizations requires inspiring, motivating and challenging the organization to achieve extraordinary personal and business results. It is a model where everyone shares in success and rewards. This requires agility to ignite action and adrenaline at all levels, and a strong belief that the best days are ahead (and not in the past) for the organization, its leaders, and its teams. Building stronger leadership connection agility throughout an organization and among its leaders requires a transformation of values, beliefs, and habits, resulting in the commitment to redefine success each time an extraordinary result is achieved.

To build stronger leadership connection agility requires leaders to believe and commit to reaching their full potential. This requires focusing on improving weaknesses rather than ignoring them. In the last several years, it has been suggested that leaders should not focus on recognizing and improving weaknesses but focus only on strengths. I could not disagree with this more. To combat this flawed thinking, Genius Leaders need to constantly remind themselves that they can improve weaknesses in themselves and other leaders in the areas of change, innovation, creativity, leadership, communication, strategic thinking, and problem-solving. These are not gifts or talents; they are skills and competencies, which can be developed and improved with the necessary commitment, training, and coaching.

To suggest that leaders forget about weaknesses and focus only on strengths is ineffective in the end because the question that goes unanswered is "What has been improved on if you have not improved weaknesses?" The conclusion that I share with audiences and groups I consult and speak to is that strengths are already strengths, so it is unlikely they can be significantly improved on. But the courage to identify weaknesses and improve them is where one will find untapped potential and newfound opportunities for business and personal growth.

This thought and mindset is for leaders and organizations that have no agility to address leadership issues, and it completely undermines the countless stories of improvement in people's weaknesses that have resulted in extraordinary success. Consider this: if Michael Jordan had ignored his weakness of not being a good team player, and had weak connection agility with his team, if he never improved his team connection agility and only focused on his ability to score more than 50 points a night, he would have never won several NBA Championships with the Chicago Bulls. The approach being touted on "focusing on your strengths and ignoring your weaknesses" would have cost the Bulls six championships. It was Michael Jordan's improvement in his leadership connection agility that won those championships. In fact, if you review Michael Jordan's stats, when his leadership connection agility with his team went up, his points per game went down, creating more team engagement, commitment, and connection, resulting in the extraordinary success of winning six championships. If Tiger Woods did not focus daily on improving his weaknesses in driving the golf ball consistently and increasing his putting accuracy percentages, he would not be recognized as one of the greatest golfers who has ever lived.

Creating an Environment of Leadership Connection Agility

It is important for Genius Leaders to maintain the mindset of creating and fostering strong leadership connectivity environments that, through time, become habits and are performed unconsciously.

How many times have you heard, "Leaders need followers"? A strong leadership agility connection environment operates under a single principle—that leaders do not lead followers; leaders lead leaders!

I remember at one point during my career leading a team comprised of finance, operations, and information technology professionals who helped me understand the concept of creating an environment of leadership connection agility. In 2002, there was a mandate called Sarbanes-Oxley, a bill enacted as a reaction to a number of major corporate and accounting scandals, including those involving Enron, Tyco International, Adelphia, Peregrine Systems, and WorldCom. These scandals, which cost investors billions of dollars when the share prices of affected companies collapsed, shook public confidence in the nation's securities markets.

As a result of this mandate, a leadership opportunity was created in a company for which I applied, and ultimately accepted, with oversight of Sarbanes-Oxley. Who says government does not create jobs?

During the process of interviewing for the position, I asked one of the C-level executives what he felt my major challenge would be in the new role. There answer was, "This position is like herding kittens that won't follow you." He went on to describe the business owners, employees, and teams who had to comply and implement the new regulatory requirements as being lost and all over the place, "They're like a herd of chaotic kittens. These 'kittens' need a strong leader with agility." He went on to describe how silos, politics, and territories were challenges for the organization.

Several weeks into the role, it became painfully obvious that it was not the so-called "kittens" that were all over the place; it was the leaders who operated in chaos. I had to rely on an awful lot of agility to work with varying leaders' styles, personalities, and motives. Because the process to comply with Sarbanes-Oxley was already under way, being run by another leader in the organization in addition to his full-time job, many of the leaders were frantically calling meetings to try to find out what needed to be documented, tested, and certified to comply with Sarbanes-Oxley.

As I observed this environment, the mindset that "followers need leaders" came to mind. The current environment projected arrogance, superiority, and elitism, and made it difficult for the "followers" and "leaders" to exchange information and ideas and to develop strategies on how to comply with the legislative mandate. In multiple instances, during those meetings scheduled by C-level leadership, you could see that there was a significant divide between two distinct groups: the leaders and followers were split into separate camps. This was so strong in the fabric of the culture, you could watch how the weak leadership connection played out in the lunchroom. Rarely could you find leaders in the organization sitting at a table with "followers." In fact, many of the so-called leaders did not eat in the cafeteria. The culture was so divided that one human resources initiative was to somehow get leadership to eat in the cafeteria with their employees. Because this could not be achieved any other way, they started a program called, "Lunch With the Executives," which created even more division when nobody participated except the executive who started the program. There was a significant weak leadership connection that would require significant agility to improve.

On the Sarbanes-Oxley front, not much was completed after several months, and progress was dismal. After discovering the lack of empowerment, commitment, engagement, and trust was the result of leadership not establishing connections and demonstrating agility in meeting the mandate, I recommended to C-level leadership that we begin to empower those viewed as "followers" with formal positions as "leaders," and they agreed.

Simply put, we made everyone who participated in the Sarbanes-Oxley activity a business lead, meaning they were empowered to lead and represent their business interests. Leadership is not a position or title, but rather a mindset. As a part of the strategy to empower people to become engaged, I asked each person on the enterprise team to be the Sarbanes-Oxley leader for their functional area. The Sarbanes-Oxley leader was not a position, title, or formal role noted in the human resources job description database of titles and grades; it was simply a mindset. If you have not asked someone to be a leader, I would suggest doing so. Being asked to lead is a compliment, and people sure do like it better than being asked to be a kitten or follower!

With approval from the CEO, I moved forward and implemented the model, creating leaders of business areas responsible for Sarbanes-Oxley. I witnessed a significant increase in engagement, accountability, and commitment. To address the trust issue, I suggested we do something creative and establish a Sarbanes-Oxley Golf League made up of all of the officers, directors, managers, professionals, including the CEO, to build relationships and foster trust and engagement. It was amazing to witness how relationships that were bruised became healed; and how disengagement transformed into engagement, simply by creating an environment with strong leadership connection agility.

A challenging process that appeared to be insurmountable turned into one of the greatest achievements of the organization, the leaders, and their teams. It was this experience that cemented my long-held belief that when people are treated as followers, they follow, but when they are empowered to be leaders, they lead.

What was the underlining issue? The issue was connected to change, and in order to implement change, leaders have to connect to leaders. The organization's culture and its leadership system viewed non-managers, staff, and rank-and-file employees as "followers." There was significant resentment and resistance to change from employees. In turn, the "followers" did not engage, exchange or, for that matter, enter into the process of change. Change is ultimately what Sarbanes-Oxley was all about. People in critical positions who were treated as followers felt a weak leadership connection and, as a result, were dropped from that leadership network. The mindset that comes with the philosophy, "Followers need leaders," is a weak leadership connection and disconnects the engagement of the mind, heart, and hands of professionals; it creates an attitude of superiority and ego, causing morale and employee participation to suffer. By defining, demonstrating, improving, and creating a culture of strong leadership connection agility, the new empowered leaders became engaged, committed, and accountable for making the Sarbanes-Oxley initiative a huge win for the entire organization.

Summary

If you want to get to a state of influence and significance, begin to lead based on a value system that empowers others. To redefine success, accelerate business results, achieve extraordinary results and create leaders, you must believe leaders need leaders, not followers.

The Agility App constantly reminds leaders that there is a genius and leader in everyone, and of the importance of creating an environment with leadership connection agility. Genius Leaders use the Agility App to create a culture that challenges the old leadership joke: "If you are not the lead dog, your view never changes." Genius Leaders create an environment of opportunities where everyone is a "lead dog," and the view always changes, because you are leaders, not followers!

6G Leadership Coaching is the art and science of retraining your brain through meditation, thought, action, and repetition. In this chapter, you will complete the exercise to immediately grasp and put into action the concepts we have discussed.

Here are 10 ways to use the Agility App daily, including affirmations, action steps, and applications, on your journey to becoming a Leader of Significance. Remember, the stronger your Agility App, the greater the potential!

• •

6G-Leadership Coaching Exercise: Agility Affirmations, Action Steps, and Applications

1. Each morning when you rise, repeat three times, "There is genius in me!" Write down three things about you that differentiate you from others. *This will open your mind to setting daily goals.*

2. Identify two leaders whom you will commit to helping discover their genius. *This will help build genius-minded growth and hold each other accountable for growth and development.*

3. What leadership weaknesses do you have that you will work on to create stronger leadership?

4. As a Genius Leader, state three times a day, "Strong leadership connection agility!" *Doing this will help you unconsciously begin to project strong leadership connections throughout your organization and teams.*

5. Think about how you can create strong leadership connections by writing down three areas where you have weak connections that need improvement. *Following this action will help you define opportunity zones for success.*

6. Repeat daily: "Leaders lead leaders, not followers!" Write down three followers you will help transform to leaders. *This will begin the process of an environment of Leadership Connection Agility.*

7. During your commute home, introspectively reflect on your day. Is there a better way to manage your time and process

information that could redefine success and accelerate change and growth in the organization and its people? *Write down three things you will do tomorrow differently than you did today that can help begin this process.*

8. Repeat daily: "I have a mission statement for my life!" *This daily regimen will force you to realize that there is genius and greatness in you and will increase your confidence level to focus on achieving your mission in life. Write down your personal mission statement.*

9. What C.H.A.N.G.E. goals can you and your leaders create to help define and achieve new levels of success that other leaders will engage in and commit to? *This will start the process of igniting creativity and innovation, and challenge mediocrity.*

10. Before you leave the office each week, write down two things you can do to incorporate Ubuntu to help develop, grow, and build leaders.

• •

Take the
Genius Leader Challenge

● ● ● ● ● ● ● ● ● ● ● ● ● ● ● ●

As I write the closing chapter of this book, I ask not what is next for me, but rather what is next for others. I want others to maximize their God-given potential, and I am grateful that I have helped you discover the Genius Leader in you!

Within the 6G Leadership System, there are six networks. Your results were identified in the leadership self-assessment, and regardless of your leadership aptitude results, you have within you a well of potential to choose which leader you want to be. Whether you select the 1G–Genetic, 2G–Generic, 3G–Go-To, 4G–Growth Leader, 5G–Gateway Leader, or 6G–Genius Leader is up to you. Leadership is a choice and a result of actions, not position, title, or authority. As I look over my life, from personal challenges with schoolyard bullies to bullies in the Corporate America workplace, there is one truth and that never fails: Good leadership always wins over bad leadership.

There is something about starting to lose your hair, realizing you've gained 40 pounds since high school, or not getting off the elevator because you've forgotten your floor that forces you and most people in a middle-age crisis to ask the common question, "What is life all about and what have I done with it?" I turned to my favorite book I like to call The Script of Life, which consists of scrolls and scriptures that tell us we are born in the image and likeness of the Creator. *"Let us make man in our image, in our likeness, and let them rule over the fish of the sea and the birds of the air, over the livestock, over all the earth, and over all the creatures that move along the ground."* (Gen. 1:26–27 NIV).

Well, my hope is that you have found your answer to that question. Life is about leading. Leaders lead leaders, and in the new economy, companies are looking for leaders, not followers.

The Script of Life reveals to us that the chief architect and Creator of the entire universe designed, created, and brought to existence everything, including resources, living creatures, all things known and unknown to man. It reminds us that the Creator leads the hearts and minds of many, directing all actions with free will. Through the process of studying, researching, debating, and soul searching, I am reminded that the Creator and His Son are the essence of leadership. Because we are all made in His image and likeness, that means we were born a leader and genius.

And the questions I posed to myself, which now I pose to you, are "Are you maximizing your potential? Are you allowing the genius in you to shine? Or are you allowing someone else to disconnect your network applications of Awareness, Acceptance, Acknowledgement, Achievement, Acceleration, or Agility?"

You see, I've discovered that people with low self-esteem, personal handicaps, and bad leadership habits will try to convince you that you are not capable of leading, that you are not good enough, that your thoughts are wrong because they do not agree with theirs. If this is happening to you, then congratulations! This is a signal to you that you are on the path to becoming a Genius Leader. You are good enough.

Through this process, I have come to realize that the solution to the leadership challenge is to transform followers into leaders using a system that maximizes their potential. This is what I have chosen to dedicate my life to. I would enjoy being your friend, but more importantly, I want to be your leadership coach. I want you to win in life and celebrate what you've learned.

Perhaps you are a person of influence, or support an activity, project, initiative, process, or function, performing in the role of an individual contributor, team lead, manager, director, or C-level executive. If that's what you do, then simply put, you're a leader and there is a genius in you. Just as each snowflake that falls from the sky is one-of-a-kind and every finger has its own unique print, each of us has our own special leadership genius dwelling within. From the janitor to the CEO, we are all leaders in some form or fashion. Whether it's completing an assignment, activity, or function, individually or with teams, it doesn't matter what it is we do but how we do it. My grandfather was a janitor and an expert carpenter for more than 70 years, and he was a Genius Leader! Leadership is a mindset, and based on your subconscious belief, your well of potential is where you will operate. I invite you to take a bold step, ignore critics, and decide to act using the principles, solutions, and systems in this book to be the leader you were born to be. Take the leadership challenge.

Next are three simple unconscious habits you need to develop to begin taking action to become a Genius Leader and to sustain your connection on the 6G Leadership Network.

Habit 1: Drink the Kool Aid and See That Everyone Is a Leader

The first habit that needs to be formed is recognizing "everybody is a leader!" In short, there are many "experts" who embrace the traditional view of leadership that would suggest that everyone is not a leader, and that leadership is based solely on appointment, title, or position. Traditionalists also argue that leadership is merely a vertical-climb concept: a climb up an imaginary corporate ladder in which one matures from one level to the next, eventually elevating to greater responsibilities and oversight, never having to revisit the previous "steps" or "roles" climbed to reach their desired level of success. History reminds us of leaders who climb up and fall down their leadership ladder, because leadership is not that vertical climb on a ladder but a navigation on a horizontal sphere consisting of leadership applications that every person has within their DNA. Leadership is a natural gift at birth. The difference between a "follower" and a "leader" is merely awareness.

Habit 2: Recognizing Tomorrow's Success Requires Today's Leaders

Recognizing leadership is, simply put, only as good as the system of leaders. In order to have extraordinary success, an organization in today's competitive environment, accelerated change and overwhelming complexity cannot afford to have an enterprise of followers. The leadership concept that in order to have leadership you must have someone willing to follow and someone willing to lead is antiquated and outdated. Without being innovative, doing more with less, and becoming more effective and efficient in today's competitive world, followers will not be the competitive force that will create new ways of doing business. This will come from leaders. Traditional followers don't think; they do as they are told. If followers doing what they were told created the issue, logic suggests to do the opposite. Make it a habit to create leaders and experience extraordinary results.

Habit 3: Discover and Build Leaders With a Leadership System

Finally, every person was born with the innate talent and gift of leadership. We all operate on different leadership networks simply because of experience, training, typecasting, sub-optimization, or fear. We can all be plotted somewhere on the 6G Leadership Network System, designed to help leaders and organizations develop and grow using a common leadership development system. In today's global economy, organizations and companies need everyone to be in a leadership network. Make it a habit to build more leaders and fewer followers with the 6G Leadership Network System.

Next Gen Leader Coaching Exercise

As a result of completing this book, you have discovered your leadership potential and are now aware of other leadership styles, behaviors, and secrets. What can you do today to improve and become the Genius Leader you were born to be? Using the following 10 provocative questions to guide your thinking, develop a personal action plan that will give you the agility to operate on the 6G Leadership System Network.

1. Understanding the results of your assessment, what is unique about your leadership style in comparison to your peers?

2. What is your potential as a leader? What is your vision?

3. What do you view as your general leadership strengths and weaknesses?

4. What obstacles are stopping you from being a 6G Leader of Genius and Significance?

5. List three things you will begin changing today to get you moving in the right direction.

6. What coaching and mentoring do you need to receive in order to reach your new vision as a leader?

7. Who will be your accountability partner, sharing your leadership development goals, helping you keep track of your progress and providing you FeedForward support?

8. How will you determine success, and what does it look like?

9. How will you reward both your and others' successes?

10. Incorporate items 1–9 into your professional and personal development plan and list your monthly progress.

Summary

Organizations and leaders of High Significance understand that "leadership is everything!" If you are looking for your or another leader's success footprints, you will find them in their journeys through the Awareness, Acceptance, Acknowledgement, Achievement, Acceleration, and Agility Apps. Within these leadership applications lie the secrets of the Genetic, Generic, Go-To, Growth, Gateway, and Genius leaders.

By adopting the concepts and principles found in the six generations of leadership to discover my true leadership potential, I was able to rediscover and awaken the "Rob Mac" transformational leader in me. What transformational leader is lying silent in you, encompassing all of the talents and gifts that can enable you to become the "next generation" you? I invite you to search deep within your well of potential and release that Genius Leader in you to the world!

To join me and other leaders in the Next Gen Leader million-leader movement, please register and connect with us at *www.robertcmcmillan.com.*

Index

S

seeing leadership, 103-104

senses, six leadership, 101-108

smelling leadership, 104-105

strength zone, acknowledging your, 176-178

success, goals and, 207-208

T

tasting leadership, 104-105

touching leadership, 106

typecasting, gateway leaders and, 230-233

W

weak zone, acknowledging your, 178-179

About the Author

● ● ● ● ● ● ● ● ● ● ● ● ● ● ● ● ●

Robert C. McMillan is a transformationalist. He is a leadership coach and consultant to emerging, aspiring, and executive leaders, teams, and organizations. Robert is a highly-sought-after transformational speaker for organizations, associations, and conferences. Unlocking and igniting transformation and the genius in leaders, teams, and organizations is his purpose in life. His solutions are proven to accelerate change, increase performance, and improve financial results.

Robert's solutions are practical and rooted in two decades of leadership experience in Corporate America as a consultant and leader to Fortune 500 companies, organizations, and associations. Robert comes from humble beginnings, including a journey from positions of rank and file to the C-suite as one of the Chief Executive Directors for the world's largest conglomerate insurance company, Blue Cross Blue Shield Association, serving the President of the United States, Members of Congress, White House staff, and more than five million federal government employees.

Robert is recognized as an authority on leadership development and coaching through his groundbreaking proprietary and practical 6G Leadership System, and is the founder of the Next Gen Leader Institute and Circles of Dreams, Inc. He is the author of several books, including *Overcoming You: The Journey of Joe Braxton's Fall and Rise to a Corporate Idol.* Robert's body of work is awarding-winning and recognized by industry experts and practitioners as cutting-edge solutions to maximizing human potential, igniting transformation, and accelerating leadership growth and development.

Robert is a lifelong learner. Georgetown University recently selected him as a cohort fellow within the Institute for Transformational Leadership at Georgetown University, a community of the world's top organizational thinkers, leaders, and coaches from diverse fields and professions. Robert also matriculates and participates in continuous leadership and executive education programs at Harvard University, School of Business.

Robert holds dual Master of Business in Administration and a Master of Science in Information Technology Management from Johns Hopkins University. He earned his Bachelor of Science in Business Administration with a concentration in Finance and Marketing from Virginia State University. where he met his bride, Yolanda V. McMillan. Today they have two teenage children, Journee and Jalen, and live in the Washington, DC. area.